Newark

AMERICAN HISTORY AND CULTURE
General Editors: Neil Foley, Kevin Gaines,
Martha Hodes, and Scott Sandage

Guess Who's Coming to Dinner Now?
Multicultural Conservatism in America
Angela D. Dillard

One Nation Underground: A History of the Fallout Shelter
Kenneth D. Rose

The Body Electric: How Strange Machines Built the
Modern American
Carolyn Thomas de la Peña

Black and Brown: African Americans and the
Mexican Revolution, 1910–1920
Gerald Horne

Impossible to Hold: Women and Culture in the 1960s
Edited by Avital H. Bloch and Lauri Umansky

Provincetown: From Pilgrim Landing to Gay Resort
Karen Christel Krahulik

A Feeling of Belonging: Asian American Women's
Public Culture, 1930–1960
Shirley Jennifer Lim

Newark: A History of Race, Rights, and Riots in America
Kevin Mumford

Newark

A History of Race, Rights, and Riots in America

Kevin Mumford

NEW YORK UNIVERSITY PRESS

New York and London

NEW YORK UNIVERSITY PRESS
New York and London
www.nyupress.org

Library of Congress Cataloging-in-Publication Data
Mumford, Kevin J.
Newark : a history of race, rights, and riots in America /
Kevin Mumford.
p. cm. — (American history and culture)
Includes bibliographical references and index.
ISBN-13: 978-0-8147-5717-8 (cloth : alk. paper)
ISBN-10: 0-8147-5717-0 (cloth : alk. paper)
1. Newark (N.J.)—Race relations—History—20th century.
2. African Americans—Civil rights—New Jersey—Newark—
History—20th century—Sources. 3. Civil rights movements—
New Jersey—Newark—History—20th century. 4. Riots—New
Jersey—Newark—History—20th century. 5. African Americans—
New Jersey—Newark—Politics and government—20th century.
6. Black nationalism—New Jersey—Newark—Politics and
government—20th century. 7. Newark (N.J.)—Politics and
government—20th century. 8. Written communication—
Political aspects—New Jersey—Newark—History—20th century.
9. Newark (N.J.)—Race relations—History—20th century—Sources.
10. African Americans—Civil rights—New Jersey—Newark—
History—20th century—Sources. I. Title.
F144.N6M86 2007
305.896'07309749320904—dc22   2006101772

New York University Press books are printed on acid-free paper,
and their binding materials are chosen for strength and durability.

Manufactured in the United States of America
10 9 8 7 6 5 4 3 2

Contents

Acknowledgments

It is with heartfelt gratitude that I acknowledge the following institutions, colleagues, friends, and family for invaluable assistance in completing this book. I have benefited from well-maintained and expertly staffed research libraries around the nation. I owe a large debt to the unflinchingly professional staff at the Newark Public Library, especially to the great librarian and historian of Newark, the late Charles Cummings. At one of life's numerous moments of indirection, the late Richard Newman facilitated my residence at the W.E.B. Du Bois Institute for Research in Afro-American Culture at Harvard University, where I was introduced to the wonders of Widener Library, Loeb Library, Littauer Library, and the Harvard University Archives. In particular, I recall the generosity of the librarians in interlibrary loan and in census and statistics. I also thank the attentive staff at the New Jersey State Archives in Trenton; the Library of Congress, Manuscripts Division; the National Archives in Maryland; the New Jersey Historical Society; the manuscripts division of the Schomburg Center for Research in Black Culture; and the Wisconsin State Historical Society. I owe countless thanks to the research librarians and staff at my various institutional affiliations for their day-to-day service, including the University of Maryland, Towson University, and the University of Iowa. I received crucial institutional and financial support from Harvard University, Towson University, the New Jersey Historical Commission, the University of Iowa, and the National Endowment for the Humanities.

I benefited from very able research assistants, and I thank Scott Printz, Megan Warner, and Eric Johnson for help with data entry, documentation, and illustrations. For assistance with production, I thank Jean Aikin and Pat Goodwin in the Department of History at the University of Iowa, and the editors and staff at New York University Press, particularly Eric Zinner and Emily Park. At various stages of the book's development, a number of colleagues agreed to take time away from their work to respond to mine. I wish to thank Kenneth Kusmer, Lizabeth Cohen, Sonya Michel, David Roediger, David Gergen, Jennifer Frost, Angela Dillard, Shelton Stromquist, Linda Kerber, Waldo Martin, Nick Yablon, Paul Greenough, Martha Hodes, and Rosalyn Terborg-Penn. Since embarking on the study of political culture, I learned a great deal from engaged conversation and e-mail exchanges with all of the above, as well as a number of other scholars who took time to consider my ideas. I thank Anthony Appiah, Hazel Carby, Martha Biondi, Evelyn Brooks-Higginbotham, David Lewis, Nancy Cott, and Nell Painter for their insight. I have benefited from both brief and extensive communication with historians of Newark, and thank Clement Price, Robert Curvin, Tom Hayden, Stanley Winters, and Warren Grover. I must acknowledge my continued indebtedness to the scholarship of George Fredrickson. I recently re-read his introduction to a volume of essays that touched upon the complex issues raised by diversity in an age of postmodernism, and was humbled to see that a decade after embarking on my book I had almost (but not quite) reached the level of insight he shared in a few paragraphs, much less what he taught my generation about the role of racism in world history.

Friends and family don't ask for special recognition, but that is why I have fun mentioning them. Karen Moser (my mother), John Moser, Maryann Rasmussen, Stephen Vlastos, Kurt Jacobs, Tavia N'Yongo, Robert Reid-Pharr, Leslie Schwalm, Michel Gobat, Nicole Dombrowski, and Harry Stecopoulos added to the pleasures of life. Also pleasurable, and as crucial to sustaining my work, were the coffeehouses. I thank the café baristas at Towsontown Barnes and Noble Starbucks, Iowa City Starbucks, DOMA Café, Prairie Lights Java House, Mormon Trek Java House, The Big Cup, Peet's Santa Cruz, and the Terrapin Café.

In times of confusion and moral uncertainty, to write on the subject of civic values and public responsibility involves predictable yet treacherous pitfalls, particularly the temptation to indulge in self-righteousness. In searching for a higher plane, I have sought to draw on the wisdom of mentors, to whom this book is dedicated. In his offices at Harvard Law School, I conversed and sometimes sparred on matters of race with Professor Randall Kennedy, whose genius informed my thoughts during the early years of research. For his personal strength, commitment to multiculturalism, and faith in my abilities, I thank my friend Professor Michael Cowan. For sharing his unsurpassed knowledge of United States political history and dinner companionship, I thank Professor Mark Whitman. This book did not appear in time to be read by Professor Kenneth Cmiel, who died unexpectedly this winter. As chair of the Department of History at the University of Iowa, he not only persuaded me to accept an offer of employment, but also commented on more drafts of chapters than any other colleague. All of these learned mentors sustain my belief in the value of scholarship. Finally, I want to acknowledge the lifelong mentoring from my father, N. B. Mumford, especially his example of striving for independence even when it means living in the minority.

List of Abbreviations

The following are listed for easy identification in the text documentation:

BCD   Black Community Defense and Development
BMLA   Black Man's Volunteer Liberation Army
CAP   Congress of African People
CFUN   Committee for a United Newark
CHNC   Clinton Hill Neighborhood Council
CSC   Computer Sciences Corporation
DAD   Division Against Discrimination
ERAP   Economic Research and Action Project
FEPC   Fair Employment Practices Commission
FHA   Federal Housing Administration
FOR   Friendship of Reconciliation
HRC   Human Rights Council
HUA   Harvard University Archives
LOC   Library of Congress
NCUP   Newark Community Union Program
NHA   Newark Housing Authority
NHS   New Jersey Historical Society
NJSA   New Jersey State Archives
NPL   Newark Public Library
NPD   Newark Police Department
NYPL   New York Public Library
PNY Papers Paul N. Ylvisaker Papers
PUF   Princeton University Firestone Library
RAM   Revolutionary Action Movement
SCR   Schomberg Center for Research in Black Culture
UCC   United Community Corporation
UNIA   United Negro Improvement Association

Introduction

I moved to Newark in 1998 to fill in for a faculty member on leave from the Afro-American Studies Department at Rutgers University in the Central Ward, the historic neighborhood where several generations of black southerners had settled over a century of migration. While gathering data for a study of such migrations, I noted that many other cities had their own books—on ghettos in Chicago, the auto industry in Detroit, political institutions in Cleveland—but not my new temporary home. Some additional searching produced a bibliography of compendiums of the official Newark—lists of once famous leaders and forgotten officials; almanacs with plans for buildings and parks; accountings of the shipping, leather, banking, and insurance industries—none of which did more than mention the black population.[1] Then I discovered that the chair of the Department, Dr. Clement Price, had written his dissertation on the Great Migration and the Central Ward, but much of his work remained unpublished. The next summer, I began to read old issues of one of the largest black newspapers, the *New Jersey Afro-American*, followed up on leads in local archives around the state, and discovered some surprising issues and anecdotes in the 1940s. I was fascinated by the anonymous citizens who wrote to the editor and complained of the indignities of Jim Crow, and not in Birmingham or rural Mississippi, but in attempting to enjoy the public accommodations of New Jersey. Eventually I realized that historians had understated the level of racial caste in the northern city, and were only beginning to appreciate the impact of early forms of protest against it. My archival radar was searching for evidence of new and unseen connections between and among the settlement in the ghettos and the undocumented early civil rights movement, while on the historical horizon loomed the mass civil disobedience that would make Newark a famous hotspot in 1967.

I began to envision a different kind of political history. I wanted to return to the great American political narrative. Newark's tale of race, rights, and rioting was worth telling, but something larger was there. The adversity that the newcomers faced and the struggle for a place spoke volumes to the whole American experience.[2]

The first characteristic of Newark that struck me—something obvious today in many cities—was the prevalence of people of color. Let me say a few words, in different ways, on why this obvious demographic fact merits our attention. For one, it is not my experience, nor until recently that of most non-white people born and raised in the United States, to inhabit a city as anything other than an outsider to white hegemony. The majority of Americans enjoy worlds of white power, and yet today African Americans have won control in a number of cities. I had grown up in the mirror opposite of Newark, in a midwestern college town, Madison Wisconsin, where I was one of only a few black students in my school, residing in one of a few interracial households. In retrospect, it seems to me that middle-class conventions and racist status systems undergirded the public culture of Madison, despite its reputation for 1960s radicalism, from the exclusively white wealth in the lovely homes around the university to the marginalization of Ben's Barber Shop on the south side where I hung out with my father on Saturday afternoons. In the light of Newark, it seemed to me that the majority in Madison spoke to itself by employing a set of particular civic values that invisibly privileged whiteness. I also remember growing up in the 1970s and visiting the white side of my family in Milwaukee, another city whose face was changed by the Great Migration, but I remember this as a place defined by class to a greater extent than race. I understood that black Milwaukeeans were concentrated in poor neighborhoods, but also that my white working-class relatives lived in quite modest places, too. Our family excursions into the shopping areas explained to me that commercial zones obviously differed by status and class, and overlapped with racial segregation, and that the downtown district had deteriorated while still undergoing urban renewal. I experienced Milwaukee as something like a smaller Chicago—a city of excitement, leisure, and consumption. I also realized that other places had created more fluid and contested status systems than my hometown.

That day when I walked out of the great hall of Newark Penn Station, I could see that African Americans enjoyed a sense of entitlement and belonging, from the black municipal employees and busy professionals to the proprietors of black-owned businesses, and I realized that power and race had converged in a metropolis in a way unfamiliar to me. Here was a living legacy of the movement for Black Power that brought African Americans to their current status as rulers of the turf, for better and for worse, as I attempt to explain in the following pages. Yet my first impressions were also shaped by the tell-tale signs of urban decline and white flight. Behind the station there was a fairly well-established white ethnic neighborhood that appeared pleasant but along the big major streets I could see white men and women speed by in fine autos on their way out of town, abandoning dilapidated houses and boarded-up shops. On a daily basis I passed homeless men sleeping in the doorways of the church about a block down from the Newark Public Library, which became my second home during several years of research. There was decay and poverty, but this urban landscape did not conform to what social scientists referred to as a ghetto, or urban planners designated as a blighted neighborhood, or critics termed cultural pathology. What did this inversion of the assumptions of black subordination and white control, this territorial repudiation of white hegemony, the granting of urban entitlement to the most humbled minority ever to have entered the gates of Newark remind us to look for in the contours of postwar American history?

Newark is located in the highly populated state of New Jersey (population 8,590,300, the ninth largest), in the powerful Northeast region of the nation. Unlike the situation in several other leading industrial states —New York and California—the major cities of New Jersey were hit hard by the cycle of deindustrialization that characterized the rust belt across the nation from the 1950s onward. Even at the height of its population and economic prosperity during World War II, Newark ranked only eighteenth among U.S. cities, and has since slipped out of the top fifty. But what complicates this familiar narrative of urban decline was that between 1940 and 1970 the black population increased from 45,760 to 207,458, from less than 20 percent to more than 50 percent, again like many cities in the postwar era.[3]

Newark offers a fresh analysis of this urban growth and economic change by exploring the politics of ethnic settlement and cultural recognition alongside a new framework for understanding mobilizations for protest and modes of civic resolution. At a time when culture wars have overtaken the Cold War as a domestic priority, and when clashes of civilization overdetermine foreign policy, studying the struggles between shifting majorities and minorities in a place like Newark serves to explicate and move toward solving seemingly intractable social conflict. At a time when fundamentalism at home and abroad offer majoritarian, universal solutions to complex problems of political and moral governance, a study of the operation of democracy at its worst and at its best in Newark blazes new paths out of cultural intolerance. At a time when the metropolis suffers from and fears political violence, a historical study of a city torn apart by riots and military intervention and brought back to life with democratic elections sheds light on the possibilities of peace. Perhaps these are overly lofty statements; yet a belief I affirmed while working on this book is that to achieve peace at home in this century we must commit to a public culture in which reason and rational discourse prevail against the too-easy sway of righteousness and group interest. Communitarian deliberation and civil liberties must prevail against heroic nationalism and intellectual sectarianism. At least these are some of the aspirations of *Newark*.

Mine is not the first book to attempt a critical reconstruction of the national past by concentrating on a smaller stretch of time in a particular locale. Recently, several leading scholars have positioned New Jersey as a bellwether state to bring a tight focus to postwar America. The pioneering study of the rise of the suburbs, *Crabgrass Frontier: The Suburbanization of the United States* by Kenneth Jackson, relied extensively on research in New Jersey, and Jackson was among the first urban historians to note the postwar increase in black population in the cities, seeing Newark as a nightmare of social problems. Perhaps the most important work in postwar historiography to appear in the past decade, *A Consumer's Republic: The Politics of Mass Consumption in Postwar America* by Lizabeth Cohen, draws on research in New Jersey to map the ways in which the expansion of a consumer economy reconstructed national objectives and political citizenship.[4] What these and other big books on New Jersey-as-the-nation tell us is that we need to think again about the consequences of the rise of the social welfare state, the changes of inequality of race, the origins and causes of the conflict within and on the margins of U.S. democracy, and changing opinion registered by the electoral system.[5]

As a study in democracy, my book departs from the others on race relations in the cities in the way that it balances the voices of the ordinary folks with the role of powerful elites, and lessens the role of political economy.[6] The modern city was shaped by forces of deindustrialization, but social history also mattered. I disagree with major scholars such as Nicholas Lemann, Thomas Sugrue, and Robert Self, who have set out to explicate a historical moment they identify as "the urban crisis"—a phrase familiar to many readers of social science and general nonfiction on social problems—which they have defined as white flight from neighborhoods, transfers of capital into the suburbs, and the failure of public housing.[7] Despite their focus on the culpability of white politicians and economic forces, they argue for a conception of crisis that began and ended with the black southern migration from the South. If I were to adopt the same framework, I fear that black Newarkers would become victims listed on statistical tables. Some of the related scholarship on the so-called black underclass was motivated by the same liberal desire to stimulate new policy initiatives and increase federal spending to revitalize the inner cities. As readers of *Newark* will learn, by the 1960s this was an all-too-familiar impulse in the explosion of social science and commission reports after the riots. But then and now, the approach of centering deprivation and neglect fails to appreciate the historical impact of black political culture and initiative. The urban crisis school recapitulates the old argument that having blacks in the city essentially signified disorganization and failure. But we know from reading in the field of African American history that local communities demonstrated remarkable resiliency, creativity, and productivity that challenged power relations, from the Harlem Renaissance and self-help and benevolent organizations, to the sorts of stories that originally attracted my interest in this research, such as the early history of civil rights organizing against Jim Crow.[8]

In Newark, the majority of African Americans searched for empowerment less on the terrain of unions or by contesting consumption than through these sorts of associations, court cases, and electoral and municipal offices.[9] A few black radicals attracted a circle of followers in larger cities, but again the majority of African Americans put racial equality ahead of class solidarity, or at least viewed the defeat of racism as a necessary condition for joining struggles organized around economic redistribution.[10] To paraphrase a leading political scientist and researcher on black opinion, Michael Dawson, most African Americans defined their outlook and beliefs as liberal. They believed in rights and fair play, individualism and opportunity, and a share in the American Dream. But in the storms of intermittent white backlashes, black Americans became so disillusioned by racism that they embraced nationalism and separatism.[11] In the 1940s, what Dawson terms the "disillusioned liberals" became mobilized in New Jersey by reading newspapers, joining civic and civil rights groups, and pursuing legal claims for equal access and nondiscrimination. In the 1960s, still disillusioned, African Americans residing in ghettos and victimized by violence engaged in direct-action protest and challenged municipal government for better services, more benefits, political representation, and the like. What I am describing is not a history of heroic communist radicals in the 1930s, nor the nationalist militants of the 1970s, but persistent if continually changing networks of civic leaders and everyday folks utilizing—and in the process transforming—an urban democracy.

Historians and political scientists, legal scholars and sociologists, have created an exciting renaissance in the study of these forms of civil society, having faith in the redemptive power of public deliberation of virtues and responsibilities, beyond rights and interests. Political thinkers argue for the selfishness of liberalism and the need for communitarian politics, but few studies of the political culture consider the role of civic racism.[12] In my view, there is a possession of authority over civic values that has been related to political power and social standing, and so, not surprisingly, also white supremacy. Yet when black citizens gained more power, the reaction of many was to reject the civic tradition of sharing values with whites. In my view, this turned out to be as unfortunate as the civic racism that is examined in the first part of this book. By exploring the deeply rooted and structural biases of Newark's civic cultures, my analysis recognizes the legitimacy of race-based claims for equality to end discrimination against blacks. But in this book, I see protest for inclusion as a genuine and more popular goal among African Africans than separatism or nationalism. Establishing this second argument requires some theoretical intervention, a brief discussion of which serves as the conclusion to the introduction.

The relevant social theory is the concept of the public sphere.[13] First introduced in *The Structural Transformation of the Public Sphere* by Jürgen Habermas in the 1960s and translated into English in the 1980s, the concept of the public sphere appealed to many disciplines or fields of analysis because of its power to enlarge the analytical scope of what constitutes politics. Not only elected officials and powerful leaders qualify as political actors but so do a serendipity of associations, volunteers, and texts reflecting shifts in the nature and impact of public opinion in the larger civil society. To paraphrase Habermas, the public sphere became visibly transformative at the moment when the people joined together in associations and conversation—and in the cities such deliberation in physical spaces and print cultures greatly expanded the reach of the democracy. New research suggests that civic engagement and participation increased more in the twentieth century than many scholars had expected, specifically when taking into account a public sphere of "new institutionalism" and "mobilization theory."[14] But it is important to remember that black intellectuals have emphasized how democracy in the United States operated on the basis of segregation and exceptionalism, giving the lie to the romanticization of rational communicative action of Habermas.[15]

At any given moment, women and minorities were restricted from equal access to the means of communication—the public sphere excluded them—but they did not automatically reject the Western creation of a civil society.[16] Black intellectuals and religious leaders reconstructed a black public sphere out of the ashes of denied citizenship, fostering the rise of several phases of the civil rights movement—one in the era of Reconstruction, another during World War II, another in the 1960s. A major category of history that shaped the black public sphere was not only class, which, according to Dawson, arrived relatively late to divide black political actors (around 1970), but also the division of gender.[17] My interpretation of the impact of integration and nationalism, as well as repression by the government, spends a fair amount of time on tracing the flows of power and resistance back and forth between private and public, consumption and protest, family and citizen. In other words, my analysis constructs a geography of gender that intersected with both the operation of racism and with local acts of resistance.[18] Both men and women—white and black—enabled and constrained the advancement of minorities toward empowerment in the democracy.

Perhaps because of its racial grounding or its oppositionality, the black public sphere has been easily stereotyped as monolithic.[19] In my attempt here to examine variations in black political discourse, I draw heavily on the scholarship addressing the problem of diversity in modern democracy, particularly the brilliant writings of Seyla Benhabib and Anthony Appiah on the construction of identity. In modern political discourse, these and other scholars argue, groups mobilize through class and race and demand from the state not only economic redistribution but cultural recognition, or respect from the larger polity. This is the paradigm referred to in the debates as the move from rights to redistribution to recognition. Contemporary debates around recognition turn on the demands of advocates of multiculturalism for respect, visibility, and resources for their ethnic group, language, and heritage. At the same time, philosophers challenge the essentialist or racialist identities ascribed to the group, excavating the historical origins and variability of meanings of race since the invention of the term.[20] Importantly, contemporary philosophers challenge essentialist claims for the group from within the community—what might be termed strategic essentialism. Benhabib argues that the problem with the politics of recognition, even as practiced by the adherents of deliberative democracy, is the residual recourse to a monolithic and simplistic concept of cultural identity and "the privileging of certain forms of collective identity over other possible identity markers—let us say gender or sexual preference"—that leads to a "reification" (simplification, reductive) exclusively focused on "national" and "ethno-cultural identities."[21] For Anthony Appiah, a humane political solution to this kind of ethnic conflict takes into account the individuality of each subject in ways that satisfy a yearning for liberty in an unconstrained landscape of life.

My argument suggests that, on the one hand, the revival of black nationalism has continuously demonstrated its capacity to include a wide spectrum of viewpoints and personal identities and mobilized larger constituencies than ever before to defeat the retrenchment of white racism. On the other hand, I argue that by the 1970s the nationalist variant of Black Power ideology ultimately failed because of its advocacy of ethnic separatism, which led to the erosion of public deliberations. It also failed because of its essentialist configurations of identity, which eroded the political influence of dissenters and nonconformists. By rigidly delineating who was "in" and who was "out" of the "race," black cultural nationalists alienated dedicated activists while also discouraging many in the next generation from joining their cause.[22]

Finally, this book looks at the corruption of political alliances, and the official repression of dissent. The breakdown of democracy bred not merely black discontent within a kind of moral economy, leading to the disorderly conduct of the crowd. Among black people in Newark, the abuse of power led to the outbreak of civil disobedience. For the federal government, the aftermath of the urban disorders in dozens of cities symbolized not the collapse of democracy but the relatively less disastrous breakdown of race relations, a very familiar explanation that served to manage eruptions of inequality and the legitimacy of government, a strategy of containment as old as race itself. Indeed, in 1968 the U.S. National Advisory Commission on Civil Disorders issued the most important document on race relations in America since the emancipation proclamation—"The Kerner Commission" Report—which concluded that riots had happened because the nation was made up of two societies, one black and the other white, separate and unequal. The roots of inequality, the commission stated over and over again, reflected the persistence of racism among whites.[23] My story reminds us of the truth of their conclusion. To what extent had both this official explanation of rioting and other social science mystified the political roots and denied the agency of black Newarkers? What has been lost in the lapse of memory and knowledge brought about by the tumult of post-riot nationalism? From the excavation of each local past, new civic lessons are passed on, hopefully in ways that guide neighbors in meeting the many challenges that lie ahead of creating cities free of the old injustices and indignities, and opening a new society.[24]

PART I

Integration

1

The Central Ward and the Rites of the Public Sphere

The galley slaves of the Orient, the wretched prisoners in the
Athenian silver mines, the depressed proletariat in the insulae of
Rome . . . but never before had human blight so universally been
accepted as normal; normal and inevitable.

—Lewis Mumford, *The City in History*[1]

In 1916, the Essex County National Bank at 73 Broad Street
published a limited edition history to commemorate the 250th anniversary of the founding of Newark. The story celebrated the traditions and
virtues of the city, neglecting to mention that Native Americans had long
inhabited the land before being attacked by the Puritans who fled Connecticut. The city fathers' book instead recounted "a day in early May
of 1666 when a little fleet of two or three vessels entered the Passaic
river bearing forty-one Puritan families." It reported that the interlopers
had assured the "resentful Hackensack Indians of their intentions to pay
for whatever lands their colony should take," and that the dissident
founder, Robert Treat, henceforth ordered his group to "build homes of
logs hewn from the forest" upon the destruction of the Indian habitat.
Soon the new settlers cultivated small plots of land and erected cabins
and a church at the crossroads of the town on Market Street (originally
an Indian footpath) and Broad Street. As a foundation for their newfound settlement, in 1688 they built a public meetinghouse that also
functioned as a grist mill. In 1696 the white people of Newark received
title to all of the streets from the proprietors of New Jersey, designating
officially the public areas and lands as their private property. "From this
humble beginning upon the river bank has grown the busy, thriving city
that numbers today 400,000 people," boasted the Essex County Bank's
commemorative.[2]

This rendering of Newark's history not only conveniently erased the uncompensated coercion of Native Americans but also ignored African Americans, a particularly notable erasure given that a black ghetto had risen in the town center by the time the bank issued its book. Rather than a city on the hill, the Central Ward symbolized the prevalence of racial injustice. Though readers of the commissioned history did not learn of the debilitating poverty in the ghetto, they understood that the public sphere assiduously enforced a color line, a peculiarly northern observance of Jim Crow. By removing their presence and contributions from the collective narrative, the founding myths of the city told in the official history book disenfranchised black Newarkers in perpetuity.

Since the rise of the city and the growth of democratic government, the tradition of the myth of a Puritan founding and the arrival of generations of whites offered something powerful to the heirs' inspiring landmarks, volunteer societies, ceremonies, and tributes. According to the public record left behind, the steadily expanding black neighborhoods and their fledgling institutions more often than not acquiesced to civic invisibility. Not until the post–World War II era of civil rights and more urgently in the post-1960s era of nationalist militancy did representative inscriptions in the public sphere begin to reflect adequately both the size and needs of the community. By that time, a famous black cultural revolutionary, Amiri Baraka, had led a community board funded by the Great Society and staffed by residents of the Central Ward in a movement to change the name of Robert Treat School to the Marcus Garvey School, to honor the famous black leader of Harlem who advocated emigration to Africa. The historical transition from margin to center, from abject racial other to ethnic victor, had always involved public culture in political struggles, and the particularities of ethnic belonging and identification.[3]

The number of heated public debates over the story of a city or the naming of a public school perhaps struck some as irrelevant, but in a nation of immigrants such disagreements frequently escalated into civic wars that interrupted the comity of the cities. The contested concept of the public good referred back to the classical Greek polis, but was especially relevant to the modern United States because everyday associations served to protect the vitality of what was known as popular sovereignty. A leading historian of how urban civic culture shaped the democratic experience, Mary Ryan, has argued that the "performances of the people"—the gatherings and ceremonies, like the one commemorating the founding of Newark—simultaneously defined the city to the group and the group to the city.[4] But the people in the cities had also pledged allegiance to the American theory of pluralism—a theory that the Jewish immigrant Israel Zangwill satirically portrayed early in the century as the Melting Pot—and thus each ethnic group aspired to be naturalized as citizens while preserving a sense of national heritage. When these heritages varied by more than the other would tolerate, or when political interests collided between and among groups, various ethnic actors fought over parades and public squares on their way to campaign rallies and at the polls.

In other words, the history of white immigration and assimilation into the nation created a kind of pluralism in which political interests and partisanship almost always were positively aligned with old world ethnic heritage.[5] Whether Germans tended to downplay their heritage or the Irish fought doggedly to champion their group, each ethnic group invested in organizations and associations in order to gain political influence. From Tammany Hall across the river in New York to intermittent spurts of reform, urban governance shifted continuously to what might be termed ethnic group succession, from Puritans to Irish and Germans, to Italians and Jews. By the 1960s, the standard studies in political science and history had established that the struggles of the immigrant newcomer was a fundamental structure of the political system—that, to quote one traditional account of the urban machine, "the problem of multiple ethnic groups having to act in concert in the framework of a single government is not simple." For historians and social scientists, investigating voting habits, electoral trends, and the operation of patronage increasingly involved understanding ethnicity.[6]

Yet the story of the white arrival differed from that of historically marginal groups—not only African Americans, but Native Americans, the poor, and women—because they suffered legal and customary exclusion from public culture.[7] To say that the black struggle against such terms of exclusion originated far back in the history of Newark, perhaps as long ago as the arrival of racial slavery in the seventeenth century, is not to explain its persistence into the twentieth century. But a brief historical excursion permits a greater appreciation for the denial of rights.

From 1664 to the early 1700s, colonial New Jersey had inherited slavery from the Dutch. The southern half of the state passed pro-slavery laws, among the most draconian in the nation, and the northern part simply omitted the word slave from statutory law on matters of citizenship, tacitly legitimating chattel.[8] In 1800 the number of slaves in the state peaked at 12,422, mostly employed in rural areas for small-scale agriculture. One extant source indicated that white residents of Newark owned approximately twenty slaves in the antebellum era.[9] The total black population of Essex County, including free African Americans, numbered only 375 to 445 until the nineteenth century.[10] Despite the disruption and liberalization resulting from the American Revolution, and the popular spirit of independence that swept through the North, the state of New Jersey tenaciously clung to the peculiar institution, becoming the last to abolish slavery in the North and gradually emancipate the remainder in 1808.[11]

In the early nineteenth century, at the dawn of mass politics and so-called universal manhood suffrage (so-called because neither women nor African Americans universally received rights of citizenship), the free and the newly freed black community confronted stigmatization from whites while their civil rights declined into a state of subordination. Although New Jersey's first state constitution had granted suffrage to all men regardless of race, including all free black males, by 1820 the new movement convinced the state legislature to prohibit voting for all black residents (just as in Connecticut and Pennsylvania, for example).[12] Although a handful of liberal legislators attempted to protect the black community by defeating a bill to require African Americans to register with the government, this was the extent of black entitlement—a kind of second-class citizenship.[13]

Into the twentieth century the black community traversed city streets that were paved with civic markers of white hostility to their presence. The influential mayor of Newark, Theodore Frelinghuysen, the namesake for a major commercial thoroughfare in town (Frelinghuysen Avenue), had presided over the Newark Colonization Society, founded in 1817 (formed at the same time as the national organization), which listed a membership of some "500 contributors." The colonization movement was founded specifically to expel or deport black citizens from the nation. With a generous grant from the New Jersey legislature, local colonizationists financed a large-scale mission to relocate black citizens of Newark to Africa, Haiti, or Latin America. During the 1830s, another famous mayor, and another namesake of a major street, William Halsey (Halsey Street just off Broad, in the town's center), helped to revive a branch of the Colonization Society in town in 1838, a couple of years after the city of Newark incorporated. A few vocal black New-

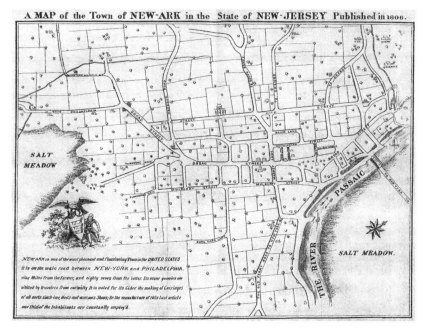

Fig. 1.1. A map of the town of New-Ark in the state of New Jersey, published in 1806.

arkers "denounced colonization," but white civic leaders empowered by their official ties to municipal and state government drowned out their protests.[14]

Black dissidents constructed and sustained a sort of counter-public of newspapers, secret societies, and fraternal associations, and sponsored ethnic ceremonies.[15] This constituted what one scholar describes as a "positive collective incorporation" that "claimed subjectivity by collectively re-appropriating that which was subject to appropriation by whites under the regime of legal slavery and the regime of racial subordination"—but they lacked both a critical mass and enough resources to mount much of a challenge to civic exclusion.[16] Into the 1830s and 1840s some groups intermittently paraded in the streets and at other times protested through their withdrawal from particular ceremonies. For a number of years, for example, black Newarkers, because of their formal disenfranchisement, refused to celebrate the Fourth of July, a once popular tradition that dually recognized national independence and the righteousness of emancipation. Thus, to explain their withdrawal from the rites of white civic culture, one angry protester was quoted as proclaiming, "We cannot rejoice in an event in which in our case is made an exception," and he insulted the "twaddle of fourth of July orators."[17]

Into the Civil War years, African Americans protested civic exclusion at home and against slavery in the South. As the white-led anti-slavery movement gained a larger following, newspapers and flyers spoke out against Slave Power, and free black men attempted to enlist in the war against southern secession in the 1860s. The state Democrats had objected to such proposals, but by 1865 some 1,185 black men from New Jersey had served in the Union Army. Meanwhile, the Democratic governor declared the Emancipation Proclamation unconstitutional, accusing President Abraham Lincoln of prolonging the hostilities.[18] In 1863 black Newarkers turned out to attend a speech by the Great Emancipator when he passed through on his way to Washington, D.C., and again on April 4, 1865, to pay their respects to the slain president's funeral train en route to Springfield, Illinois. But the whites in New Jersey had voted against Lincoln in his first term, and had the dubious distinction of casting the only northern anti-Lincoln vote again in 1864. Similarly, during the implementation of Reconstruction, the state legislature refused to ratify both the Fourteenth and the Fifteenth Amendments, which granted full citizenship through the federal government to all citizens of the states. So, for the second time in the history of the black public sphere, in the 1870s African Americans took up the cause of equal rights and organized protest, joining the convention movement that had mobilized the southern freedmen by founding a branch of the Equal Rights League in Newark.[19] Despite erstwhile black protest and the passage of constitutional provisions, the public exercise of citizenship was a construction of whiteness. Not until 1875 did the state legislature formally enfranchise black male citizens with a stroke of the pen—by simply deleting the word "white" from both the suffrage statutes and the state constitution.[20]

From the end of Reconstruction to the dawn of the modern civil rights movement, however, white citizens around the state actively resented and resisted the extension of citizenship to African Americans. In southern New Jersey, the city councils repeatedly authorized their school boards to operate separate "Colored" schools, and continued to bar black children from attending white schools nearby in their own neighborhoods. Because of this kind of conservative obstruction, the more

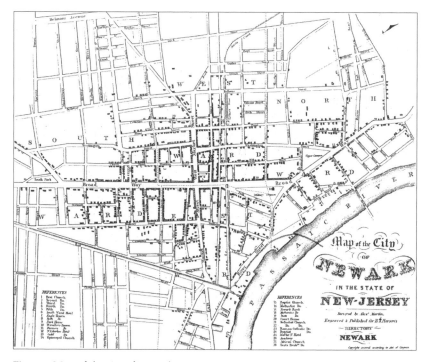

Fig. 1.2. Map of the city of Newark.

liberal state legislature passed new equal-accommodations legislation in 1883 that prohibited segregation in hotels, restaurants, and transportation. Yet, many local proprietors clung to their habits of discrimination. A second law that was passed specifically to provide for equal protection in education similarly failed to secure compliance in the white community.[21]

That was where the African American community stood: equal to whites in the letter of the law but without legal compliance or recognition of an equal place in the civic order. Into the twentieth century, the gradual increase in the black population promised to supply a larger community that could be counted on to protest the unequal treatment and to claim its rightful place on the urban mantle, a trend already evident by the 1920s in New York, Chicago, and Philadelphia, where the New Negro movement attracted militant integrationists and nationalist radicals. But in many of the medium-sized cities like Newark, neither parades nor protest nor the pace of progress increased much.

In the 1910s, even though the Great Migration came to Newark, it proved a relatively small affair of less consequence. Caused by labor shortages in World War I, ambitious recruitment, and enthusiasm for a new place, approximately 1.2 million southerners headed north for the metropolis, but the black population of Newark increased by only 22,000. In other words, although migration between 1880 and 1920 had more than quadrupled the black population of 4,477, it was still less than 5 percent of a total city population of 173,389.[22] Into the 1920s, although Newark's wartime industries attracted migrants from the south Atlantic states of North Carolina, South Carolina, and Georgia who arrived at the train station off Market Street in Newark, they settled into a dual system of rights versus rites, a political culture defined on the one hand by a legal promise to provide equal protection and, on the other hand, by a civic sphere that commanded deference and exclusion.[23]

Arriving in the city during an industrial upswing (when the national average for manufacturing value per capita was $150 and for Newark was $515), many black southern migrants nonetheless failed to make substantive, much less equal, gains in the industrial economy.[24] Compared to their predecessors, the white immigrants, who gained employment in textiles, in the manufacture of boots and shoes, cigars, clothing, furniture, glass, leather, and in oil and sugar refining, the black newcomers were concentrated in unskilled and service sectors.[25] A survey of statistics estimated that "elite blacks advanced and some prospered, but the average black[s] in Newark confronted discrimination . . . and were concentrated in the lowest paying jobs."[26] Black southerners found work in the local munitions plants, brickyards, wire factories, and in the city's major industries, including Flockhard Foundry, Coe Sette Company, and Benjamin Atha Steel. Every statistical study, however, indicated employment discrimination and occupational segregation. Although blacks constituted approximately one of every eleven workers, they represented only 3.6 persons of every 100 workers in the major industries.[27] Only 5.3 percent of the population in 1910 was black, but black workers accounted for 35 percent of male servants, 31.1 percent of porters, and 26 percent of janitors. Even at a high point of black participation in manufacturing in World War II, some 26 percent of all black males were employed as chauffeurs, truck drivers, and in delivery; 15 percent in the service sector; and only 10 percent were classified as foremen.[28] Without favors and influence in the municipality, surveys of black employment indicated that out of a population of 40,000 African Americans, the city

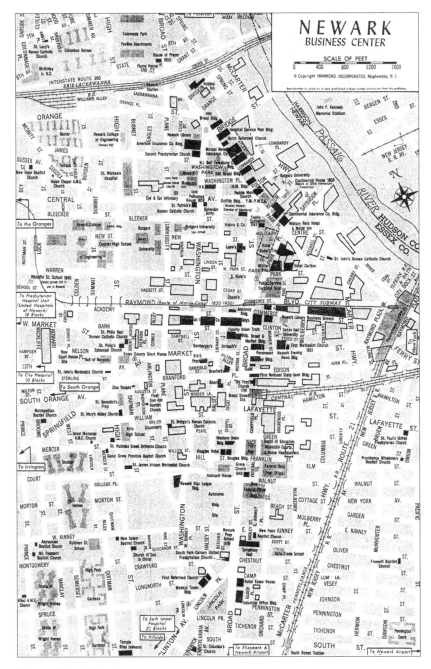

Fig. 1.3. Newark business center.

of Newark employed four black police officers, eight black school teachers, and four black miscellaneous clerical workers, and the category of "menial" accounted for 350 black employees.[29]

African-American female migrants also experienced this kind of discrimination, gaining only incremental social mobility due to increase in wages and better working conditions. They predominated in low-skill, low-paying positions similar to those they had held in the South, and in some cities, black women represented a female surplus, to use the terminology of black sociologist Kelly Miller. But in Newark the sex ratios were equal and women fared better in the economy than the national average.[30] By 1930 about 60 percent of black women in Newark found employment as domestic workers: nearly 3,367 of 5,682 domestics, and a large percentage of laundry operatives, some 299 of a total 921. The majority of these failed to make headway into manufacturing, and black women accounted for only 535 "industrial workers" in a female labor force of almost 13,000.[31] More black female migrants in Newark secured more jobs in wartime industries than in any other northern city except Detroit, but at the end of the Great Migration were the last hired, least promoted, and the first fired.[32]

The racial stratification of the economy and discrimination against the black newcomers signaled the hegemony of a public sphere dedicated to Jim Crow. Speaking of this continuity between the racial systems of the North and South, a delegate to a meeting of the black nationalist Marcus Garvey Association declared to the body: "New Jersey, as you know is north of the Mason-Dixie line, but the wind that blows [is] from the fields of Jim Crowism, and segregation finds its way into the field of New Jersey." Despite the promise of migration, black Newarkers reported "discrimination in factories," being "turned away from the door with money in your hand," and "the worst housing conditions obtain in Newark."[33] The distinguishing characteristic of the ghetto, according to Thomas Philpot, the historian of segregation in Chicago, was that "the Negro ghetto, it turns out, was [the] . . . only real ghetto." Philpot pointed out that the average white ghetto of ethnic immigrants always included at least twenty-five different nationalities, but not so for African Americans in Newark by the 1930s, for they were increasingly isolated from whites.[34] Observers described Newark as an amalgam of ethnic villages; 30 percent of the population lived in the so-called Hill Districts, a melting pot of "new immigrants," including Italians and Greeks, Lithuanians and Russians, but no group remained as confined to that area for any period of time like the increasing numbers of migrants from the South. Beginning in the 1920s, whites from the vicinity of the Central Ward moved out to better neighborhoods, to the wealthier Vailsburg, Forest Hill, Woodside neighborhoods as well as the more moderate or working-class areas such as Roseville, Clinton Hill, the Ironbound, and the North Ward. At the same time, 50,000 Jews moved into the Weequahic section in the West Ward (the area made famous by Philip Roth's novels). In the 1930s they joined an early wave of 26,000 white families departing the city for the new suburbs.[35]

At least since the Great Migration, various authorities and journalists have referred to the terrible conditions in the Central Ward, reporting that "throughout Newark there is direct correlation between areas of Negro residents and blighted housing." Of three thousand rooming houses, almost by definition the most dilapidated housing stock, most were occupied by African Americans. Although several short-lived black newspapers and concerned black citizens called attention to "a slum" in the Third Ward, the white newspaper reported that "there is no negro problem here."[36] According to Clement Price, a historian of African Americans in Newark, however, ten years into the Great Migration more than 30 percent of the city's black population had settled in the Central Ward, and by 1950 it included 90 percent of the black population of the city. With the permanent concentration of black newcomers in deteriorating housing, the migration had disappointed many blacks' expectations not only for a better standard of living, but for freedom from the constraints of segregation.[37]

By definition, the process of ghettoization encompassed all strata of the black community, for the fact was that both the poor and the prosperous faced discrimination by whites in housing and real estate, and thus all felt the confines of the ghetto wall. According to political scientist Michael Dawson, "the black counter-public is not a bourgeois sphere," because "black institutions and publics have been largely multi-class, at least up to 1970, due to the long regime of enforced segregation."[38] At the beginning of the twentieth century, the local black public sphere of elites was led primarily by entrepreneurs and professionals, who attempted to get around Jim Crow through calculated cooperation with whites, on the one hand, and by selling their services to average black folks in the Central Ward, on the other. In other words, the elites helped themselves as they served their brethren by investing in what historians refer to as the institutional ghetto. According to the historian of this ghetto formation in Cleveland, Kenneth Kusmer, the black working class lost ground in areas of service work that depended on white patronage, and the black elites became more dependent on whites for capital and supplies. A few remaining groups in the middle class protected their menial service positions as barbers and servants, but in areas where white immigration sharply increased they lost ground.[39] Although historians have found that "whites only grudgingly relinquished their power . . . and continued to own most of the businesses," black retail establishments had grown to approximately 25,000 stores across the nation.[40] Black entrepreneurs in Harlem owned over 350 stores, including meat markets, confectioners, grocery stores, even automotive repair shops, and of the fifty leading black insurance companies today, approximately thirty-five were founded in institutional ghettos.[41]

The paradox was that the institutional ghetto reflected unjust exclusion from many of the privileges of the city, and yet the experience of segregation collectively strengthened the black community to cope with the travails of white racism.[42] In Newark, the upwardly mobile and civic-minded joined various fraternal groups and lodges, such as Negro Masons and the Alpha Lodge, whose members included a baker, music teacher, school principal, engineer, machinist, and coachman, to build rudimentary, modest institutions for self-help. Black businessmen opened a bank for the community in the Central Ward, the People's Finance Corporation.[43] They formed professional societies—Negro Funeral Directors of North Jersey, the Newark Barber's Protective Association, the Modern Beauticians Association—but rarely chose to deploy their services or pool their resources in the cause of overt, visible challenges to the system. Rather, like any group of entrepreneurs, they pursued their own economic self-interest in selling goods and services, cooperating with white suppliers, professional societies, and officials in municipal licensing, zoning, and regulation. But the community suffered from a dearth of activism. According to Price's research, "there is little indication that blacks were permitted to participate in Newark's social and political life," and less indication that the elite fathers of the community had developed a successful strategy for uplifting the masses in the face of so restrictive a system of Jim Crow.[44]

The closest rivals of the conservative or accommodationist elites for the leadership of the Central Ward were the new reformers trained in the social sciences. The major white reform agencies, such as the Salvation Army, Goodwill Home, and the Red Cross, refused to lend a help-ing hand to the vast number of needy blacks in Newark. Unlike the elite conservatives in search of social control, the black social reform com-munity demonstrated real altruism. Among the most prominent was William Ashby, a descendant of slaves born in Newark who graduated from Lincoln University in Pennsylvania and from Yale University. After receiving a Master's degree at Yale, Ashby interviewed for a position at the National League on Urban Conditions (later National Urban League, NUL) in New York, and became a founding member of the Newark branch. He solicited donations from a major white philanthro-pist, Mrs. Felix Fuld (owner of Bamberger's Department Store, the only retailer to employ black clerks), to help finance the construction of a four-story building on 58 West Market Street (at the cost of $14,000) to serve as the headquarters of the Essex County Urban League.[45]

Ashby and the other social service professionals shared a moral bias against vice and unruly behavior with the entrepreneurial civic leaders, warning the migrants fresh off the sharecropping plantations to avoid the treachery of big-city prostitution and liquor. The NUL established a number of travelers' aid programs to help black female migrants locate rooming houses and employment. In addition to local settlement houses and a loose network of social workers, the Essex County League of Col-ored Women Voters hosted dinners and uplift meetings, and sponsored outreach programs that helped to integrate the new migrants into the Central Ward.[46]

Despite their dedication to service and messages of racial uplift, nei-ther the social welfare workers nor the middle-class volunteers were able to prevent the rapid deterioration of conditions in the ghetto, and few black workers in the poorer sections of the Central Ward responded with much in the way of organized protest. By contrast, public demon-strations and civic engagement swept through the streets of Harlem and Brooklyn, ranging from the civil rights demands of the newly founded National Association for the Advancement of Colored People (NAACP), to nationalists, to new organizations with black socialists from the Caribbean. But perhaps the most radical alternative to the mainstream institutional ghetto was the group of Marcus Garvey nationalists who called for racial separatism and a mass exodus "back to Africa." The Newark branch of Garvey's United Negro Improvement Association (UNIA) opened offices on Lackawanna Avenue, and sources show a membership of one hundred members sometime around 1922. But when these Garveyites reported to the national convention, they criticized the community in Newark for its lack of political motivation, accommodationist attitudes, and preference for the pleasures of the nightlife.[47] Both Father Divine and the Moorish Temple, progenitor of the Nation of Islam, attracted large followings in the Central Ward, and the enthusiasts staged the occasional public procession. But their collective actions, parades, and public meetings usually called for uplift rather than a demand for equal rights or more resources from city hall, and drew upon a tradition of self-help.[48]

The resulting insularity of black organizations led to the neglect of popular mobilization against social injustice and perhaps even encouraged its own kind of accommodation. Black workers who gained a better foothold in industrial employment avoided the local unions, confirming what many observers of New Jersey politics claimed to be the virulence of anti-labor sentiment. In big cities like New York and Detroit, workers demanded fair employment and equal accommodations, but in Newark the record of the unions proved mixed at best. While the white ethnics gained ground in the Newark chapter of the United Auto Workers (UAW) and the Congress of Industrial Organizations (CIO), they constructed new areas of leisure and official ceremonies that excluded black workers. The CIO had supported a civil liberties board that filed a suit against a proprietor of a Newark restaurant for discrimination against a black patron.[49] Particularly in Newark the CIO represented the lily-white trades of building, printing, and transportation.[50] The Essex County CIO and other "labor groups" publicly endorsed candidates for local and statewide offices, usually at private ceremonies and parties, but they consciously maintained an exclusively white off-the-shop-floor public sphere.[51] Local black workers viewed the unions with suspicion, particularly after reading a newspaper report that the American Federation of Labor rejected a plea by A. Philip Randolph for the elimination of the color bar.[52]

White newcomers too felt the stigma of the suspect stranger, but less so in the labor organizations and unions than in the local Democratic clubs or nominating committees of the Republican Party. As early as 1873, a group of immigrant Italians arrived in the First Ward (an area of 250 acres on the north side of the city) and established enclaves and a few shops along Boyden Street. The area, popularly known as a "colony" and as Little Italy, grew rapidly in the era of the so-called new immigration, increasing from around 407 in 1880 to more than 27,000 in

1920. Meanwhile, more and more Italian newcomers settled in the Iron-bound district in the East Ward, on Fourteenth Avenue, and in the Silver Lake District. But in the First Ward in particular the 30,000 or so immigrants wished to re-create their old world customs. They attended one of a number of Catholic churches, and patronized thriving commercial areas where they observed rituals of heritage "in numerous cafes, restaurants, pizzeria ovens, music stores, and open-air clam and oyster bars."[53]

Yet like many African Americans in the Central Ward, the Italian immigrants also confronted prejudice from better-off whites, particularly from the Irish, their immigrant predecessors. The natives of the city easily stereotyped the Italian neighborhoods—which some reports indicated also included a "handful of Negro families"—as "evil and torturous." They portrayed them as a tradition-bound community that enjoyed festivities in the streets, and collected on porches where they were "gay and exuberant."[54] Like African Americans, members of the Italian community suffered insults because of their distinctive appearance and unknown cultural practices, and also their Catholic religion. Italian American writers sometimes referred to their own unique physical gifts, and even self-identified as "colored" and their constituency as the "colored vote."[55] If the Great Migration stimulated anti-black sentiments and the crowding of northern ghettos, the rapid influx of Italian and other European migrants mobilized what historians term "one hundred percent Americanism," a xenophobic grassroots backlash that ultimately resulted in the passage of immigration restriction legislation. In response to deepening racial hostilities, the Italians, like African Americans, established separate businesses that catered to the taste of the neighborhoods, and both groups established and maintained special services to help assimilate the new arrivals into the city.[56]

Both Italian Americans and African Americans suffered disproportionately from the downturn of manufacturing and decline of consumption in Newark during the onset of the depression in the 1930s. As the number of Italian-born residents decreased from 30,587 to 26,140, the average incomes for Italian Americans lagged behind those of the native born, but they formed the majority of the membership of several local unions, according to newsletters published in Italian and English.[57] While Italian Americans slowly and unevenly overcame anti-immigration sentiments, black southern migrants still experienced similar prejudice in the city. Before the depression, a variety of industries sent recruiters south to sign up African American laborers from Alabama, the

Carolinas, and Tennessee, but now many of the same white civic leaders who once welcomed industrial workers called for monitoring the balance of racial groups. They demanded an end to advertising on southern billboards and the cessation of recruitment campaigns. In response to the cooling atmosphere, a writer from the Newark Urban League cautioned that "we must be fair that my people do not get the mistaken idea that an attempt is being made to run all the colored people out of town."[58] But white officials countered with a so-called Negro drain on a shrinking pool of social services, and the press reported that the "Overseer of the Poor . . . contacted six Southern Governors in hopes of gaining their assistance in an anti-migrant scheme." Black workers accounted for a tiny number of skilled workers—559 non-white construction workers, 15 professional workers, 197 craftsmen, and more than 1,000 laborers, 1,100 service workers, and 3,800 female service, domestic, and laundry workers, according to the census reports. But white fears of labor competition continued unabated.[59]

In light of this and other sources of white hostility, what might be called a bifurcated or dual public sphere gained hegemony over the political terrain of the city. The city operated on a pattern in which marginal groups tended to withdraw into their own realm of cultural activity rather than move freely in and out of public spaces. By the 1910s Italian associations raised enough money to build a statue of Columbus in Washington Park, and they began to lobby for an official holiday to recognize the greatness of the Italian adventurer and supposed original discoverer of the nation. When immigration peaked in the 1910s and World War I brought news of Europe home to Newark, some fifteen thousand Italians marched through Newark on the anniversary of the liberation of Rome. The Catholic Church also served as the institutional foundation for public culture of Italian Americans, accompanied by such mainstays as the Red Cross and the Memorial Day parades.[60] Folk anthropologists and religious historians see these public rituals, especially the emotional commitment to Catholicism, as a tactical performance in the maintenance of "highly visible corporate identity by means of a very public religious life," and argue that "this is well understood by local politicians, who prominently march as invited guests."[61] As Italian Americans observed their faith they deftly wielded ethnicity and civic activities to advance their interests in the public sphere. Their stores and shops, churches and professional offices, marked with their names and those of their national heroes, served to imprint a distinctive Italian culture on the commercial thoroughfares.[62]

Every year, thousands of North Ward Italians marched along Wright Street, Pennsylvania Avenue, and Broad Street to Washington Park on Memorial Day. The generation of immigrants who preceded them, the Irish and Germans, had succeeded in the city by cooperating with the local political elites and pursuing their ethnic affinities throughout the neighborhoods.[63] To follow their pageants of empowerment, the Italian middle class built the Newark Opera House and paid tribute to their Italian civilization.[64] But every year Italian Newarkers also celebrated "I Am an American Day," with a parade and dinner at the Military Park Hotel or Branch Brook Park.[65] They convened a conference of the Nationality Groups that extolled the virtues of their theory of cultural pluralism by which "Americans from every corner of the globe belong" to the nation.[66] This was the dual function of what were known as the "civiceers"—to express pride in Italian heritage and to assimilate into the mainstream.[67]

After several decades of this kind of maneuvering for position in the political machine, the Italian Americans gained ground in the traditional ward system of loyal patrons and bosses.[68] While some were joining the First Ward Civic Clubs to promote political networks, the Columbus North Ward Club observed the golden anniversary of its incorporation.[69] They sponsored the movement to designate Columbus Day a national holiday, since its passage into law in Newark in the early twentieth century had attracted growing numbers of Italian residents to parades and festivities, reaching more than 15,000 in the 1940s. The Italian American mayor formed a Columbus Day celebration committee that met in the conference room at Newark City Hall, and chose this site for the destination of the parade, inviting the governor to address the crowd.[70] By the mid-1950s the congressman from Newark, Hugh Addonizio (who would win election to the office of mayor of Newark), announced that he would introduce a bill on the first day of Congress to declare Columbus Day a legal holiday, with the same status as Memorial Day or George Washington's Birthday. The legislation spearheaded the offense against the McCarran-Walter Act, trumping the legacy of anti-Italian nativism—what the headline termed "hate"—with ethnic pride. By 1955, Rep. Peter Rodino had shepherded the measure through committee and won its passage into law, designating October 12 a national holiday. In Newark, celebrations filled the streets with an estimated 25,000 Italian-American, many of whom were officially recognized as citizens from a different shore but now commanded substantive political clout in their new homes.[71]

But on the eve of the U.S. entry into World War II, the historical precedence for black advancement out of the ghetto and into the urban democracy proved not to be Italian American machine politics but Jewish American civic protest. With the rise of Adolph Hitler in Europe in the 1930s, the Jewish community gained new ground in the public sphere through challenging the status quo and utilizing radical forms of protest, particularly in pickets and rallies. From a base estimated at about 65,000 in the Central Ward, Jewish labor and religious leaders organized massive public demonstrations and boycotts of German-made goods in the department stores. With publicity from *The Jewish Chronicle* that focused opinion on the threat of anti-Semitism, hundreds of Jewish residents marched in parades and walked in pickets of Bamberger's and Kresge's department stores to demand they remove German products from their shelves, and sustained protests against Sears Roebuck, S. H. Kress, Hoffman LaRoche, and Kraft Food Company until they agreed to the terms of the international boycott. Some stores honored the boycotts, and some, like Woolworths, refused to stop purchasing German products. For the most part, Newark's Protestant elite remained indifferent, as did most African Americans, and not until late 1938 did the white civic leaders speak out against anti-Semitism and the rise of Hitler. The African American community did so somewhat later.[72]

In the first period of population growth, the era of Great Migration, the African American community suffered great burdens of political and economic discrimination, but rarely responded with organized protest or resistance like other ethnic groups. There were a few important exceptions. In 1938, black Newarkers picketed the Grand Five and Ten Cent Store on Springfield Avenue in an action sponsored by a group that is mentioned only briefly in the newspapers, the Newark Negro Council, for refusing to hire black sales personnel. This group was affiliated with the National Negro Congress, a communist and labor organization. The *Newark Herald News* ran a story celebrating the assertiveness of the militant protest, for "never before have Negro citizens been so solidly behind a movement for racial betterment." An observer of their successful picketing of a department store interviewed by the local African

American newspaper optimistically predicted the strike signified that now "the Negro at last is dropping his slave psychology."[73] In some ways, the pickets of the store, as well as a brief campaign for "Don't Buy Where You Can't Work," helped to energize the community. But at its height the group attracted no more than forty members and perhaps a couple of hundred supportive bystanders.

The nationalist historian Komozi Woodard has argued that the ghettos fostered the beginnings of black nationalism, and that "ghetto oppression had become a national oppression for black Americans."[74] Although many scholars locate the origins of an effective protest ideology, a culture or sphere that mobilized the community, in the great traditions of radicalism, in Newark the movement sustained remarkably classic political ideas. It would take the Second World War, with the massive propaganda campaigns disseminated in times of disruption and flux, to begin to challenge and reform the political consciousness of the Central Ward.[75]

2

Double V in New Jersey

As shipments of supplies to the allied forces left the Port of Newark, African Americans responded to mobilization for war in unexpected ways. The once passive civic leaders and society newspapers boldly invented what was known as the Double V, a cool turn of phrase that imagined a connection between victory against fascism abroad and the defeat of racial discrimination at home.[1] The slogan helped to give coherence to the first major civil rights demonstrations since Reconstruction—one led by an army of ordinary citizens who publicly called on the ideals of democracy to challenge inequality in accommodations and employment.[2] In some ways, the dynamics of the movement were as significant as the eventual achievement of legislation in a handful of states and some progress made by the federal government. In the past, the random activist or union organizer planned a march or convened a conference, dispersed information, and gathered support for reform. But the Double V campaign increased in scope and reach with the expansion of a new print culture that spontaneously awakened a powerful sense of entitlement among black Newarkers.

The rising consciousness prompted a resident of Long Branch, New Jersey, to write to the national headquarters of the NAACP to inform them of an untenable contradiction between the legislated rights of equal protection and his experience of discrimination. "We in New Jersey have a civic problem for which we would like suggestions on how to solve. Negroes in New Jersey are discriminated and segregated in public places in spit [sic] of the fact that we have a Civil Rights Bill."[3] He referred to the fact that the New Jersey legislature had prohibited discrimination in public accommodations on the basis of race.[4] But his civic problem was that the public appeared to endorse separate facilities, despite the law. In Newark the majority of theaters, department stores, restaurants and coffee shops, swimming pools and public baths, hospitals, and the downtown YWCA (but not the black Central Ward

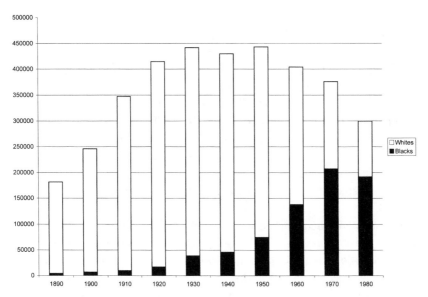

Fig. 2.1. Newark: Population and racial composition.

YWCA) publicly observed Jim Crow, the name that whites invented to designate segregation.[5]

By the beginning of the 1940s, once one or two individuals began to demonstrate against the refusal of service or separate seating areas, black editors and reporters ran their stories, in turn inspiring new initiatives in the community.[6] In the process, the African American newspapers activated currents of social change through new forms of circulation—and here the term refers to *circulation* in a double sense. First, on the eve of war, the circulation of newspapers had increased to an all-time high. In 1940, an average of 1,276,000 black newspapers was purchased each week; by 1943 the number was 1,643,311; and by the end of the War it was 1,809, 060.[7] It was estimated that four million black citizens read the weekly newspaper. The literacy rates for African Americans in Newark had climbed steadily since the turn of the century, and by 1930, 13 percent of white immigrants but only 5.7 percent of black Newarkers reported illiteracy.[8] In New Jersey, African Americans read the *Newark Herald* and the *New Jersey Afro-American*, both based in Newark.[9] Robert Queen, a native of the city, not only edited the *New Jersey Afro-American* but also the *Pittsburgh Courier*.[10] At the height of the war, reportedly 30 percent of African Americans in the nation read the newspapers in barrooms, barber shops, and at church socials as well as at fraternal and political organizations, contributing to additional possibilities for mobilization.[11]

The movement for Double V was sustained by another process of circulation: the complicated and expansive route through which the civil rights message circulated. The black print culture, by documenting discrimination first in cities, then in the nation, then on the battlefields of Europe or northern Africa, and back again, constructed a new public sphere. The rise of a black public sphere linked the immediacy of local violations of state equal accommodations laws to the nation and national propaganda, and this orientation against racism to the moral righteousness of the global war against fascism. The rise of the black newspapers and their popularity signaled the final ingredient in the making of a mass protest movement—that is, the arrival of a critical mass. Between 1940 and 1950, the black population of Newark increased to the point where it crossed the threshold from passive accommodation to mutual support in the face of Jim Crow, from 45,760 to 75,637, or from 10.7 percent to 17.2 percent of Newark residents.

Both leaders and editors exposed the violation of the principle of equality—and located the nation's capital as a site of and for political change. In 1941, the black labor leader A. Philip Randolph had visited the White House to meet with President Franklin Roosevelt, and threatened to lead a mass march on the city unless he delivered comprehensive anti-discrimination legislation, something like a federal civil rights bill. Rather than risk a disruptive protest on the capital mall, the president signed an executive order that banned discrimination in the defense industries. Several years earlier, however, a talented black performer had first protested for equality in the federal government, sealing a kind of route of identification in the popular imagination between the nation and the neighborhoods.[12] The elegant spectacle occurred on Easter Day 1939 in Washington, D.C., with the famous contralto Marian Anderson singing "God Bless America."

The travails of the opera singer began in February 1938 when the president of the Daughters of the American Revolution (DAR), the civic association dedicated to preserving the ethnic heritage of the descendants of New England patriots, rejected several written requests from the music department of Howard University on behalf of Anderson to reserve a performance date in Constitution Hall. The DAR had built the hall in 1929 to host their annual congresses (and to be otherwise available for rental by the community in the capital). It had not been reserved on the date that Anderson requested to perform. When they received her application, the DAR announced that they rented to "whites only."[13] After this incident, several officials from Howard University requested a room at Central High School in Washington, D.C., and this time the Board of Education rejected the application based on its policy of segregation in the public schools. Back in New Jersey, the *Newark Herald* reported that the eminent African American lawyer Charles Hamilton Houston organized a picket in D.C., and formed the "Marian Anderson Citizen's Council," which reportedly attracted 1,500 members.[14]

Newarkers devoured news of every turn in the plot of the Anderson controversy, charging that "the Daughters of the American Revolution barring Miss Marian Anderson from giving a recital in Constitution Hall in Washington, D.C. is by any line of civic reasoning, downright foolish, ludicrous and vulgar."[15] The leading black politico of the Central Ward, Irvine Turner (who would be elected the first black member of the city council), announced the first organizational meeting of his version of the Daughters of the American Revolution—one that was "improved" because it was reserved for the "Newark descendants of slaves who fought in the days of 76."[16] Even before the nation had officially entered the war, the black press already drew on foreign policy and events from abroad when it repeatedly referred to the DAR not as true Americans but as "fascist."[17] In Washington, it was Eleanor Roosevelt rather than President Roosevelt who challenged the DAR—she resigned from the organization, as did more than two hundred members that year. As a gesture of the president's support, the White House invited Anderson to sing at a special concert on the capital's mall, an event which the singer vividly described as a "crowd stretched in a great semicircle form the Lincoln Memorial around the reflecting pool." Instead of singing German opera at Constitution Hall as she had planned, Anderson chose to perform the national anthem, a portion of which was filmed for movie-house news reels and all of which was transmitted on radio across the nation. In effect she upstaged the DAR with her display of patriotism in a subtle message on the evils of racial segregation.[18]

If Anderson's performance served to raise the consciousness of the nation, the *New Jersey Afro-American* followed up by reporting on local stories about the glaring contradiction between the nation's goals and its record of racism. While the New York–based National Urban League referred to "the irony of American criticism of Hitlerian racial concepts . . . [when] the Negro's plight is unchanged,"[19] back in Essex County, a black physician, Dr. Hilton, complained that he was refused a cup of coffee at a local restaurant, Kriegl, owned by a Jewish proprietor. At a time when Jewish leaders in Newark had organized boycotts against German goods, the contradiction in Jewish racism was not lost on the city. The waiter, Lester Kurtzman, reportedly told the black customer, "I have orders. I won't serve you because you are colored." "Jews should be the last to practice discrimination on any other group," asserted the district attorney. The court awarded the plaintiff $100 in damages and $40 in counsel fees. Back in the days of accommodation, African Americans tolerated this kind of racism when they were refused service, despite equal-accommodations legislation. Now the militant black newspaper proclaimed that wartime patriotism dictated new customs: "This is not Germany but America."[20]

African American editors and reporters discovered that vivid discussions of anti-German propaganda helped to sustain local activism against discrimination, and so they ran more headlines, first-page features, and regular columns on the fascist implications of racial discrimination.[21] By informing their audience that "Hitler's *Mein Kampf* discriminated against Negroes" or that the Nazis had passed laws that prohibited intermarriage not unlike southern antimiscegenation statutes, black journalism turned Jim Crow practices into an evil enemy.[22] Local groups protested the segregation of Baltimore theaters, picketing daily "in protest against the Hitlerian technique."[23] In far-flung places such as a Wisconsin restaurant, a group of black travelers demanded equal treatment. "We speak for the masses of Negro Youth . . . before we go out on Foreign field to fight the Hitlers of our day, we want to get rid of all Hitlers around us."[24] By 1942, not only moderate newspaper editors but black radicals, including the increasingly effective Communist Party in the cities, joined a critique of racist capitalism with a call for unity and mobilization against fascism. The National Negro Congress, including thriving branches in New Jersey, were influenced by publications from the Workers Library on *The War and the Negro People* that echoed mainstream black journalism: "full unity must now be clinched speedily," but warned against "left anti-imperialist moods." The fact was that black radicals had changed position from labor agitation and protest of economic inequality to advancing an agenda of prowar antiracism, or in the words of a socialist treatise, "a war of black and white, of brown and yellow men and women against the 'racial' theories of the Nazis."[25]

The newspapers and periodicals not only promoted civil rights but trumpeted consumption for black Americans at a time when wages began to climb with the rising rate of black employment in wartime industries. As black women watched the performances of Marian Anderson, they observed a woman whose style and refinement were legendary. When black women demanded entrance to a civic club or equal treatment, they followed Anderson's example by protesting segregation in a place that rightfully belonged to all female residents of the city. Just as they consumed Anderson's elegant triumph over the racism of the white women in the DAR, they pioneered protests against discrimination in other venues frequented by women in the cities, particularly in the department stores. The major East Coast department store chain, Bamberger's, had employed black sales personnel since the 1920s, but a number of establishments on Broad Street in the downtown center randomly observed Jim Crow segregation, and the press reported that stores "refused to extend to blacks the usual courtesy of allowing patrons to try on garments before buying them."[26]

By 1947 Newark boasted a thriving retail sector, including the A & E Department Stores at Hawthorne; B. Altman & Co. at 576 Central Avenue in East Orange; Altman's Department Store on Broadway; and Bamberger's on Market. But the segregated stores included the Kresge's Department Store at 508 Broadway, and the 5 and 10 Cent Store on Broad Street.[27] Some of the local black journalists monitored the quality of services and protested where they could, reporting: "A subtle line in the S. S. Kresge . . . on the eve of the Christmas shopping rush when three young Newark socialiti sought to eat in the luncheonette of the store." After moving to a what appeared to be "reserved section," according to the story, "the three seated themselves at a table . . . when a waitress came over and said, 'You can't sit down.' " Like the waiter who refused to serve a cup of coffee to the black physician, the waitress blamed her superiors for the policy (either truthfully or lying from embarrassment). At one point the shoppers told the waitress that they had previously received service in the reserved section, and then the manager appeared and denied that he issued the order "not to serve colored." In response, the black newspaper's first line of attack was to expose these customs of racism, reporting in a headline: "Downtown Color Bar Revealed."[28]

Another line of attack was to send undercover reporters to test the policies of the public accommodations available to black customers. When the *New Jersey Afro-Herald* reported on another test of Kresge's policy the following week, "she [a black reporter] seated herself at the tables and was ignored." But later she was "seated at a table again and was served promptly." They interviewed the assistant manager and he claimed that they had served all customers but admitted that the store encouraged "colored to use the counter service in preference to table service." At another point, it was revealed that the store posted signs demanding that African Americans sit at the counters, because reportedly "the manager stated that bankers, office workers and downtown workers ate in the luncheonette whether they shopped in the store or not." Noting their assumption that Jim Crow served the civic duty of the city, the manager announced: "It is felt that for the good of all they should be discouraged from seeking table service." By the mid-1940s, an increasing number of black victims of discrimination were impelled to sue for their mistreatment in stores and restaurants. Indeed, in 1949 the famous performer Lena Horne sued Caruso's Restaurant, located in an Italian neighborhood on the north side, for refusing to seat her racially mixed party. The discourtesy was probably intended as a slight against the black community as a whole. Horne sued and won the $500 lawsuit.[29]

In the towns heavily impacted by wartime mobilization, the rising consciousness flowing back and forth from city to nation, from battlefield to home front, inspired more everyday protest against the indignities of Jim Crow. At least 20,000 black New Jerseyans enlisted in the armed forces, with some reporting to the local Newark draft board #22. Many African Americans were passed over for service, however, reportedly at twice the rate of rejection for whites.[30] When in service, African American soldiers confronted yet more Jim Crow barriers and wrote to the *Pittsburgh Courier, Chicago Defender* as well as the *New Jersey Afro-American* to complain about their experiences. From Sioux Falls, a black soldier reported on accommodations that were "very Jim Crow," and pleaded that his statement "gets into the AFRO and all the colored papers right away. It may just be the very thing to help us."[31]

Black soldiers also complained of segregated entertainment at the USO facilities and in the canteens, not only in bases at home but also in Europe and Africa. In Newark, plans to build a segregated USO drew crowds of picketers, and the group reportedly won a number of concessions from the military, including the promise that the next facility would employ an integrated staff. In response to this kind of local and national protest against the Jim Crow army, the armed forces gradually implemented a new policy that prohibited the racial segregation of entertainment facilities.[32] The deepening patriotism among civilians and soldiers alike reinforced the multifaceted black consciousness that continued to demand enforcement of equality before the law, and by 1945 the victory against the evils of fascism and Nazism inspired President Truman to issue executive order 9881, outlawing racial and ethnic discrimination in the armed forces. The president also appointed a civil rights commission that introduced a number of domestic initiatives spelled out in the pamphlet *To Secure Our Rights,* while back in New Jersey the papers reported that Republican senator Albert Hawkes had proposed, on the floor of the U.S. Congress, a federal law to ban lynching.[33]

Ultimately as influential as President Harry Truman's legislative initiatives, none of which survived conservative southern opposition and filibustering in Congress, were the liberal state legislatures outside of the South in New York, Massachusetts, Pennsylvania, Minnesota, and Illinois. In New Jersey in 1938, an African American member of the state assembly who represented Newark and Essex County, Frank S. Hargraves, introduced a new bill to create the Urban Colored Commission, to be charged with investigating the health and living conditions of African Americans. Hargraves was a physician who migrated from North Carolina and wanted the new commission to examine civil rights violations. He later helped to legislate a bill, armed with strong mechanisms of enforcement, to outlaw racial discrimination in public accommodations. He modeled it on the Fair Employment Practices Commission (FEPC) legislation that President Franklin Roosevelt had signed several years before. Many white liberal and African American legislators rightly emphasized the FEPC as a priority for workers, and Hargraves's Urban Colored Commission closely monitored complaints of discrimination in wartime industries. According to their records, the commission considered complaints of discrimination against Monsanto, Warner Webster, United Parcel Service, and Newark Metal Manufacturing, among others, and consulted with the National Urban League.[34] In 1942 Hargraves helped to establish the Division Against Discrimination (DAD), which would be responsible for investigating grievances against segregated public accommodations.

The first offices of the DAD were located in the same building that housed the Urban Colored Commission in downtown Newark. From this base in the social welfare community, the DAD kept records of complaints and investigated cases. For example, in its first year the organization recorded complaints from "46 Negroes and 2 Jews," and the numbers climbed to over one thousand by the end of the 1940s, many of which were resolved by entering into a kind of binding arbitration.[35] When the parties in the matter proved unable to reconcile, the DAD employed an attorney to sue in the state courts. Although some historians attribute the remarkably rapid expansion and enforcement of equal accommodations to the later Omnibus Civil Rights Act in 1949, which combined antidiscrimination with employment protections, Frank Hargraves, not Grace Freeman of the later legislation, deserves priority. Hargraves pioneered passage of the first modern "civil rights" act, a term publicly associated with equal accommodations, back in 1945. In fact, when Freedman's legislation of 1949 came to the floor, some black leaders were opposed because they cautioned that the focus on employment discrimination could distract from the enforcement of equal accommodations. Since the days of pickets of the local department stores sponsored by the National Negro Congress, the massive and persistent Double V protests sustained by the press, and the work of the legislature, the black leaders and liberal allies maintained a long view of the black struggle for equality: "No phase of discrimination directed at the State's urban colored population has a wider or more dangerous influence than discrimination in public places."[36]

At the same time, a white reaction and populist efforts rose up to defend the old racial customs. Much of this racism surfaced in the civic culture—amid and between popular understandings of the letter of the law and publicly contested meanings of neighborly obligation. Many whites resisted a discourse on racial equality in public accommodations, and many attempted to preserve local ways as legitimate civic custom. The dimensions of this civic contest symbolically congealed in the politics of blood donations during and after wartime mobilization. In a nation at war, blood represented a dense symbolic site—perhaps *the* civic material—something that conjured up the connections between family and soldier, service and duty. The symbol of blood triggered a chain of meanings—corps, corporal, corpuscles—constituting the metonym of the national corps and the patriotic body. But this civic material ultimately revealed the dimensions of the racialized body, either honored by inclusion in the nation as reward for service or excluded from the public realm by observance of civic racism. For whites, especially white women, joining volunteer efforts of the Red Cross constituted a major mobilization effort, with plans announced in the Italian press to gain 20,000 members in the city. African American civilians desired to transport their blood overseas, save injured soldiers, and fortify the struggle to save democracy, yet whites sought to thwart their participation by rejecting the blood of black people.[37]

The Red Cross was founded in the late nineteenth century to rescue victims of disasters or emergencies, and the first blood bank was established in England in 1921. Soon, a New York operation opened and the head offices moved to Washington, D.C., to assist the allied war efforts by the beginning of the 1940s. The African American research physician Charles Drew headed the blood plasma collection division. Ironically, Drew was seriously injured in an automobile accident in North Carolina after the war, refused medical attention when he arrived by ambulance in the emergency room, and died from complications.[38] Equally if not more important than the actual plasma were the activities and associations of the Red Cross, because it was a major venue for voluntarism, and perhaps the most important civic institution, except for the church, for the Italian American community.[39] Italian American newspapers granted the organization free advertisement as a public service, featuring ads in English and Italian. The essence of the Red Cross was the feeling of connection between local members and the soldiers overseas; the Newark chapter advertised its annual blood drive with the slogan, "Your Red Cross is at His Side."[40] During the war, some 9,000 Newark volunteers donated over 2 million hours of service and 59,133 pints of blood; so-called Gallon Club members numbered 531.[41] White schoolchildren constructed picture books and participated in letter-writing campaigns with children in European nations.[42]

So important was the Red Cross to the public life of the nation that the NAACP continually pressed and negotiated with the national board to adopt a policy of integration. Before the war, black leadership attacked discrimination in Red Cross operations in rescue and emergency relief, and by 1939 the Red Cross announced its infamous policy of refusing to collect blood from African American volunteers, claiming this was the preference of commanders in both the army and navy.[43] In response, black newspapers and the NAACP deluged the Red Cross with complaints, and they soon amended their original policy by deciding to collect plasma on the basis of segregation. Despite pleas in the press and from leaders for total integration, the Red Cross announced that "in

Fig. 2.2. The Italian American community actively supported the Red Cross and granted it free advertising space in the community newspaper, running announcements in both English and Italian. (The *Italian Tribune*, March 1952)

deference to the wishes of those for whom the plasma is being provided, the blood will be processed separately so that those receiving transfusion may be given plasma from blood of their own race." The blood issue was controversial enough that it split the leadership—the highest ranking black officer of the Army, General Benjamin Davis sanctioned separate facilities—but clearly the rank and file demanded nothing less than equal treatment.[44] The NAACP decided to fight against the practice of separation of blood, which they soon connected to an ongoing protest against Red Cross service clubs for soldiers in Great Britain.[45] Meanwhile, the Newark chapter of the American Red Cross rarely referred to the intense conflicts over segregation in printed advertisements for programs, and the annual reports celebrated a series of successful blood drives, collecting a record high of 14,496 pints of blood in 1945. Their publications featured glossy pictures of Red Cross activities, but pictured only whites. The one exception concerned the blood plasma activities, where the editors published a photo of a black nurse lying beside a white nurse, dressed in immaculate white uniforms, donating blood plasma. The photo seemed to want to reassure its readers that the Red Cross employed both black nurses and white nurses but that plasma collection remained separate.[46]

Some whites, including high-ranking officers in the armed forces, supported the policy of Jim Crow blood because it would cause a shortage of African American plasma, offering yet another justification to curtail the enlistment of black soldiers.[47] Writing to the NAACP, the director the Red Cross argued that segregation represented the will of the majority and that acceding to their wishes fulfilled the requirements of the

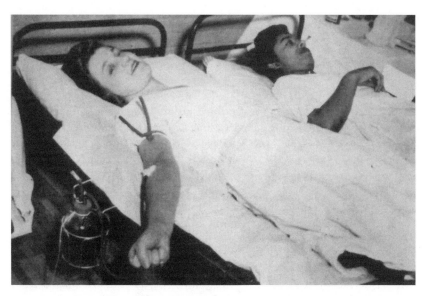

Fig. 2.3. The Newark Red Cross traditionally ignored the issue of race and the controversy surrounding blood donation, except for this rare photo of an African American nurse. It reassured readers that both black and white staff are available to perform the transfusion of blood in accordance with the policy of racial segregation. (*Annual Report of the Red Cross of Newark,* 1943)

democracy. In response, the president of the NAACP, Walter White, picked up the Double V rhetoric, and replied that even the president rejected "a doctrine [which] savors more of Hitler's theory of a 'master race' than of a democracy."[48] Yet in conducting a major blood drive in 1945 for 200,000 pints of blood, their publicity hedged on the question of accepting African American blood at all.[49] In protest of their exclusion from this mobilization for war and in rejection of biological racism, African Americans collected blood through alternative organizations, such as the Blood Transfusion Betterment Association of Newark, and from 1944 to 1945 a mobile unit from New York visited the state's industrial sites, including New Jersey Bell, Clark Thread Company, and Ballantine Brewery, for African American donors.[50] In the print culture, black opinion challenged the stigma on blood and asserted that no "factual basis" existed to support segregated plasma, particularly since blood flowed freely between the races in civilian transfusions.[51] The NAACP discredited Red Cross policy as "absurd and unscientific prejudiced" and as "intolerable at a time when we are fighting Hitlerism with its grotesque race theory . . . which happens to be in accord with the nonsense about racial blood."[52]

But many whites preferred the separation of the blood—even relative liberals who distanced themselves from the policy's connotation of biological racism. By not mixing the blood of men abroad, and by repressing the spectacle of the white nurse giving plasma to the black soldier, the whiteness of the nation was sustained even in the turmoil of war and ethnic genocide. To a large extent, the national prohibition against miscegenation remained untouched by the Double V rhetoric. After allied victory abroad, black soldiers were marrying German women, who birthed "Brown Babys [*sic*]."[53] "Hitler called them 'semi-aped,' but German frauleins find Negro GIs likeable and human," trumped the papers. The black press also wondered, "But what ideas about equality will the Negro GI bring home?" If miscegenation was tolerated in Germany, would it return to the United States, influence black veterans and their black supporters, and lead to black protest against segregation at home, or even result in a surge in black/white marriages? World War II introduced America's race problems to Britain, and its response varied from tolerance to some racism, but it rarely proved more progressive than stateside.

When the Red Cross officially ceased segregating domestic plasma in 1944, the local politics of civic segregation intensified. The South had always obsessively forbidden black/white sexual relations, and now, several years after the war, the NAACP discovered that in some cases the Red Cross was still labeling blood plasma with the race of donors to appease southern members.[54] Even before the anti-Hitlerism discourse so prominent in the black newspapers and the national repulsion against Nazi racism, liberal social scientists such as Franz Boas had discredited the argument, leveled by southerners since the heyday of nineteenth-century American ethnologists, that blacks were biologically inferior. The Double V campaign had further persuaded broad sections of the public to repudiate civic racism, and even southern white supremacists downplayed biology when justifying a return to their caste order.[55] Among white ethnics in the cities, many supported equality before the law and equal treatment of customers and even workers, at least to the extent that they sacrificed little and benefited much from the new enforcement of fair employment and equal accommodations. But Italian Americans and other immigrants refused to give up their whiteness, which, as recent arrivals, insecure civic engagers, and in-between citizens, remained a precious resource.[56] According to sociologists at the time, the leading indicator of ethnic assimilation was the rate of marriage of immigrants outside their ethnic group, and the group that had seemed to cherish most their allegiance to the Red Cross, the Italian American community, demonstrated a remarkable preference for marrying their own kind. In a study comparing Italian, Romanian, and Slovak immigrants and in a detailed analysis of Italians in Newark, researchers found that they desired marriage within the group.[57] Second to their own ethnicity, Italians preferred northern Europeans—British, Germans, French—and, according to a dissertation on Italian Newark, "Jews, Negroes, and Orientals were definitely excluded from their choices."[58]

Another civic material that complicated further advancements of Double V ideology against civic inequality and in which urban northerners still deferred to the southern ways of Jim Crow concerned public waters. This time the question of racial mixture raised more than a symbolic threat of blood mixture, for desegregating swimming pools involved the potential for extraordinary intimacy between the races. Public bathing was among the most significant formal rituals that citizens shared in the civic culture. The sport of swimming was slow to organize in the United States, and was promoted in the 1940s primarily by civic organizations, including "Athletic clubs, YMCA, YWCA, educational institutions, national associations for boys and girls, the American Red

Cross." "It is a duty to teach personal hygiene, sex hygiene, community hygiene, first aid, and swimming," one guide explained. A 1958 volume of *Physical Education* published a story, "How I Have Included Christian Emphasis on Teaching Young Boys to Swim," by Richard Peterson, who testified that teaching swimming to young boys instilled the virtues of Christianity.[59] Most swimming pools had arrived in the United States at the height of the Gilded Age, built on the estates of the Robber Barons, such as George Gould's Georgian Court pool in Lakewood, New Jersey. In the postwar era, a growing industry installed pools in affluent suburban homes and municipal parks, supplying the intensely competitive swimming clubs located in areas that attracted black and white customers. In postwar culture, the swimming pool was frequently featured in Hollywood films and was associated in the popular imagination with the so-called pin-up girl; in several popular Hollywood films the sex symbol Marilyn Monroe modeled swimsuits at poolside, expanding the boundaries of acceptable sexual display to encounters with more explicit sexual fantasy.[60]

Against this rising tide, New Jersey's beaches and bathing houses enforced racial separation and inequality. Since the turn of the century, the city of Newark had provided public bathing facilities for residents without modern plumbing, seven of which remained open into the 1940s, including the Clifton Avenue Baths and Montgomery Street Baths in white ethnic neighborhoods.[61] During the war, some complained of the poor conditions of the Morris Street and the Wilson Street pools, and around 1945 the Bureau of Public Baths reported that four new swimming pools had been built, one of which was designated for use by African Americans, the Hayes Park West Pool. It was built in honor of Freddi French, a "Negro Mess attendant" who died overseas. These modern amusements were popular during the sweltering, humid Newark summers, and receipts collected in 1945 totaled $19,176.[62]

During these years, despite the construction of a new civic culture of equality and the legal enforcement of equal treatment for African Americans, at least in public accommodations by the state government, whites in New Jersey employed various methods to maintain de facto segregation in the waters. Before the courts ruled definitively on the matter, pools and beaches observed systems of Jim Crow eerily similar to the days of Nazism. The City of Long Branch attempted to segregate municipal beaches by requiring bathers to buy permits and wear actual badges or tags. Black bathers discovered outside of the area indicated by their official tags, were fined. Although the city justified the system in the name of controlling beach congestion, the black newspaper believed that the plan was nothing less than Jim Crow segregation.[63] In response, African Americans in Long Branch founded a branch of the NAACP, and an angry member, after applying to use the two beaches reserved for whites, filed suit to challenge the ordinance. She prevailed against the segregated beach in the Supreme Court of New Jersey the following year, but the Court rejected the ordinance on narrow grounds.[64] Thus some pools continued to discriminate on the basis of race and color. Nonplussed, black residents planned an excursion to the beach on the Fourth of July, "without fear of being shunted off to some Jim Crow section."[65]

Across the state, similar local contests over public obligations in the civic realm arose from something as innocent as children's play. In a southern New Jersey town, when three colored boys bathed, their unattended clothes were doused with water by someone opposed to their presence. The press interpreted the incident as an act that "was evidently done to impress their [group], in going in the pool was displeasing to some persons," and reported that "the recreation commission closed the pool." Here the writer espoused a simple but incisive theory of public ceremonial democracy: "Public swimming pools owned and operated by the public have from time to time, been the source of so-called 'racial difficulties.' The difficulties arise as long as some selfish, ignorant, bigoted individuals will try to use the property of the public, as if it were their individual property."[66] By the mid-1940s, left-oriented youth groups influenced by the Double V campaigns, such as an organization called American Youth Democracy based in New York, came to New Jersey and challenged pool segregation in Paterson.[67]

In Asbury Park, about an hour's drive from Newark, the coming of war had brought defense industries and a small stream of African American migration, and in response white residents attempted to impose segregation in housing, in the Red Cross, and in swimming pools. But the black residents protested that they "resent being set apart as does any racial group." They organized to protest the operation of a Red Cross plasma center in town, when they had been told "the Red Cross does not welcome colored blood donors. We aren't taking blood from any colored people today."[68] When they organized a local chapter of the NAACP, whites and blacks in Asbury Park had to decide on the issue of integrated public swimming. Whites again preferred segregation,

Fig. 2.4. In the postwar era, the new Human Relations Commission issued reports on interracial cooperation, featuring a photo of black boys swimming with white boys. The accompanying caption called Newark "lucky" for escaping the race riots that erupted in Detroit and other cities. But the editors stayed clear of depicting any sort of physical intimacy between blacks and whites of the opposite sex. (*Report of the Newark Human Relations Commission,* 1953)

whereupon local black residents filed suit.[69] The state Supreme Court of New Jersey continued to hear cases on segregation in swimming, and in the late-1940s it finally ruled definitively that pools and private clubs must integrate.[70] Because suburbanization drew white residents out of Newark and municipal finances dipped, in the mid-1960s the public pools were closed, leaving inner city youth without adequate recreational facilities.[71]

At the end of the war, African Americans and white liberals felt a burst of pride at the accomplishments of the Double V campaign. In

1947 the mayor addressed a citizenry that "prided itself upon the fact we have been free of any so-called 'flare-ups' in the domain of interracial relations." Newark enjoyed the benefits of harmonious race relations in the public sphere, particularly in comparison to the outbreak of racial violence in Harlem and Detroit in 1943. In 1953 the Newark Human Relations Commission released its annual report with a photo of black and white boys in a public swimming pool. Side by side, two youngsters dove in, cheered by an interracial contingent of friends on the deck. To picture swimmers of the opposite sex as well as different race—of black men and white women—still proved beyond the limits of permissible representations, for at all costs the city wished to avoid racial disturbances. Although random complaints showed that there were areas of noncompliance and dissatisfaction, the mayor assured all that Newarkers had "cooperated splendidly in civic endeavors and patriotic demands."[72]

3

The Construction of Integration

From the end of the war until the conclusion of the civil rights movement in the 1960s, the efforts of African American citizens to enjoy civic equality foundered at the gates of the family residence. Mutual enjoyment of public facilities—the restaurant or swimming pool—was infrequently the site of racial conflict any longer, in part because the law definitively demanded access for all. When the occasional proprietor attempted to discriminate, like the case in 1967 of a white barber who refused to cut the hair of a black customer, the state supreme court rejected his appeal on the basis of equal protection (holding that barber licenses subjected them to state antidiscrimination statutes).[1] But white New Jerseyans, and most Americans, refused any further mingling of the races in peacetime, and a nation at war with communism proved less amenable to the sort of strenuous dissent by blacks that had fueled the 1940s Double V movement. The white foes of equality resisted the directive to integrate children in the public schools handed down by the Supreme Court in the landmark decision *Brown v. Board of Education,* which overturned the late-nineteenth-century principle of separate but equal. To maintain de facto segregation of the putatively private sphere, most whites kept African Americans from their neighborhoods.

In New Jersey and in many leading industrial states, the politics of white supremacy reconstructed the metropolitan landscape, dividing the dense inner city (dropping to only 16 percent of the state of New Jersey), including Newark, Trenton, Camden, and Jersey City, from the modern urban fringe (which increased to 59.9 percent of the state). The city of Newark still boasted a population of more than 400,000, but the numbers had already started to decline, and the suburban population in surrounding Essex County had increased eight times in the postwar years.[2] These suburbs encompassed eighty-eight square miles of new residential development that attracted thousands who fled the cities.[3] Across the nation, publicly backed initiatives and private investment financed more

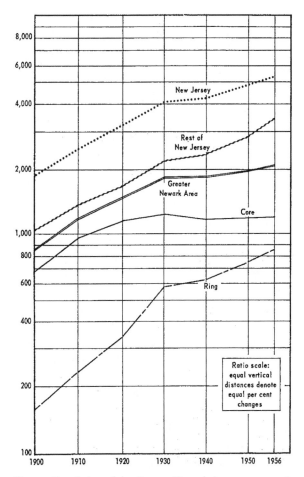

Fig. 3.1. Population of the Greater Newark Area, 1900–1956.
Sources: 1900–1950, Census of Population: 1956, New Jersey, U.S. Dept. of Commerce; 1956, GNA, Rutgers-BERC.

than 20,000 firms that constructed 400,000 dwelling units reportedly worth more than $2 billion.[4] As whites left behind the social crises of cities and the rampant corruption in government, they passed new laws in the suburbs that promoted the construction of more residences, prioritized low taxes and minimal regulation, and encouraged commercial projects under a more libertarian system called "home rule."[5]

The suburban boom promised to fulfill the American Dream of the good life, but now cities were "less desirable as a place to live," in the parlance of urban planning.[6] Since the 1940s, the State of New Jersey had forecast uneven growth due to the relocation of manufacturing out of cities, the growth of dynamic service industries in suburbs, and the surging retail sales in regionally based shopping malls.[7] In 1956 the state projected an increase in per capita income in the Greater Newark area, including both suburbs and the so-called inner city, of 12 percent. But when they subtracted the income averages for the inner city population, the growth rate increased to 39 percent. The suburbs enjoyed a 37.3% increase in per capita income, while that in the inner city declined by 6.2 percent, pulling down the income of the state to 4 to 5 percent below the national average.[8] The wealthy, in the meantime, got richer, as suburban incomes increased at the rate of 150 percent of the national average, while workers and the poor in the core of Newark were left with only a 13.7 percent increase.[9] According to statistics from the New Jersey Department of Labor, 70 percent of the state's population with the lowest income lived in the urban core.[10] Postwar prosperity was symbolized by "brisk, modernistic business districts . . . [and] middle-class self-sufficiency" but the inner city suffered from "moderate absolute losses in population, number of dwelling units, and employment." This dualism of white suburb and black city was featured in a long essay published in a 1956 issue of *Atlantic Monthly* that described Newark as "a vast scrawl of Negro slums and poverty, a festering center of disease, vice, injustice, crime."[11]

Into the postwar years, as the conversion of the national economy followed unequal paths of growth and decline, the fate of the cities hung in the balance. In response to worsening conditions, in 1949 the Congress passed landmark federal legislation that allocated massive spending (two-thirds matching funds and low-interest loans) for renewal of commercial zones and new housing stock for older and deteriorating areas which planners declared to be blighted. But the operation of race relations and political interests varied from city to city, mitigating the success and impact of the new policies. Newark's housing stock had slowly expanded since the 1920s, when an average of 3,250 privately financed dwellings went up each year, but construction slowed to less than 300 units annually during the economic collapse caused by the Great Depression. Under the New Deal, the federal government financed more new housing in part to ameliorate social problems and relieve local governments from excessive costs of "police and fire protection."[12] By the 1940s, the Federal Housing Administration (FHA) allocated more than

$1 million to New Jersey (second only to California), which ranked seventh in loans to banks and builders (just behind large states like California and New York).[13] At the beginning of urban renewal in Newark, the number of buildings lacking hot water or a private toilet and bath was more than 7,200 of 124,000 dwellings, and black residents undoubtedly bore the brunt of these deplorable conditions.[14] As black migration from the South increased into the 1950s, the newcomers arrived poised to take advantage of a vastly improved infrastructure. But they confronted discrimination in most types of housing, which perpetuated patterns of geographical separation established in the Great Migration. Despite the new obstacles to the good life, despite lax or nonexistent enforcement of equal protection laws in the North, black protest had faded into the past of Double V, replaced by an insidious spread of segregation and acquiescence to prejudice. In the era of affluence, a token segment of minorities advanced onto the liberal terrain of tolerance and benefited from improvement in racial attitudes. Black Newarkers negotiated new opportunities for wealth and class mobility, but they did so in the midst of a growing black underclass that lost opportunity.[15]

If postwar liberalism and prosperity promised infinite possibilities, in the 1940s and 1950s, even the most advantaged black Newarkers still confronted obstacles of race. By 1945 an estimated 5,600 African American veterans had demobilized in Newark, approximately 90 percent of whom intended to reside there permanently. Some 38 percent of respondents to a federal government survey took up residence in rented rooms, trailers, or cabins, some with their relatives, and some were "doubled up" with another family and other temporary situations. When they applied for the housing that the federal government constructed for wartime workers, most of the local municipal administrators had reserved the better units, such as Bradley Court (with a rent of $46.48 per month), for whites only, and assigned the black veterans a lower grade, with the poorest units, such as the F.D.R. Homes (with a rent of $35.37 per month). These varying conditions corresponded with a racial gap in the average income (2,738.00) of residents in the housing. The all-white Bradley Court reported the highest average income ($3,369) and the F.D.R. Homes reported the lowest ($2,338).[16] Because of the severity of the housing shortage (the city vacancy rate was less than 1 percent), black veterans had few options, and the federal government's own reports implicitly acknowledged segregation in housing markets when calculating occupancy by categorizing *"units available to Negroes."* And

	Developments	Units
Belleville	9	289
Bloomfield	17	757
Cedar Grove	22	905
Livingston	25	1418
Maplewood	1	20
Montclair	1	24
Newark	2	24
North Caldwell	1	31
Nutley	5	76
Roseland	1	20
Short Hills	1	5
Verona	12	421
West Caldwell	10	366
West Orange	24	915

Fig. 3.2. Veterans Administration in fifteen Essex County municipalities: Housing developments by VA mortgages. *Source: Newark News* (4-24-56)

even with new federal programs that at least as formal policy were nondiscriminatory, no government agency had directly challenged the segregation that the reports documented. When federal investigators asked black veterans hypothetically if they planned to rent or buy, 46 percent chose the latter, yet they had low expectations. Only 9 percent, or 540 African American veterans' families, believed that they could actually overcome the innumerable obstacles to buying a new home.[17]

In the meantime, both black and white veterans enjoyed their stay in modern public housing units—at least until their incomes exceeded the official maximum and they were required to move into private housing. But when both black and white veterans applied to the Veterans Administration for loans to buy single-family residences, black applicants faced additional forms of discrimination. Most veterans believed they could carry a mortgage for $6,000 and make monthly payments of $45 (including taxes, fire insurance, and utilities), but few of the respondents actually purchased homes, in part because the Veterans Administration had always tolerated racial discrimination.[18] As financial analysts noted in a study of banks making VA or VA-FHA combination loans, a program which had declined because of competition from private lenders, the VA did not collect information on the racial background either of applicants for mortgages or of the successfully financed home buyer. But an investigation conducted by the *Newark News* in 1956 exposed racial bias in the lending practices of the VA in Essex County. The survey showed that the majority of recipients of the loans resided in two all-white areas or zones (totaling some 2,700 loans to buyers).[19] By contrast, African American home buyers received only fifty-five loans; in every case the loan was made to purchase property near the core or inner city, rather than in the convenient and economically mobile suburbs.[20]

Yet even when prospective black buyers were able to obtain a loan, most white realtors rarely showed them nice properties in the white neighborhoods. They were taken instead to the declining or transitional areas, which in turn many banks had considered too risky to finance. Since the 1930s, federal loan agents had downgraded such areas in Newark (the Home Owners Loan Corporation assigned them the lower ratings of B, C, and D) because of the immigrant background and the interracial character of the environs. Moreover, in every major city undergoing renewal, particularly in the transitional areas of racial diversity, many whites had already fled to the all-white suburbs. Whites left areas of blight, a designation similar to an area that is condemned and signified deterioration. They also affirmed the principle of civic racism that black move-ins into white areas constituted moral and racial contamination. If black move-ins compromised the civic value of a neighborhood, many whites feared a commensurate decline of their property value.[21] Some whites also sought to escape what were perceived as uppity black neighbors. In a collection of salesman logs for the popular suburban tract development Levittown in Camden, New Jersey, a white buyer reportedly questioned the motives of those who "seem to get a great deal of satisfaction out of going where they are not wanted."[22] White home buyers reported various fears and anxieties about racial integration—"Doesn't want any Negro next door," "Cancellation because of Negro situation," and "Very disturbed about the situation"—and even forfeited their deposits or contracts rather than move into integrated neighborhoods. In the words of one white visitor of Levittown, racial integration always promised "to mushroom in one place and begin a systematic downgrading of a neighborhood."[23]

To protect their investment, established white neighborhoods agreed to abide by various restrictive covenants or clauses in deeds that prohibited an owner from transferring property to buyers with specific characteristics, usually that of an undesirable minority racial or religious background. In a pivotal but at the time little noticed decision, *Shelly v. Kraemer* (1948), the Supreme Court had ruled restrictive covenants to be unenforceable. Historians of housing have documented their continuation and prevalence in suburban growth, dubbing the long-term effects of the illegal observance of these and other racial inequalities "American apartheid."[24] While sellers and buyers of suburban homes cooperated in racial exclusion despite legal obligations to the contrary, for many years the white landlords in the cities also openly discriminated against black renters, including documented cases of racially segregated listings in newspapers and real estate agencies that advertised a "white couple preferred" or an apartment for a "Colored G.I."[25] Although research into the FHA has demonstrated a level of complicity with local Jim Crow, especially federal deference to southern housing agencies, the Newark Housing Authority (NHA) followed the intentions spelled out by the Supreme Court in *Shelley*.[26] While the FHA dispatched its own accountants to investigate racial bias in loan practices in New Jersey, the director of NHA, Louis Danzig, announced that "integration" was "the official policy" and promised to base selection of applicants on "need" rather than race (or on other illegal distinctions or religious belief, color, national origins, protecting the immigrants from Southern and Eastern Europe).[27] If the local compliance reflected politicians' interests in gaining federal dollars and thus the doling-out of patronage, black residents accrued the benefits of equal protection. In the early 1950s, the NHA reported that "nine Negro families are being moved" into formerly all-white residences, and that other families were integrated into Hyatt Court in the Ironbound Section, and Stephen Crane Village, and Bradley Court on the west side. The three predominantly black projects (F.D.R. Homes, Felix Fuld, and Baxter Terrace) were officially opened to white residents, but relatively few white families moved there because of an overall decline in their demand for public housing.[28] The *Newark News* reported that African Americans, less than 15 percent of the population, occupied between 23 and 24 percent of the 3,009 units by 1950.[29] Five years later, according to a social science study of urban renewal, "there were more Negroes than whites in public housing, and the flight of white tenants showed no signs of slackening." By the 1960s, the ratios changed from 77 percent white to 66 percent black occupancy in seventeen projects.[30]

Most whites of the upwardly mobile classes planned to buy a tract house or better, and leave for the suburbs. Yet they continued to support federally subsidized urban renewal projects and public housing in the old neighborhoods in the city. The veterans and wartime workers had enjoyed their stay in the modern units, and turned over the premises to civilians who showed some sort of special need, such as families displaced from blighted neighborhoods by ongoing renewal projects, or large families with low incomes (households that moved out earned an average annual income of $3,221 and those who moved in earned $1,850).[31] Five years after the wartime workers had moved out, most of the 11,627 residents were from moderate and low-income backgrounds.[32] There was an increasing concentration of black residents in particular areas that foreshadowed the rise of all-black housing projects and laid the foundation for the so-called Second Ghetto that had arisen not from discrimination in rentals but from the housing agencies that planned new buildings in ghettos, rather than dispersed them more evenly across many diverse neighborhoods.

For a few potentially transformative years, however, the new developments and constructions positively impacted the racial and class geography of many cities.[33] Newark's housing units offered the low-income renter an extraordinary improvement over the dilapidated stock in Central Ward neighborhoods. The policy of nondiscrimination caused the dispersal of black residents from the poorest ghettos into predominantly white neighborhoods, providing unprecedented access to first-class municipal services (garbage removal, traffic and street lights, parks and recreation), and the best schools. With the completion of a half-dozen more constructions and more integration, the composition of several working-class or lower-middle class medium-sized neighborhoods achieved something approaching racial balance. In other words, the percentage of African Americans in these once predominantly white neighborhoods gradually increased to closely match the black percentage in the city population. By 1957 Newark's black population increased to 18 percent of the city; to approximately 17 percent in Roseville; and 24 percent in North Newark. The figures for the Jewish neighborhoods in the South and West Wards proved even more promising. It was primarily in the wealthy neighborhoods where whites adamantly rejected the integration of black residents (whether or not they moved into public housing or attempted to purchase a single-family residence), and not surprisingly few black residents moved into the best Protestant and old immigrant neighborhoods such as Vailsburg.[34]

Early on at least, most Italian Americans supported the construction of public housing, although not necessarily the accompanying administrative commitment to racial integration. At a time when whites greatly exceeded—and the foreign-born almost equaled—the number of

Neighborhoods	Percentage Negro, 1950	Percentage Negro, 1958
North Ward		
Forest Hill	4.00	2.00
North Newark	12.00	24.00
Roseville	4.00	17.00
East Ward		
Central Business	35.00	46.00
Iron Bound	7.00	14.00
Central Ward	63.00	85.00
West Ward		
Vailsburg	10.00	43.00
South Ward		
South Broad	20.00	61.00
Clinton Hill	8.00	44.00
Weequahic	2.00	16.00

Fig. 3.3. Dispersion of the Negro population in Newark, 1950–1958.
Source: Harold Kaplan, *Urban Renewal Politics: Slum Clearance in Newark*, p. 149.

African Americans (with the census recording a foreign-born population of 70,600 compared to a black population of 74,200), most whites could feel safe and secure in supporting more public housing, especially if they believed that City Hall tacitly approved various mechanisms to segregate unwelcome groups. Additionally, more Italian Americans had landed key positions in the housing agency, and foreign-born males accounted for more than 64,000 construction workers. The Italian American community envisioned new construction to house the future waves of immigration, and in the 1950s, both the City Council and U.S. congressmen lobbied for the easing of citizenship requirements to facilitate immigrants' applications for public-housing.[35] Some whites objected to renewal plans because they threatened to destroy historic buildings and community institutions, and historians of the Italian American community have argued that they felt "uprooted and displaced, virtually returned to immigrants in their new homeland" by renewal projects, and that many mourned the loss of commercial life along Eighteenth Avenue, with its shops, restaurants, and bakeries. But political leaders reminded the community that in exchange for "local color," they would enjoy "first class housing," with all the modern conveniences of toilets, plumbing, and central heat.[36]

The construction of integrated public housing fostered a liberal commitment to racial integration that particularly influenced two predominantly Jewish areas, Weequahic/Dayton Street (59 percent Jewish) and

Clinton Hill (42 percent Jewish). Many of these older Jewish families had originally immigrated into the Central Ward, established ties with the African American community, and felt a sense of affinity with the hard knocks of ghetto life and lower status in the civic culture. As one government study speculated, perhaps too optimistically, Jews and blacks "empathized religiously as God's suffering servants and secularly as oppressed minorities."[37] According to a leading scholar on black-Jewish relations in Newark, Sherry Ortner, Jews "wanted to be Jewish but they also wanted to fit in," and by the mid-1950s there were no "groups socially higher than the Jews of Weequahic." Looking back at the mobility of their parents, a cohort of Jewish children who came of

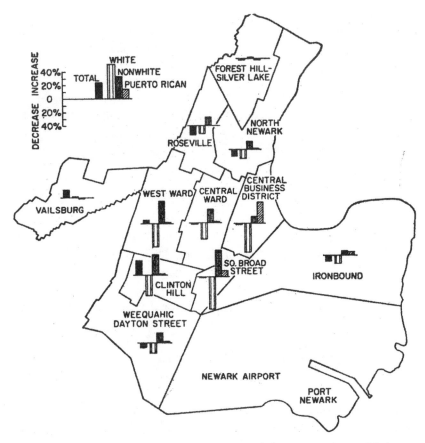

Fig. 3.4. Population changes in Newark's neighborhoods, 1950–1958. *Source*: Market Planning Corporation and Newark Central Planning Board.

age in the integrated schools and social milieu of the Weequahic section also remembered a residual of racial ambivalence. One son recalled that after "I did my first year of high school at South Side High, . . . My parents wanted me out of South Side" because of the number of black students, and, as he recalled, "it is clear in retrospect that my parents were moving away from that."[38] Despite their remarkable welcome of black neighbors, Jewish families maintained the civic boundary of marriage. Into the 1950s, most Jewish families rejected interracial dating in the name of preserving ethnic identity, and Jewish families refused to invite a black friend of their children from high school to dine in their homes. Black students recalled feeling overwhelmed by living as a minority for the first time, and yet "wouldn't say that it was prejudice." "There were some that I did speak with . . . but never usually invited to each other's home." Of nineteen African Americans whom Ortner studied, the majority reported feelings of alienation mixed with feelings of greater than usual tolerance, and in some cases real acceptance by whites.[39]

But the construction of a new housing project in the Italian American North Ward brought forth visible signs of hostility that eventually snowballed into a white resistance to the NHA. Around 1952 the NHA announced a new plan for Columbus Homes, which originally enjoyed enthusiastic support from Italian elected officials and Italian societies in the public hearings.[40] The NHA deliberately named the 111 clearance acres in the Old Third Ward after the Italian icon Christopher Columbus, and scheduled a Columbus pageant and christening ceremony for the opening.[41] The staging of civic events with an Italian character, such as moving-in ceremonies featuring local Italian celebrities, processions including banners with pictures of Christopher Columbus, and an honorific in the name of the Star of Italy awarded to a local physician, helped to build support.[42] The Columbus Homes project proceeded smoothly enough, according to reports in the dailies, because the NHA had not forced them to comply with the antidiscrimination policy. Many whites in the North Ward tended to "see the NHA as 'the Negro's agency' or as the agency that has hastened the racial invasion of white areas." But the agency head, Louis Danzig attempted to play both sides of the racial divide, assuring whites of their safety from the "Negro invasion" and promising blacks a fair share of the new housing units. When white liberals and civil rights organizations demanded what was termed open occupancy, some local Italian Americans formed a group

Fig. 3.5. The rise of urban renewal brought modern housing to Newark, such as the new Columbus Homes, but also introduced the disruptions and adjustments of racial integration. The Italian American community initially attempted to stop black residents from moving into the North Ward. (Courtesy of the Newark Public Library)

that opposed both black applicants and white quotas in the new project, similar to the hostile opponents of integration in numerous northern cities.[43] Talking out of both sides of his mouth, Danzig promised the inclusion of black residents in a future cohort, while at another time he publicly repeated his adamant refusal to "commit himself to a strict open occupancy in Columbus Homes" in the face of growing Italian American protest. Eventually, the NAACP and other civic organizations called for an official investigation, and Danzig was summoned to testify before the state civil rights commission, where he assured officials of his compliance with policies of nondiscrimination. For a time, more black residents moved into white areas of the city.[44]

In response, most white ethnics tolerated the slow, matching integration that characterized dispersal into the South and West Wards, and into some of the older housing units in the North Ward (where the percentage of blacks in the area increased each decade). Again, for a time, despite their dislike of too much diversity, Italian Americans in the North Ward elected city council members who campaigned on the benefits of urban renewal, and they actually voted down a couple of candidates running against the housing projects.[45] In other words, at this point in the 1950s, most Italian Americans remained invested in the larger administrative culture of the city—revealed in memos, policy statements, and press releases—that circulated in and out of City Hall in an effort to promote racial harmony and implement integration. In their official capacity, white administrators spoke of the "values of non-segregation" to be inculcated in the staff of the NHA.[46] Thus they used the term "integration" not only as a legal measure but as a policy keyword, an operating concept. As the number of public housing units increased, the city administration recognized the necessity for accommodating personal attitudes and what they often termed "prejudices." If the city likened racial tensions in the predominately Italian neighborhoods to an "armed camp relationship," they projected optimism on the feasibility of integration in the Jewish areas, especially Weequahic.[47] So seriously did the administration take the problem of creating harmony among the races that they commissioned a race relations survey, a kind of technology of opinion that both recorded and introduced racial attitudes in the public sphere.

A national marketing firm won a competitive bid to conduct a citywide survey of race relations and proposed to complete four thousand interviews, based on a research design crafted in a series of meetings at City Hall.[48] The city had publicly announced that the objective of the project was to measure attitudes toward racial diversity in order to implement one of the buzzwords of the moment, that is, racial integration —or in their conception of the racial phenomenon, the "rapid advance in many spheres" of black residents. Cognizant of impediments of prejudice to neighborhood diversity and equal opportunity, the city administration fashioned a policy "to inhibit the growth of a situation out of which such crises could develop."[49] There was something both naive and insufficient in this conceptualization, largely because of the absence of a critique of political power. Speaking only of racial attitudes without recognizing the struggle between ethnic groups for power at City Hall obscured the vested interests aligned with ethnicity in the political machine that perpetuated racial segregation and economic inequality.

To avoid, in effect, racial conflict of the sort that erupted in Detroit and Chicago over public housing, the city government introduced the Mayor's Commission on Group Relations. The civic body served to support fair employment practices by promoting educational campaigns for racial harmony, involving religious, labor, and civic leaders. Progressive labor activists such as August Meier, who belonged to both the Congress of Industrial Organizations and the NAACP, continued to make presentations to labor leaders on their activities concerning race and to secure federal legislation that extended the Fair Employment Practices Commission (FEPC) established by 1940s protest.[50] Meier became conscious of racism back in those Double V campaigns and was influenced in particular by the protests against segregated blood plasma, and now advocated race-based civil rights. Labor union involvement in race issues remained sporadic and included a few public forums on human relations. The United Steelworkers sponsored a public screening of "Burden of Truth," a film that depicted "a Negro family and the problems they face in climbing the ladder of economic and social success."[51] Another spree of initiatives were led by a consortium named the Newark Presbytery, comprised of some forty-eight churches that convened meetings, promoted events, and circulated petitions for fair and open housing. These and other progressive whites served as liaisons to other interracial groups in the area, such as the Essex County Intergroup Council and the Essex County Joint Council for Civil Rights, which conferred with and advised city officials.[52] Even the conservative *Italian Tribune* dutifully reprinted antidiscrimination legislation and ran stories that denounced employment prejudice against the dark worker.[53] Across the river, the Italian American mayor of New York City assailed discrimination and biased attitudes ("libel" and "defamation") against Sicilians.[54] The Italian mayor in Newark kicked off a week-long series of informational events on fair employment, including Bamberger's department store's "window display with Brotherhood and Fair Employment," made with materials donated by a local arts school. He also issued a directive to stores and other places to post an announcement that "Newark Employers Hire on Ability, Not Race, Creed, or Color."[55]

Thus the principle of racial integration gradually defined a major strand of a developing postwar urban liberalism. More resolutely than at any time since the Civil War, a new consensus had come to denounce the peculiar social customs of the South, and many whites in the North admired the new protest of Martin Luther King, Jr. Northerners took the side of the Supreme Court, the National Guard, and President Dwight Eisenhower when the South resisted federal mandates to integrate on the basis of race. But meanwhile, the North was unselfconsciously drawing invisible but assiduously observed color lines against black applicants in professions and refusing entrance in white neighborhoods to black home buyers. And, paradoxically, the same black Newarkers who had once stood for the Double V movement now abandoned their stance of protest. Perhaps, like the lucky few who moved into Weequahic or received veteran's benefits, they had experimented with a measure of cultural assimilation to attain the benefits of the American Dream. But the total number of families living on $3,000 per year or less was still 27.4 percent for non-white families in Newark. By the 1960s, after fifteen years of economic prosperity and major transfer and matching payments to the cities, more than 27 percent of African Americans still reported an income below $3,000, compared to only 10.8 percent of white families. Almost 38 percent of whites earned more than $10,000, but less than 17 percent non-whites did. The white population earned the highest personal incomes, and black and Puerto Rican families the lowest.[56]

In other cities, protest had persisted, new groups formed, leaders spoke out—so why the apparent passivity among black Newarkers? In Oakland, California, the unions launched a general strike in 1946; in Harlem radicals sustained innovative protests; in Detroit the United Auto Workers encouraged shop-floor radicals.[57] And in Newark's Clinton Hill, a community group formed to rehabilitate and improve the housing stock, to promote better schooling, and to control the effects of urban renewal. These neighborhood associations clearly had ties to organized labor, but they preferred upwardly mobile black homeowners over the lower working class pouring in from the Central Ward renewal projects. In fact, the Urban Colored Commission, the social welfare group organized during the war, had declared that "the trade union movement" did not play a noticeable role in civil rights or employment discrimination.[58] Most mainstream organizations during the anticommunist hysterics, like the Newark NAACP, felt new pressures from the government to expose and repress radicalism and to demonstrate their loyalty to the nation.[59] In at least one meeting, NAACP members discussed the "steps to be taken to secure the Branch against the infiltration and undue influence of Communists and their fellow-travelers."[60] And in 1952 the Executive Board suggested that "such steps be taken," which it was "considering in detail."[61] Back in World War II, Newark was widely considered to be an energetic center of civil rights, but postwar liberalism was polite and passive.[62]

Even as the economic pressures on black neighborhoods increased, the black newspapers that mobilized readers had declined both in influence and numbers. By 1960, the circulation of the *New Jersey Afro-American* dropped from 14,031 to only 5,452, while the *Newark Record* and the *Newark World Telegram* and a number of smaller African American publications completely stopped production. By the 1950s, the black migrant population overwhelmed more than refortified the Central Ward. In less than a decade the black population doubled, from 68,316 to 142,600, while the white population declined by almost 100,000, from 348,856 to 255,800.[63] Though the black middle class increased in both size and influence after the war, many chose to move into the so-called service suburbs, such as Orange and East Orange, taking with them the kind of background and capital that had once sustained black protest in the ghetto. By 1970 the area next to Newark, classified as "urban fringe," East Orange, became the largest black suburb in the nation, signaling the arrival of real class cleavage and social difference within the black community.[64] Meanwhile, black occupational mobility lagged behind white mobility throughout the decade—of more than 51,000 non-white employees, the majority fell into the categories of operatives and kindred workers (16,971), laborers besides farmers (7,942), and service workers, besides private household workers (5,505) and drivers and deliverymen (4,072). Black male underrepresentation persisted in the categories of growth and mobility, such as sales, construction, retail trade, managers, and mechanics and repairmen.[65] Since the 1950s, social scientists identified a cultural malaise in the black community, a psychological depression arising from isolation and divergent values that afflicted the so-called Dark Ghetto, to use the term in the title of a major book by Kenneth Clark.[66]

Against the backdrop of a diminished black public sphere, the banality of middle-class conformity, and a civic culture uncomfortable with dissent, the Newark NAACP actually attracted new members. Since the

1940s, the branch leaders continuously attempted to extend its influence by corresponding with government officials and through national lobbying. Some members wrote letters to support President's Truman challenge to the appointment of an alleged racist as the director of Civilian Defense, and to commend housing officials for their antidiscriminatory "stand on public housing."[67] A local culture of civility flowered in municipal meeting rooms and forums, reinforcing the NAACP's approach of working within established channels and seeking cooperation through them. They boasted 425 senior members and approximately one hundred in the Youth Council, but the group labored under the image of elitism, referred to by one author as "the silk stocking set." Although they were seen as provincial, key members regularly attended regional and national conferences, and heard national speakers on labor and legal strategies.[68] On the one hand, the black elites moved within a relatively rarefied world, worshiping at Bethany Baptist Church and St. Philips Parish, socializing in clubs like Jack and Jill and the Smart Set, and throwing the annual so-called cotillions or society dances. But close observers of the black elite commented both on their small number and the relative mildness of their snobbery. Compared to the Philadelphia Cotillion, for example, their galas appealed to Newark's "masses." One longtime resident recalled that the women who headed the events displayed a more common and popular orientation, and that this "is what put her over in Newark. She geared her club to the children of the hardworking domestics."[69]

Many in the black middle-class retained a sense of civic responsibility, but few were affected on a day-to-day basis by the harsh realities of discrimination and the stigma of ghetto isolation. From their perspective, many of the burdens of racism had been defeated by the passage of state-level equal protection legislation, and the remaining major racial problem was unequal access to public education. Although committed to the realization of the promise of *Brown v. Board of Education,* few elites recognized the extent to which spatial integration was crucial to attaining the Court's liberal vision of equality. Since the late 1940s, several branches of the NAACP in New Jersey conducted a major investigation into allegations of bias in the public schools. They reported on abysmal conditions and the continued enforcement of officially recognized Jim Crow practices in middle and high schools. By the 1950s in Newark, the school board and other groups in the government dismissed the finding as well as more recent charges of racial bias in the hiring of top administrators. In response, the members of the NAACP publicly pleaded for the "elevation of Negroes to administrative positions in the school system."[70]

Although the board of the Newark NAACP appointed a housing committee to take action on urban renewal, few historical documents or sources reveal meetings or even correspondence with the NHA. In other cities, African American leadership successfully influenced equal employment on construction projects, and the Harlem activist Jesse Gray had led a major rent-strike campaign that demanded both appropriations for low-income families and the passage of legislation mandating the takeover of privately owned buildings.[71] But Newark's polite and conventional members of the NAACP remained naïve about power and the need for political influence, as members adjourned their meetings on housing problems with a resolution merely to ensure that "anti-discrimination laws are properly administered." The board acknowledged in a memo that legal integration was "only a beginning," but they failed to intervene in the planning process. Volunteers in Clinton Hill had organized and stopped a renewal project, but no members of the NAACP had even attended public hearings or formally objected to emerging patterns of racial segregation in announced constructions. At a time when Italian Americans demanded that particular candidates of "Italian extraction" serve on the board of the housing authority, African Americans in the Central Ward pulled fewer strings.[72]

By the 1950s, both white and black middle-class residents organized to reform corrupt machine politics and construct a new system of five wards to replace the older electoral map of fifteen voting districts. Thus the white Jewish and Protestant progressives and elites formed the Charter Commission, which won approval from the voters in 1954, and drew up a government plan. Theodore Pettigrew, president of the Newark branch of the NAACP, was the lone black member.[73] But a familiar black politico from the Central Ward, Irvine Turner, filed a suit against the Charter Commission because its original draft of a ward map failed to produce a black representative, even from the majority-black Central Ward. In response, the commission compromised and redrew the wards, turning in a map that the Democratic Party supported and suburban Republicans opposed, and which gained overwhelming approval in the fall referendum. When the commission turned to identifying candidates

Fig. 3.6. Irvine Turner was the first African American elected to the city council in 1954, serving for sixteen years with renowned skill and charisma. In the 1960s Turner broke from the political machine by publicly demanding more housing for the Central Ward.

to run in the upcoming elections, they hand-picked African American Roger Yancey to run against Turner in the Central Ward. Born and raised in Newark, a graduate of Barringer High School, and a former student at a seminary in Virginia, Turner launched a spectacular campaign in which he literally wrapped himself in the American flag and drove around the neighborhoods with a bullhorn, singing the national anthem.[74] In the midst of rumors that Yancey was paid to abandon the race, or that opponents intimidated him so much that he fled, Turner handily won a seat on the City Council and served as the consummate politician of the people for four terms.[75]

However, the Italian American candidates lost their hold on political power, capturing only one of the five wards and going down to defeat in the mayoral race. Once the Italian incumbent, Rudolph Valani, fell to the Irish candidate, Leo Carlin, the rhetoric of fair employment and nondiscrimination faded from the pages of the *Italian Tribune,* and with it apparently the neutrality of many white ethnics. Slowly, the slippage between support for public housing in the Italian American neighborhoods, some of which depended on their expectation of de facto and under-the-table segregation, conflicted with the legal implementation of urban policy.[76] The local civic culture was trumping the laws on the books. To the extent that the federal mandate of attempting to achieve integration impinged on local preferences, the unhappy whites in the North Ward publicly attacked Danzig and organized counter-demonstrations against the relocation of black residents. By the time of the

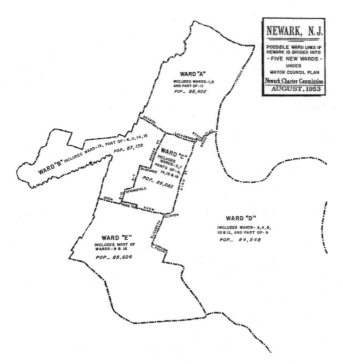

Fig. 3.7. Possible ward lines if Newark is divided into five new wards.

next election, the Italian-born percentage of the population of Newark had increased from 28.8 percent to 37.4 percent, barely outpacing the black population, which had sharply increased from 11.6 percent to 34 percent. By the 1960s, Italian Americans re-organized and regained their influence at City Hall by capturing a number of vacancies left by the flight of Jews, Irish, and white Protestant voters. Some of the leaders questioned the successes that NHA claimed for their projects, and the *Italian Tribune* wondered if the construction in some "blighted areas" truly justified the "hardships thus imposed upon the citizenry" and if such a wealthy city should consent to "so many low cost housing projects."[77] Eventually some reservations about public subsidies turned up a notch—into white resentment of integration.[78] They protested implementation of "the integration program. . . . The way many see it, this is an outright infringement on the rights of people to live and do as they see fit." Although city officials and the Italian American rank and file continued to endorse fair employment practices, on the issue of integrated residence the editor invoked the aphorism "that no man convinced against his will is of the same opinion still."[79] It was not surprising that in 1956 a correspondent of African American bureaucrat Harold Lett discovered a publication of the "White Citizens' Council" of Jackson, Mississippi, on the doorsteps of a suburban home in New Jersey, for on matters of custom and in private attitudes, the racial outlook of northern whites had converged with the publicly repudiated southern racist.[80]

The NAACP appeared helpless in turning back the tide of resegregation and even popular black leaders accommodated city hall. Before elected to the city council, Turner had served the Irish and Jewish machines, and attempted to increase his political leverage for the black community in what one scholar described as an "underworld system that gave jobs to black men as number runners, in black social clubs, and in prohibition liquor."[81] By the 1950s, the black community had learned to expect housing from the government, which was one reason why the NAACP criticized Turner's patronage-style politics, accusing him of corruption and of pandering to the poor. When no new housing projects were planned, Turner reportedly challenged "city officials, laborers and builders," and publicly criticized taxes on FHA loans, the major source of financing for African American home buyers, which at 40 percent were astronomical compared to the national average of 14 percent.[82]

Name of Project	Named For	Date Opened
Cellis Austin Apartments	Board Member, Prudential Insurance	1931
Douglass & Harrison Apartments	Abolitionist and Actor	1935
Stephen Crane Village	Writer	1940
Pennington Court	Prominent Family	1940
Seth Boyden Court	Invetor	1941
James Baxter Terrace	Principal of Colored School	1941
John W. Hyatt Court	Inventor	1942
Felix Fuld Court	Civic Leader	1942
Franklin D. Roosevelt Homes	President	1946
Joseph P. Bradley Court	Justice of Supreme Court	1950
Otto E. Kretchmer Homes	President, Peerless Imperial Company	1953
Archbishop Walsh Homes	Archbishop	1953
Rev. William P. Hayes Homes	Negro Clergy	1953
Christopher Columbus Homes	Explorer	1955
Stella Windsor Wright Homes	Black Social Worker	1960

Fig. 3.8. Low-rent housing projects in Newark. *Source*: Compiled by G. Cahalan (July 1967).

Turner never wavered in his obedience to Jewish and Irish higher-ups in the machine, but at one point he uncharacteristically threatened to defy patronage protocol and lead a rent strike in the Central Ward.[83] Turner's political style proved the tragedy of the old adage, too little, too late. Despite massive redistribution across the urban terrain induced by the rise of public housing, the new generation of African Americans replaced rather than integrated with whites. The segregation index for Newark in 1940 was almost exactly the same, 74.9, thirty years later. According to the segregation index, in order for the black population to achieve a totally "natural" distribution in neighborhoods, 77.4 percent of all African American residents would be required to move into white neighborhoods. Compared to many cities, Newark enjoyed a relatively low figure—every other northern city exceeded the Newark segregation rate, from 95 percent in Chicago to 82 percent in Pittsburgh. In part because of the success of the first generation of public housing that integrated many neighborhoods, the statistical formulas still reflected the benefits of the original construction of racial dispersal. But Newark experienced above-average segregation in the categories of concentration, centralization, and unevenness. In other words, by the 1960s Newark was a city of many ethnic groups, but most African Americans still resided in the central area, the Central Ward, Broad Street, or the Lower Clinton Hill. It was a city of two or three major ghettos, rather than a series of rigidly segregated neighborhoods.[84]

Project Areas	Original Population	Total Acres	Clearance Acres	Fed. Grant $000's	City Share $000's	S&P Blight Declaration	Part I HUD Final Approval	Acquisition Started	Construction Started
1. Branch Brook R-3-1	702	20.4	11.7	2,304	1,151	6/25/52		project completed	
2. Broad Street R-3-2	433	22.6	13.4	2,970	1,483	6/25/52		project completed	
3. Old Third Ward R-6	13,000	224.9	111.3	21,447	9,916	4/5/55	2/5/60	7/20/60	8/20/64
4. Newark Colleges R-45	2,658	57	34.3	10,099	4,799	6/3/59	8/28/61	4/17/63	4/7/64
5. Newark Plaza R-58	91	50.7	31.9	10,518	4,755	12/16/59	12/26/63	11/13/64	5/17/65
6. Educational Center R-50	184	23.7	20.2	2,724	856	7/1/59	12/16/63	11/4/66	11/4/67
7. Hill Street R-49	141	12.9	8.2	4,309	2,024	7/1/59	9/7/61	7/20/62	9/18/64
8. South Broad R-52	1,380	42.4	26.3	7,878	3,714	7/1/59	9/1/61	7/20/62	10/3/64
9. St. Benedicts R-123	693	35	14.6	6,465	2,996	1/16/63	1/6/66		
10. Essex Heights R-62	2,289	47.3	31.6	7,248	3,260	2/3/60	8/14/62	6/7/65	
11. Essex Heights (2' Stage) R-141	950	14	10.3	4,540	1,410	10/16/63	6/23/66	deferred	
12. Lower Clinton Hill R-38	6,250	78.2	13.3	3,953	1,822	7/23/59	9/29/61	6/2/64	6/13/67
13. Central Ward R-32	6,447	94.6	57	15,487	4,835	12/18/57	7/22/66		
14. Fairmount R-72	4,464	84.8	50.1	12,695	3,937	2/16/61	6/16/65	1/28/66	5/11/66
15. Medical Center R-196	3,163	54.2	47.8	17,321	5,389	1/18/67			
16. St. Michaels R-156	1,400	46.3	21.2	10,000	5,807	2/19/64			
17. Industrial River R-121	1,575	1528.5	542.6	27,025	12,153	9/5/62	10/14/66	9/10/65	5/6/66
TOTALS	45820	2437.5	1045.8	166,983	70,307				

Fig. 3.9. Summary of urban renewal projects, 1952–1967. *Source: Urban Renewal in Newark*, 1968, Newark Public Library.

Racial isolation had increased dramatically in forty years, from 22.8 percent in 1930 to 78.3 percent in 1970, meaning that African Americans were less and less likely to encounter different groups of folks and experience multiple ethnic cultures on a daily basis.[85]

The first wave of urban renewal had countered segregation by dispersing residents of blighted areas into the first fourteen projects erected between 1940 and 1955 in every major white neighborhood. However, on Turner's watch, new public housing contributed to more and more resegregation, and the warning signs of black concentration and isolation returned with a vengeance. Housing reports indicated that neighborhoods that suffered from high poverty rates in 1950, even when a new project was built, declined even further over several years by an average of 8 percent.[86] Subsequent proposals for plans that mixed middle-class and low-income housing failed when the state legislature refused to appropriate funds.[87] By 1965, the NHA announced a ten-year plan that predicted a shortage of at least 10,000 units, but of twelve new public housing projects slated to open in the late-1960s and 1970s, only University Gardens (first named University Court) proposed middle-class, low-rise housing, and nonetheless bordered between two emergent ghettos, and Zion Towers proposed a 265-unit, twenty-eight story structure for the middle-class neighborhood in North Weequahic. By contrast, the completion of the Hayes Homes and Stella Wright Homes inaugurated the rise of the Second Ghetto and the eclipse of optimism. The very housing projects that once had achieved an integrated balance between white and black residents tipped to majority black between 1955 and 1965, and the majority-white projects—with names like Seth Boyden, Stephen Crane, Archbishop Walsh, and Columbus—had remained white, despite the initial push for dispersal and integration. By 1966, a series of major news stories by local reporter Douglas Eldridge on the "ratio changes in Low-Rent projects" announced the failure of integration—the old veterans' housing, the Bradley Court, had 94.7 percent whites (perhaps a majority were elderly), and Stella Windsor Wright had 98 percent non-whites.[88]

The rise of the Second Ghetto reflected the racial bias of the City Council and the mayor in the administration of housing. Although the mayor's racial-attitude survey indicated that a clear majority of whites rejected "further encroachment" by Negroes into white residential neighborhoods, a majority of African Americans from all economic backgrounds felt their housing reflected a "a real deprivation."[89] Barring

Location and Units	Sponsor	Date Started	Percent Completed	Esitmated Occupancy
Third Ward				
High Park Terrace	Jack Parker	Sept. 1968	92 pecent	Sept. 1969
Brick Towers	Bricklayers Union	Sept. 1968	68 perent	Dec. 1970
High Park Gardens	Jack Parker	Sept. 1968	70 percent	Dec. 1976
Hill Manor	Newark Community Housing Corp.	Sept. 1969	—	Dec. 1970
Central Ward				
826 Units	Newark Housing Authority	1970 HUD	—	Dec. 1972
Lower Clinton Hill				
Mt. Calvary Homes	Mt. Calvary Baptists Church	Sept. 1965	95 percent	Dec. 1969
Avon Heights	Metropolitan Urban Renewal Assoc.	App. Pend	—	—
Coop Garden Apts	Metropolitan Urban	Sept. 1970	—	—
Educational				
Elderly Homes	Mount Carmel	Sept. 1970	—	—
University Gardens	Jack Parker	Sept. 1968	—	—
Lincoln Towers	Lincoln Housing	HFA 1968	—	Dec. 1970
Zion Towers	Zion Towers Corp.	Sept. 1968	10 percent	Dec. 1970
440 Elizabeth Avenue	Elizabeth Corp.	Sept. 1968	25 percent	Dec. 1970

Fig. 3.10. New public housing projects, 1969–1970. *Source: Summary of New Public Housing Projects* (1970), Newark Public Library.

blacks from the suburbs clearly was the new frontier of civic racism, a carryover from World War II resistance to mingling in water, mixing blood, and forbidding miscegenation. But it was the rise of the Second Ghetto that ruined the dream of affordable and equitable housing for all. In opinion polls, black Newarkers reported that they felt renewal had improved the quality of life in the Ironbound (78 percent agreed), West Ward (69 percent agreed), and Weequahic (68 percent agreed), and "a large number of black residents told of their aspirations to leave their current neighborhoods" but also their desire to avoid "encounters [with] hostile whites" in suburbs where they felt unwelcome. According to a survey, some 65 percent of black Newarkers fully intended to stay in the city to enjoy their hard-won rights and exercise the privileges of civic inclusion and the rites of the public sphere.[90]

At some point in the late-1940s or early 1950s, the Urban Colored Commission in the state legislature either received or wrote a memo entitled simply "The Third V: What the Negro Citizen Can Do." The document outlined a new tripartite political campaign. If the first V symbolized victory abroad in the war, the second V for victory over "imported or home grown fascism," the third "V symbolizes the Negro's victory over himself." All of the basic black institutions that comprised the public sphere—lectures, sermons, pageants, plays, editorials —needed to be summoned to the cause of community building and an "intra-racial crusade." The remarkable political tract called for cooperatives, credit unions, schools, as well as the policing of the newly identified moral threats of political demagogues and underworld figures. After a long campaign of demanding integration, the "Third V" testified to the resurgence of protest energies that would gather force and mobilize fresh forms of dissent in the 1960s.[91] Despite their reputation for elitism and the limitations of their legal-based approach, the NAACP continued to recruit and train the type of volunteer who later ventured south to organize for civil rights. Some later returned north to protest in cities against the very economic and political ills that worsened and festered in postwar Newark.[92]

4

The Limits of Interracial Activism

In the 1963 March on Washington at the Lincoln Memorial, the same landmark where Marian Anderson had protested her exclusion from Constitutional Hall by the Daughters of the American Revolution, Martin Luther King, Jr., summoned the iconography of U.S. nationalism, from the Gettysburg Address to the National Anthem. The moving refrain of his historic speech, "I Have a Dream," celebrated the promise of the American Dream but questioned the greatness of a nation that had reneged on its commitment to equality for all. King continually returned to the tragedy of a racist society in which mobility meant climbing from one ghetto to another, larger one, and where blacks in the South could not vote and in the North had nothing to vote for. In Newark, tens of thousands watched King on their televisions, and the Essex County branch of an innovative protest group, the Congress of Racial Equality (CORE), had dispatched five buses of volunteers to the capital.[1] The historic rally for jobs and freedom—contested and diverse—signaled the wider scope and more radical direction of protest, and the emergence of a national civil rights movement.[2]

Since the 1950s, thousands of volunteers and demonstrators had built the southern movement from a series of successful boycotts into ongoing mass resistance. The Student Non-Violent Coordinating Committee (SNCC) attracted both white and black youth who would lead local groups in support of equal accommodations and register them to vote, but recent reports had raised questions about future progress. A number of the groups had collapsed under pressure from within, due to cultural differences and unconscious white racism. Some black members broke away to experiment with still inchoate conceptions of black power, while many returned home to the North in search of new causes in New York, Philadelphia, and Chicago.[3]

U.S. cities had long been home to do-gooders and reformers: the "charity agent" of high morality in the Victorian city, and the neighborly college graduate in Progressive-era social settlements. But the figure of the new activist appeared on the scene at a moment of political inventiveness that defined the 1960s. They utilized direct action tactics that pressured and disrupted the operations of the government, and they envisioned themselves as advocates of the neediest, seeking to identify with rather than uplift the community.[4] Rather than the bodily sacrifice required of black demonstrators in the South, the northern groups shocked the customers of restaurants or middle-class professionals at corporations, parading arm in arm, chanting shoulder to shoulder. The black and white activists embodied precisely what most whites still feared— black and white together. By the mid-1960s, the northern branches of CORE leveraged this uncomfortable publicity or controversy into bargaining power in negotiations with government officials and corporate executives for equal treatment. Another group of radical activists, the youth of the New Left, eschewed these volunteers as too conventional and beholden to the middle class, and emphasized day-to-day interactions with the oppressed. Organizing around different axes of black-white cooperation, the Students for a Democratic Society (SDS) mobilized ambitious plans for what they called "an interracial movement of the poor."

In planning and carrying out direct-action demos, the white volunteers learned from black volunteers, and vice versa, and in the process created an interracial public sphere that rejected much of the polite civility inherited from the 1950s. The new activists challenged the orthodoxy of civic groups that privileged meetings with government officials, and questioned municipal authority, thriving on confrontation and political dissent with the establishment. It was the planning and execution of each demonstration that introduced instructive clashes over race and class. In some circles, the younger black activists adopted the new militant rhetoric of black power and withdrew from white groups, and some of the black integrationists fought bitterly with black militants. The students of the New Left had studied the classic texts on building a class movement, only to confront the verities of racism in daily organizing in the inner city. Members of CORE took stock of the achievements of the direct-action movement, experimented with racial separatism, and in the process lost much of its base membership. At a time when radicals searched for revolutionary movements, the process of interracial activism contradicted any sort of easy uncoupling of racial discrimination from the crisis of poverty.[5]

Thus around 1961 the civil rights movement officially arrived in Newark, when what were known as the Freedom Riders and their well-wishers gathered at Military Park to send off the demonstrators destined for Chattanooga, Tennessee.[6] The Freedom Riders demonstrated against Jim Crow in interstate travel, and signaled the revival of CORE, which was founded in the 1940s by a small pacifist network, the Friendship of Reconciliation (FOR). They had planned to establish a race relations project for "federated local groups" to "voice nationally" the cause of "abolishing the color line," and designed a flexible structure that permitted the branches to experiment but required new members to pledge "the CORE philosophy" of nonviolent civil disobedience and interracial cooperation. By the 1960s, with the publicity surrounding the Freedom Rides, CORE expanded with large national headquarters, regional offices, and more than a hundred branches.[7] On the day of the ceremony the founders of Newark's Essex County branch, Rev. Joseph Randall and Rev. Homer Tucker, depicted the interstate journey not as an insurgent disruption but an exercise in humanism and "an experiment in love," recalling the spiritual idealism in the founding of CORE.[8]

Yet the valorization of protest against southern Jim Crow deflected attention from the national scope of the race problems and particularly eroded the memory of the quite recent struggles around Double V in Newark. The fact was that civil rights in the Central Ward had not kept pace with rising expectations, and the local leadership of CORE seemed to ignore discrimination at home. A rabbi from East Orange proclaimed it did "not matter what color or creed" but that the attendees had faith in "the future of Democracy," and the members in the suburbs praised the program, calling for a "Freedom Riders' Week," to reinforce the public's commitment to their civic duty of nondiscrimination in public accommodations. But by 1960, more than fifteen years after the victory of Double V in the state, perhaps such paeans to these modest objectives served to distract the public from the crisis of inequality signified by the growth of the Central Ward ghetto, not to mention the persistence of discrimination in real estate, employment, and accommodations in the suburbs.[9]

In the early 1960s, both the local and national operations of CORE had grown by recruiting a diverse membership in northern states like New Jersey and tapping into the churches, high schools, and regulars of the Democratic Party and the NAACP. The charismatic national chairman, James Farmer, frequently made excursions to Newark from the headquarters in New York to address the Mayor's Commission on Group Relations or the African American fraternal order Bethany Lodge Number 31, and on occasion crowds of reportedly two thousand or more attended. But some observers also reported tensions in several chapters between recent recruits and the older members.[10] At a meeting in Teaneck, New Jersey, to discuss the "northern Negro," an unidentified spokesman reported that the younger people had taken a strident and "uncompromising" stance on matters of what he vaguely referred to as "methods," referring to new militant rhetoric associated with black nationalism.[11]

One of the reasons that the Essex County CORE survived the turmoil of prolonged internal conflict was the dedicated and talented leadership of Robert Curvin. Born and raised in Newark, Curvin graduated from Rutgers University, served in the army, and worked for the Essex County Welfare Board as a caseworker. As a college student, he had searched for a role in the civil rights movement, and decided to join the Newark branch of the NAACP, but then felt somehow dissatisfied. He was later recruited into several leadership training programs both locally and in New York, and was active in matters of civil rights and urban renewal politics.[12] Curvin joined CORE around 1960–1961 and soon stepped into the chairmanship at a time when many branches deliberately selected African American leaders. From 1963 until he resigned about four years later, Curvin attempted to reorient Newark's agenda away from the Freedom Rides by addressing local problems of discrimination and employment. Because of his focus on local struggles, one former head of the branch wrote to Farmer to criticize Curvin's tepid enthusiasm for fund-raising for the southern campaigns.[13] Despite his mild insubordination, Curvin was elected to the post of regional vice president, the titular head of CORE chapters in the Northeast, and he gained both leadership experience (from regular attendance at regional and national meetings) and greater stature in Newark.[14]

Soon the attendance at weekly meetings exceeded that of the NAACP, drawing as many as 200–300 casual members and perhaps 40–50 committed regulars, about one-half to two-thirds of whom were black. An extant membership list for 1964 indicated 71 black members in a total group 108, and many of the white members considered more committed identified themselves as Jewish. Some had worked previously in the local NAACP, and others were moved by the courageous defiance in the South.[15] Also, the physical proximity of Newark to currents of radical activism stimulated interest in Essex CORE. In 1964 six members from Newark participated in major demonstrations organized by Brooklyn CORE at the World's Fair, including a stall-in that attempted to prevent attendance at the Schaeffer Pavilion, a brewery, because of its record of racial discrimination in employment. Members of Newark CORE experienced firsthand the events of Freedom Summer in 1964—the flowering of grassroots activism in the south—when a contingent of the Mississippi Freedom Democratic Party traveled across the state en route to Democratic National Convention in Atlantic City, attracting a crowd at a local rally. Meanwhile, Essex County CORE sent volunteers to aid activists in Trenton at demonstrations against urban renewal, and another contingent to support boycotts of several breweries in New York City.[16] Encouraged by the activism in the South and in major cities, the burgeoning Newark branch, to quote one new member, envisioned a movement in which "whites and Negroes could work together in a militant, but non-violent, way to achieve integration on all levels: housing, employment, schools, etc."[17]

Essex County CORE initiated major demonstrations against Jim Crow accommodations similar to the Double V protests twenty years before, using strong rhetoric and principled arguments for equality, fair treatment, and integration. But like the new urban grassroots activists in other locales, they increasingly focused on discrimination by employers and industry.[18] Like Seattle CORE, which had reached an agreement with the A&P Supermarket chain, and Detroit CORE, which negotiated an agreement with several construction companies, Newark activists pressed for compliance with fair employment.[19] Again, their protest built upon the civic culture constructed into the public sphere by the postwar coalitions of white liberal and religious civic leaders, such as the Newark Business-Industrial Coordinating Committee, and black uplift groups like the local Newark Urban League.[20] In 1963 CORE led a major campaign against the building trades by picketing the all-white construction crews at Barringer High School and at the Rutgers University Law School, forcing the city and the university into negotiations to hire more black construction workers. In response, the mayor established a new apprentice program that involved a significant percentage of black workers.[21]

They also organized major actions at the White Castle diners in Newark and in the suburb of Orange, staging sit-ins not only to demand equal treatment for black customers but also fair employment practices for black applicants. The interracial activists went driving through the all-white suburbs, and stopped at each restaurant to form picket lines and display placards that demanded "More Jobs Now," "White Castle Shames Orange," "We Want Black and White Castle," and "Bigotry in Business Equals Bankruptcy."[22] The staging of CORE actions not only disrupted the civic routines and commerce of the suburbs but also advocated interracial unity that frequently angered hostile white spectators. Although black members led many of the actions, whites accounted for one-half to two-thirds of demonstrators. But when black customers crossed a picket line, the black demonstrators admonished them: "Negro, You're not ready for freedom yet."[23] So radical was the spectacle of real integration in white suburbs—of black activists appearing alongside white activists—that whites sometimes physically attacked demonstrators. Like their southern counterparts protesting at bus stations in the South, Essex CORE remained dedicated to nonviolence and turned the proverbial other cheek. On one occasion, a firecracker was thrown at the activists, but they proudly remained passive and sang southern civil rights ballads, "We Shall Overcome."

Originally founded by pacifists, CORE strongly criticized manifestations of violence in rhetoric or deed. The leadership rejected pleas for assistance from the Deacons of Defense, the southern militant group associated with Robert F. Williams (who had advocated the use of guns against white opposition as early as 1959), and publicly denounced the Black Muslim movement and Malcolm X as evil, racist, and undemocratic.[24] In the South, CORE members sent to investigate conditions spoke of intimidation and violence by southern whites, and when asked to identify "problems with the Negro community," activists listed "fear, apathy" due to "much KKK, City Council Activity." By contrast, perhaps as few as one in every hundred northern demonstrations resulted in a violent attack on an activist, and police repression remained largely undercover and covert.[25] In any case, the CORE demonstrations succeeded, and it was reported that White Castle officials announced new hiring policies that promised opportunities for black applicants.[26]

The Essex County CORE turned from the outlying areas and suburbs to targeting major corporations that had offices in the downtown area, and by the end of 1962 it had started a major campaign against Newark Bell Telephone that had occupied long hours of planning.[27] The copious notes recorded by former NAACP secretary August Meier, who now commuted to meetings of CORE from his post as a professor of history in Baltimore, suggest complex, intense negotiations largely facilitated by Richard Proctor, another veteran of the NAACP. Their strategy marked a new level of effectiveness. As the rank and file hit the sidewalks of Market and Broad Streets at Bell headquarters, the Employment Committee (Proctor, Meier, and Curvin) entered negotiations with corporate executives. In one of the most infamous campaigns, the local members initiated a "phone-in." As the volunteers coordinated a series of strikes in which members telephoned the phone company all at the same time, jamming the switchboards, they sent representatives to demand minority hiring and training.[28] In the past, Newark Bell had hired only 208 black employees, most of whom (203) were operators, although their spokesmen maintained that lack of jobs accounted for the relatively low number. The company denied charges of discrimination and pointed to a recent article that appeared in the black press which commended their record on minority hiring. But Meier, Proctor, and Curvin publicly challenged such statements. According to CORE investigations, they had hired only a few black female employees in traffic, accounting, and commercial, and fewer black men in the engineering and plant operations. Although Bell officials claimed that they recruited from a diverse pool of high schools, advertised in the black press, and announced a cooperative program with the Urban League, they employed only one African American in management and one secretary.[29] In investigating not only the percentage of black employees but their rate of placement in management and in promotion, CORE demonstrated a sophisticated appreciation of the dynamics of corporate racism. They exposed Newark Bell's hiring practices to a public that appreciated the ideals of King and desired compliance with the antidiscrimination law. At one point, CORE's employment team called for quotas, and the Newark Bell representatives announced a comprehensive plan to hire more black employees at all levels.[30]

After these and other successful campaigns against formal discrimination, some of the local branches experimented with new tactics of militancy and radicalism. The chair of the Bergen County CORE, Shirley Lacey, began to call for more black visibility, and other branches opened store-front operations in downtown ghettos.[31] The newer membership declared the need to reach out to the truly needy in the community, which they abstractly defined in terms of the "community" or the "poor," and the national leadership launched a new agenda that prioritized the "grass-roots" in efforts toward "becoming a more inclusive group socially and economically," according to literature distributed at one of the annual national meetings. CORE moved cautiously toward the more militant southern-based SNCC, with whom they shared a "non-violent spirit," as one member wrote in a letter.[32] It was the younger and newer black members who wanted to work with the masses rather than struggle as itinerant practitioners of civil disobedience around the state.[33] Yet Curvin continued to believe in the efficacy of the carefully planned direct action that shifted locations and issues, and once explained that "if you are going to have a demonstration and it is communicated to our organization, the people that are going to be dominant in the demonstration are your constituency"[34] He felt that the new debates around militancy and authenticity missed the point of the deeply organic nature of direct action tactics, which he believed had really engaged the "people that know you, that are involved in the issue."[35]

But black and white activists increasingly disagreed over actions and rhetoric, and after 1965 or so that gap widened. When Bergen County CORE had waged a major campaign against segregation of public schools in Englewood, a middle-class and predominantly white suburb in the north of the state, they conducted an all-night sit-in at the Board of Education to protest. Police arrested eleven of the demonstrators. But the white members from Englewood felt betrayed by the vehemence with which black demonstrators attacked discrimination in their town. Some whites accused black members of usurping control of the branch, and alleged that protesters had "fostered an atmosphere of hate, vilification," and at one point a white member complained that one of the militants had compared Englewood's situation with violent clashes in Little Rock, the famous southern town where President Dwight Eisenhower had mobilized federal troops to escort black high school students. If the suburban whites still had faith in the potential for racial redemption of their community, despite the depth of Jim Crow, many black activists rejected any sort of moderation of their anti-white rhetoric.[36]

Not surprisingly in this context of rising anti-white sentiments and questioning of the ideal of integration, when CORE eventually opened a new office in the Central Ward its membership declined. Black members recalled that whites felt alienated and were dropping out. Also, the national planning committee of CORE had "changed a good deal," according to Curvin. White membership in the committee was reduced to only one, while the Newark chapter itself "was disintegrating during the latter part of 1967." Yet, in the midst of racial deterioration, the remaining members mobilized a major demonstration against urban renewal in the Central Ward. Still, "there were a few whites left" in the Newark membership.[37] Curvin explained the dearth of whites both in terms of the rise of black militancy and as a paradoxical effect of the success of integration. "Public accommodations had been basic for non-violent action, making CORE the vanguard."[38] But with successful desegregation and expansion of employment opportunities, the organization lost its relevance to the larger movement. Curvin encountered the view that the traditional direct-action campaigns did not necessarily address the "basic problems facing the masses of blacks."[39]

Essex County CORE had pioneered new forms of confrontation against discrimination, but perhaps the overriding commitment to the black middle class—the fact that many members had full-time jobs and lived in better neighborhoods—prevented a more complete transition to grassroots community organizing. In a provocative thesis about the group, Margaret Shapiro argued in the 1970s that "CORE's base had almost entirely abandoned Newark for the suburbs," and that its distance from the masses effectively hindered the development of a class-based social movement.[40] On some level, CORE's ongoing demonstrations against the telephone companies belied these charges, for the fact was that a number of working-class black women gained employment as the result of persistent protest by committed integrationist organizations. It is true that between 1960 and 1970 the rate of black suburbanization out of Newark increased—as black settlement in Montclair rose from 11 to 37 percent and in East Orange from 20 to 26 percent, and in fact Curvin once described CORE as a group of "the emerging professional."[41] Yet the statistical evidence from the period 1940–1960 indicated that most African American men who earned college degrees earned "substantially less" than white men with a high school education. In 1940, for example, black college graduates had earned 45 percent of what white high school graduates earned, and in 1960 an African American college graduate still earned only about $16,372 per year compared to $27,493 for a white college graduate.[42]

Black middle-class activists suffered from white racism to the same if sometimes not greater extent than more isolated poor black southerners and ghetto dwellers. Thus striking a blow against employment discrimination also defined the front lines of radicalism. It is true that when CORE declined to stage a major protest against urban renewal and disrupt a housing agency in Trenton, their critics noted that one of their members was employed by the very agency against which they planned to demonstrate.[43] While CORE groups in Harlem and on the West Coast resorted to increasingly militant actions, Newark CORE seemed to lose both direction and interest in protest, and news stories of CORE demonstrations appear infrequently after 1965. The more radical veterans of SNCC such as Phil Hutchings rarely participated in CORE activities, precisely because they were viewed as suburban and middle class.[44] At the same time, one report suggested that a number of "charter members of CORE" had "dropped out because it was too conservative," and that the radicals "w[ere] always talking about Black Power, Black Action, direction with gun in hand."[45] In addition, Curvin once argued that "the great success in many of the employment campaigns paradoxically caused a decline [in members' interest in that issue]."[46]

The integrationists like Curvin defended their commitment to nonviolence but did not always respond gracefully to the pressure tactics of the blacker-than-thou faction within CORE. When Curvin attended a conference convened to debate the adoption of what was vaguely referred to as the Black Power program, he recalled his anxiety that "no one had any programmatic idea on the meaning of black power." At one point, he even asked the convention to "define what the term Black Power really means." One meaning that materialized was the marginalization of white members. Curvin recalled that the housing activist Jesse Gray, the very figure once heroicized by leftist white radicals, delivered a "fiery speech" punctuated with anti-white rhetoric.[47] At one point, Cliff Montaro, the son-in-law of national chair Floyd McKissick, privately approached Curvin and said, "Gee, Bob, I didn't know you were so conservative." In response, Curvin reportedly told Montaro, "Gee, Cliff, I didn't know you were so stupid."[48] As CORE declined to a low-visibility group of minimal influence by 1967, perhaps one important legacy was the rising stature of Curvin, who had gained a considerable following as a community leader, despite his feelings of alienation.[49]

During the period in which CORE emerged and declined, the white youth in SDS fanned out into the cities and declared their commitment to a new movement for the poor.[50] If it was true that CORE had suffered from a kind of conventionality and middle-class respectability, the white youth in SDS confronted unexpected complexities of race that continuously tested their class-based activism. Like the vision of a beloved community illuminated by Martin King, the young activists imagined they could transcend social injustice. They rejected the American Dream, and flouted the values of the postwar mass consumer society, sacrificing traditional careers and suburban family life to live and work among the nation's poor. Intellectually attuned, sophisticated, well read, the activists followed radical intellectual traditions, as well as using their experience in the southern civil rights movement. If they escaped the stifling effects of bureaucracy by forming alternative communities, in Newark they confronted unexpected alienation and anger in poor black neighborhoods. Yet even in their own retrospective studies and personal historical accounts, few white activists reflected critically on their distance from them and black ghetto dwellers, or between leftist radical thought and the realities of racial oppression. From the beginning, they misunderstood the complex processes of cross-racial identification and failed to overcome some of its limitations.[51]

The new interracial movement for the poor started in 1962 in Ann Arbor, Michigan, with the drafting of the Port Huron Statement, the SDS manifesto, and formation of the Economic Research and Action Project (ERAP). The New Left debated the so-called Triple Revolution of "massive government spending on public works, education, housing, public power, and tax," and planned to establish contingents of ERAP in the major cities.[52] If the SDS group at the University of Michigan prized theoretical rigor, "having the best ideas," as one student declared, the new ERAP groups put ideas into practice on the ground, in the service of pressing the civil rights movement into a mandate for planned economic redistribution.[53] Despite their focus on class and radical economics, even the best activists misunderstood black poverty.[54] They wrote to Michael Harrington for advice, requesting copies of his bestselling book on the poor, *The Other America*, published in 1961, and studied the so-called Community Action Program model that stressed moral uplift and disciplining of beneficiaries in preparation for the delivery of government funding, and rejected its elitism. They had studied radical sociology and the older Chicago School models of urban poverty, both of which assumed a level of psychological or cultural deficit.[55] According to a few pieces explicitly dealing with economic systems, the New Left did not see poverty as a cultural problem or a matter of behavior, but neither did they show much appreciation for the intersection of race and class, of how deindustrialization and the rise of the suburbs had combined to marginalize black urbanites. Even as white activists set out to move into the inner cities, many still believed that their only problem was to mobilize apathetic whites, and early planning was stuck on the fact that "whites can't be organized."[56] To their credit, unlike most white liberals, who assumed that poor people suffered from a culture of poverty, and, according to historian Alice O'Connor, "disconnected the Poverty problem from urban restructuring and urban politics," the white youth influenced by the civil rights movement in the South intended to listen to the poor.[57]

Before they departed for Newark, the white volunteers had expected to organize working-class whites only to arrive at the predominantly black neighborhood of the Lower Clinton Hill in the South Ward. One of the stars of the student movement, Tom Hayden, later remembered the day I "found myself looking for the first time at the black ghetto of Newark," a sight that left him feeling "unbalanced," an appropriate enough impression for a young leader about to spend three years balancing between a theory of social democratic class politics and the everyday barriers of race. As more of the young white activists arrived, a newspaper feature recounted the apocryphal story of the students' double surprise, not only that Clinton Hill was all-black but also that "they found that the major issue would be housing; they had thought it would be unemployment."[58] In any case, they rented a flat, opened a storefront on Ridgewood Avenue, and established the Newark Community Union Program, or what became known around town as NCUP or "encuf" (and also as SDS or Hayden's group).[59]

The newcomers first met with a group of white progressives in Clinton Hill, most of whom were well aware of SDS through mutual contacts in New York and planned to recruit them to a labor-oriented program for job training and unionization. These white progressives had established the Clinton Hill Neighborhood Council (CHNC), headed by Stanley Winters, a professor of history, and Stanley Aronowitz, a nationally renowned labor organizer. The CHNC had successfully brought together civic, church, and synagogue leaders for better education and more school funding, promoting the civic ideology of "Better Human Relations." The CHNC spearheaded a campaign to stop an urban renewal project scheduled to clear and develop a favorite local park, and demonstrated for additional funding to improve the local teachers.[60] Winters and the CHNC initiated a new project based on the old industrial unionism goal of promoting job training and union membership for upwardly mobile African Americans but the NCUP volunteers who headed out into the neighborhoods reported that residents "don't like to talk about their unemployment, but will often discuss other problems." In fact, surveys had indicated that although many black Newarkers experienced racial discrimination in employment, they were more concerned over housing discrimination—31 percent identified unfair housing but only 3 percent issues of employment.[61] There are no clear-cut reasons why the average black resident responded positively to white organizers when they talked about housing, and ignored employment, but a likely explanation concerns past failures of unions to treat black workers with respect. When a new jobs and training center opened around 1964, for example, a black representative from the National Urban League explained the failure of black neighbors to enroll in the program by pointing out that "these people have been denied jobs so long that they just don't have the experience. You tell them now that jobs are available and they think you are kidding."[62] But rank-and-file white unions proved unreliable and essentially too conservative for the progressive mobilizations. When NCUP attempted to recruit the Hospital Workers Union 1199 to join a demonstration against the treatment of Mary Grace, an African American woman who was evicted and arrested for demanding basic repairs to her apartment, the union eventually backed out.[63]

Despite the young students' discovery of new issues and their considerable success, they wrote to the national office to confess their anxieties, doubts, and fear of failure. Day after day, the middle-class residents of Upper Clinton Hill had slammed the door in their faces, and observers charged that NCUP activists "were absent and uncommitted."[64] The activists replied sincerely that "we are happy here," and that "we are inspired by the morality of Port Huron, the vision of America in the New Era, and the political potential of Newark."[65] And by the end of the summer, they began organizing on housing issues in the Lower Clinton Hill. This area experienced the influx of African Americans when the NHA converted a retirement home into a public-housing facility for residents from the Central Ward displaced by renewal. From 1950 to 1958, as the black population of Newark increased by approximately 40 percent, Clinton Hill's share increased from 4 to 12 percent. As the Lower Clinton Hill threatened to tip to black residents, realtors attempted to convince Upper Clinton Hill residents to sell to them at low prices so that they could turn around and find blacks to buy at inflated prices.[66] Since the publication of the recent race relations survey, it had become public knowledge that black renters paid more than whites in the African American neighborhoods (Central Ward, Central Business-South Broad, West Ward, and Clinton Hill). By far the largest number of property holdings, up to 90 percent in the Central Ward, listed so-called absentee landlords who resided in the wealthy suburbs. African Americans owned a few buildings, but the vast majority comprised "earlier immigrant strains" and "substantially Jewish and Italian."[67] Because of this disparity in ownership in the neighborhoods, a number of black tenants in poor neighborhoods attempted to pressure landlords and bring suits, but studies of code enforcement in Newark, and in other major cities, showed that the experienced landlords absorbed fines as part of their routine expenses, while authorities criticized the codes for failing to improve the living conditions.[68]

One of NCUP's first truly independent actions were the "fix-up squads," which combined civic duty with proactive housing demonstrations by gathering neighbors to repair buildings, clean up public spaces, and promote a sense of community responsibility. The groups working in the poorest areas initiated a clearinghouse for rental properties and a center for counseling in tenant-landlord disputes. Despite the need for housing reform, traditional civic leaders like Winters distrusted the motives of Hayden and the other NCUP workers. Winters saw them as youth with a lot time on their hands who just "moseyed around."[69] In some ways, Clinton Hill epitomized the confused, ambivalent response of middle-class northern white liberals to the arrival of the race problem in their own backyards. As white immigrants and upwardly mobile workers, they voted Democratic and professed faith in the ideals of equality and the image if not the reality of integration. Yet their civic culture also stressed home ownership as the basis for fulfilling mutual obligations and affording a kind of respectability. In the South, in the face of integration, whites joined the Ku Klux Klan and other extremist white supremacist groups, but liberals predominated in upwardly mobile Clinton Hill.[70] CHNC campaigned to push back public housing and further integration of the poor, while the students in NCUP started with "We Declare War on Rats, Roaches, and Ridiculous Rents," and sponsored a "NO RENT FOR RATS 4RS RALLY" that challenged landlords to meet renters' demands for better maintenance and fair prices.[71]

Hayden, Carl Witman, Carol Glassman, as well as Eric Mann, Mike

Zweig, and a dozen others started to look for ways to organize black residents, and many found their way into rent parties or so-called "sip" parties, and fashioned pragmatically a community-based agenda.[72] Rather than leading or planning, the activists created new agendas simply by following the famous pioneer of civic organizing Saul Alinsky. He employed strategies of block organizing and building a sense of neighborly efficacy in the working-class areas of Chicago, but the New Left youth had preferred direct action, revolutionary-style commitment to the practice of democracy.[73] They associated Alinsky with the "old CIO organizing days and left tactics: Machiavelli for the poor," they quipped in a newsletter.[74] In turn, when Alinksy met Hayden and Carl Witman when they began organizing in Newark, he reportedly criticized their methods as "doomed to failure."[75] At one point the tension between the older progressives and their civic agenda and NCUP's unruly activism erupted into a crisis of bitter disagreement and forced a showdown. Representatives from both sides addressed a plenary session of the various block groups, presented their agendas, and then polled the audience. Not surprisingly, the CHNC won the vote of confidence, but not by as much of a margin as many had predicted. In the aftermath, Winters remembered that they lost several activists to NCUP, including black residents such as Jesse Allen, who helped to bridge student actions to the local black community.[76]

On the rebound, the activists in NCUP searched for support and enlisted the charismatic national civil right leader Bayard Rustin, who spoke on their behalf at a rally early in 1965.[77] Although local leaders accused the young activists "of dividing and disrupting the community," Rustin assured audiences that they are "approaching the problem correctly."[78] He reiterated a belief in the efficacy of the tactics of grassroots organization and advocacy (which of course he had helped to invent) in closed meetings with the students, according to a classified report by an undercover police officer. The official said that "Rustin advised the people at the meeting to contact all landlords and to organize block by block. He stated a lot of homes should not be demolished but improved."[79] Despite encouragement from the veterans of the civil rights movement, their deployment of direct action tactics encountered stiff opposition. In one case, for example, opponents posted anonymous flyers that alluded to Rustin's conviction for homosexual conduct, labeling him as "Convicted Criminal . . . [who] served 60 days in jail on a morals charge" in an attempt to undermine the NCUP movement.[80]

From 1964 to 1966, the activists mobilized residents to protest for better housing, including effective code enforcement, inspection offices, stricter regulations, and in the process, in the words of one activist, they "develop[ed] lots of leadership."[81] This daily organizing achieved considerable success. Simply blocking an eviction meant mobilizing as many as two hundred residents, and by the end of the summer the student volunteers managed to organize a series of rent strikes.[82] In one action Hayden was arrested and charged with assault and battery and threatening to harm an older woman, as disclosed in a case filed by a landlord the group had targeted.[83] According to the activists, while Hayden was leafleting, he confronted the landlady and the two argued about the treatment of her tenant, and she hit Hayden. At that time the property owner, "Mrs. Hayes," summoned the police, and charged Hayden with assaulting her. He was arraigned the next day. "Meanwhile," according to the NCUP notes sent to the national office, "the neighborhood rallied to Tom's defense and began making phone calls to the police stations urging his release." About ten hours later, a group of local residents and South Ward city councilman Lee Bernstein arrived at the precinct to release Hayden. When a week later the case came to trial, the woman recanted her testimony and Hayden was exonerated. In referring to the incident the NCUP slogan of the week quipped, "He hit her in the pocketbook so she hit him with it."[84]

In forging informal connections in neighborhoods rather than working exclusively through a branch of an organization, the activists cast a wider net that appeared to draw in roughly equal numbers of women and men in the community. Middle-class African American women had joined the Upper Clinton Hill association to picket in various demonstrations, such as a campaign to prevent the establishment of more liquor stores in the neighborhood. But NCUP recruited poor black women, pressing many into leadership responsibilities. As a group with a number of leading white feminists, NCUP recruited an African American woman, Terry Jefferson, to work on the staff, and their first visible actions around housing involved Mary Martin, who had demanded repairs on her apartment, and the extermination of "rats and roaches." She refused to pay her rent and was evicted, and NCUP launched a protest campaign on her behalf.[85] NCUP also advocated for Ida Brown, an African American resident of Clinton Hill, who refused to pay rent in protest of substandard conditions and untended repairs. After she informed the landlord that she intended to buy a home, vacated the premises, and moved in with neighbors in the upstairs apartment in the same building, the landlord ordered the removal of her possessions from her apartment. He reported Brown to the health department for allegedly "overcrowding" the apartment, and moved to evict. According to the NCUP version, the landlord and police "arrested her and pushed her to the floor," "they argued," and "a detective behind her pushed her . . . and the two of them fell down the stairs." But the landlord told police that Brown hit him, and she denied the accusations. Brown was arraigned in court on charges of assault in January 1965, and the judge set her bail so high that she was forced to await trial in prison.[86] At the time, only one of the four municipal judges in Newark was African American, and he reportedly sat in traffic court.[87]

Joining local activism with national publicity, NCUP and the leadership of SDS spearheaded the so-called Hayden-Brown Defense Fund that claimed to receive donations from and sponsorship by famous civil rights figures from Rustin to A. Philip Randolph, and white radicals from Harrington to Paul Goodman. This campaign became more spectacular as both local and national newspapers featured a shocking photograph of Brown, a middle-aged woman, being dragged by police to a patrol car. After NCUP managed to convince the judge to dismiss the charges against Hayden in the phony assault case, they regrouped to support Brown's case through several appeals. But the judge in Brown's case warned NCUP that any agitation in or outside the courtroom would adversely affect sentencing. Then the judge sentenced Brown to one year probation and payment of fines. "The judge told her that she was being used as a tool by others to further their ends," reported the incredulous activists. After the sentencing, members of NCUP campaigned against the landlord and published his address in their newsletter, letters, and telegrams of protest.[88]

Although they strongly identified with the oppression of African Americans, the young white activists failed to work hard enough to comprehend black anger and the dynamics of racial resentment.[89] At one point they characterized the new black militancy surfacing in the cities as an attempt "to liberate hate," and at another they dismissed cultural nationalism as merely the "black" ideologies "of the new militant middle-class Negro leadership" appealing to "the usual psychological justification." They criticized nationalism for failing to meet its own professed ideals of advancing the interests of the community.[90] As they continued to concentrate on housing issues, the white activists encountered more poor black women but sometimes approached the community in ways that probably alienated some or irritated others. At one point, Connie Brown, a white NCUP member, recalled that the "central issue of the development of a radical movement was the forging of a new identity," but if black residents cooperated on housing, few endorsed the construction of "new" identity. At one point Hayden declared that NCUP wanted to "organize, first, around the feeling of being poor and powerless, rather than being black." At another point Hayden declared that the black community had never engaged in serious and effective political action, and with these remarks betrayed not only the class orientation but a kind of cultural bias that obscured his and the group's vision of how to build an interracial movement.[91]

Only by establishing closer ties to their neighbors did the white activists advocate effectively. In one action in 1965, white demonstrators recruited black activists and together put their bodies on the line, storming into the mayor's office and staging a "lie-in" in which they lay down and refused to heed requests by the Chief of Police to move. Blacks and whites advocated on behalf of residents for a traffic light at an intersection that had been the scene of several serious auto accidents. When their request was delayed with red tape, an inch-high headline read: "Youth Invade City Hall."[92] NCUP also concentrated on the recruitment of legitimate community members to the group, including a resident from the Virgin Islands whom they called "the most promising community leader we've come across yet."[93] They "talked to him about everything from housing to garbage to Cuba and he has really grown to think strategically and take responsibility for the functioning of the block group." In another series of actions, they recruited a young "house painter and good artist," who was "really hot on doing something about the schools," and planned to make him the facilitator at the next meeting.[94] By identifying local, organic talent for leadership roles, NCUP facilitated interracial cooperation. After the black activist Jesse Allen bolted from the old Clinton Hill organization, it was humorously reported in a newsletter that students were "sorry to hear that Jesse Allen is having trouble with his wife. She does not like the idea that he gave up his work to work on stuff." NCUP joked that Jesse would receive a salary of eighty dollars per month to keep his wife from going to the police and filing for desertion.[95]

Despite gaining the trust of some poor black residents in Lower Clinton Hill, NCUP sometimes misunderstood and to a certain extent neglected the issues of utmost concern to the larger community. To that extent, the white activists negotiated unevenly the line between community insider and resented stranger. Like African Americans pouring into the city, the student activists were ostracized by the public. The deputy mayor was quoted as saying that the group was "from New England, New York and the Midwest. Those are not Newark citizens. They are outsiders."[96] The reporter Douglas Eldridge wrote on "a small militant group that was stepping up efforts to arouse" that belonged to an avowedly "racist" national organization—an antagonistic introduction to Newark, to say the least.[97] The group routinely suffered "crank phone calls, property damage, and threats of bombs and beatings," they wrote. Vandals smashed the windows of the NCUP headquarters, an anonymous phone call warned of a bomb on the premises, and the press reported on "a history of threats and harassments."[98] When Hayden and Norman Fruchter, a film director who eventually produced a documentary on the group, were dining out, an aggrieved landlord entered the establishment with a "strongly built male" and "threatened" the activists.[99] A year after arriving, NCUP was asked to leave its premises on Ridgewood Avenue because the landlord succumbed to "pressures" that were "placed on him."[100]

But NCUP had infrequently targeted police brutality, which had become a contentious issue that topped the black political agenda. However, in 1965 the white students inadvertently took on the police in one of their most important actions. NCUP came to the assistance of a black customer in a Klein's department store, Clyde Wright, after he was beaten by the security staff in a basement for allegedly stealing a sweater and a pair of women's shoes. As it happened, Wright was a relative of black NCUP member, Jesse Allen.[101] The beating of Wright received as much publicity as the Ida Brown legal case, and the group organized national demonstrations against Klein's. For months they leafleted the entrances to the store—"Clyde Wright Was Beaten Bloody in S. Kleins Dept. Store"—and sympathizers posed as store customers, selected merchandise, and refused to pay at the sales counter in the name of Wright.[102]

In combining retail discrimination with a case of totally unjustified brutality, the Wright assault publicly joined a growing chorus of dissension among African Americans against victimization at the hands of the police.[103] If NCUP staged a trial in a radicalized public sphere, the opposition chose to protest with false publicity, distributing an anonymous flyer with a large question mark drawn in the middle. It asked the question, "Who are the Outsiders In Our Neighborhood? Do-Gooders Or No-Gooders. Let's Keep Our Neighborhood Safe For Our Children." It was signed, "Clinton Hill Council for Better Harmony," an apparently nonexistent organization. By January 1965, an unidentified group distributed some five hundred bogus newsletters, including a block-style scrawl, handwritten heading, an amateur typeface, and a fake headline: "Clyde Wright Wrong: Admits Guilt In Klein's Case." It went on to report that the recanted testimony "slightly disappointed" and that Wright was "telling people that he was really guilty of shoplifting." If Wright had indeed lied, had the students suffered a terrible setback by investing so heavily and publicly in Wright's innocence? When the students discovered the counterfeit newsletters, they retaliated by issuing a newsletter that corrected the false story, and another that solemnly reported on the conviction of Wright. They recirculated the fake newsletter with a disclaimer headnote that warned "below is the counterfeit newsletter."[104] After Wright was convicted on charges of theft and assault, and a conservative judge sentenced him to prison, NCUP received more physical threats, their landlord was pressured to evict them, the office windows were smashed, and more members were arrested. Even CORE, which had refused to recognize NCUP, sent a letter in support of the "right of the community to organize and to present its grievances to the political structure."[105]

Yet historically evaluating the importance of NCUP remains as controversial here as it was in 1965. Some major studies on postwar cities tend to minimize the white progressive youth, and historians of black nationalism barely mention Hayden or some of the less famous figures in Newark. Most works omit postwar white progressive organizing from the standard narratives or interpretations of African American political thought. Even the integrationist Curvin recalled that "Hayden was not very significant in the larger scheme of things. He was important in the Clinton Hill Section." The sense was that Hayden and "the SDS kids" were temporary sojourners whose commitment to social justice for local people was not nearly as deep as that of natives of Newark, especially black people in the community. To what extent, however, was Curvin correct in concluding that "in the scheme of black politics, it would be hard to say they were a very significant force?"[106] A quarter century before, Hayden asked how he himself could "speak for the Negro citizens of Newark?"[107] At the same time, the white youth questioned Curvin's popularity, leadership style, and the depth of his grassroots support.

There were signs of change in the rising winds of black dissent in the spring of 1965, just months before the Watts riots exploded. The new head of CORE, Floyd McKissick, signaled the new direction of the organization at the annual conference on "The Black Ghetto: An Awakening Giant," when he advocated the enlargement of the long-term strategic focus from southern towns to northern cities, and stressed the new cultural identity of Black Power and running black candidates for office.[108] Up until the end, however, even though Curvin did not embrace the separatism advocated by the black militants, the membership of Essex County CORE turned to grassroots organizing and weeded out white members.[109] At the 1966 CORE national convention, delegates voted to support a public statement in favor of racial separatism, and Curvin publicly dissented, sounding more like a member of SDS: "The poor both black and white can participate in the running of the country."[110] For a moment in the civil rights movement, interracial activists reinvented politics—they emphasized local grievances, energized the ordinary citizens with exhortations for change, and in the process literally confronted democratic institutions.[111] NCUP facilitated the numerous cross-racial political encounters in ways that reconfigured the public sphere. In the South, civil rights workers would distribute flyers individually, and in clandestine ways, but even the boldest activists hesitated to go public. When an NCUP flyer announced a "May Day Rally For Peace"—a celebration of international communism—at Military Park on a Saturday afternoon, double-billed with the appearance of a black candidate for the U.S. Senate speaking on racial equality and on the Vietnam War, their publicity creatively mixed symbols of black militancy and radical New Left. The call "It's Time To March" and the ubiquitous phrase "PEOPLE HAVE GOT TO BE RESPECTED" had boldly crossed the color line.[112]

At a time when Newark's survey of race relations indicated that 65 percent of whites reported that they "would accept Negroes only as speaking acquaintances," and a mere 15 percent would accept them as close friends, the young white activists and black volunteer neighbors enjoyed real affections and mutual respect, enacting an exemplary model of interracial trust. There was a moment when diverse activists could stand together. But eventually one of the factions that had remained latent and more isolated in the public sphere in 1965—the progenitors of black nationalism—not only rose to dominate the platform but eventually demanded that the white activists move into the wings.[113] Years later, Tom Hayden testified before a congressional committee that "youth" was more important than "economic class"—a far cry from the Ann Arbor neo-Marxist revolutionaries—but such was the idealism that had inspired a powerful protest against the housing authorities and the police in Clinton Hill. Despite their moving commitment to the people, they would not lead the next stage of the movement.[114] The famous observer of American politics Alexis de Tocqueville wrote that "the liberty of association has become a necessary guarantee against the tyranny of the majority." With the democratization of the public sphere, new forms of citizenship that promised to cohere around multicultural factions and diverse interests, not racial polarities, gained more ground than ever before. Perhaps substantive pluralism and nonviolence, and respect for human dignity and personal empowerment, could prevail over racial conflict.[115]

5

Brutal Realities and the Roots of the Disorders

At dusk on July 12, 1967, two Newark police officers, Vito Pontrelli and Oscar De Simone, stopped John Smith's yellow taxi. The officers were white, Smith was black. Bystanders later testified that the police physically attacked the taxi driver without any provocation, but Smith was still charged with assault and battery, and resisting arrest. The initial police report indicated that "Smith became loud, profane, and abusive" and classified him as a conspirator in the disorders that erupted later that evening. The police and district attorney, however, eventually dropped the felony charges and citation for operating a motor vehicle with a suspended driver's license. (Having changed residence frequently, Smith could plausibly claim his ignorance of the revocation.) The other taxi drivers radioed news of the police beating across town and shuttled public housing residents to a planned demonstration, while rumors circulated that Smith was dead. In truth he had sustained a broken rib on the right side of his chest and was awaiting arraignment in a holding cell. Over the next five days, the most devastating riots in the history of New Jersey exploded in the Central Ward—costing twenty-six lives, injuring hundreds and destroying millions of dollars worth of property.[1]

Two days after ordering the withdrawal of National Guard troops, Governor Richard Hughes announced the appointment of seven white and four black members to a commission charged with the investigation of the civil disorders.[2] The following spring the Governor's Commission released the *Report for Action*, which proved to be a remarkably comprehensive summary that emphasized three causes of the riots: lack of political representation; police brutality; and worsening social conditions. For the first category, the commission identified inequities in the political system that reflected "not simply how many black people are appointed to, or hold, high position, but whether the administration as a whole is responsive to the black community."[3] For the second category, they subpoenaed testimony from both black and white witnesses who testified on the excessive force and unbecoming conduct of law enforcement. The commission blamed years of such abuse for causing "the real breakdown in community relations." For the third category, they cataloged a set of issues that would become dominant or hegemonic popular explanations of the riots—segregation, economic distress, and psychological alienation.[4]

The *Report for Action* obviously served to restore the authority of the government at a moment of crisis. The authors powerfully set the terms of the debate, establishing both the origins and ultimate meaning of the disorders. Their solutions involved more state and federal spending to ameliorate the volatility of the problem areas. If the commission affirmed faith in a failing liberalism and the efficacy of the government, it legitimated an unprecedented level of state intervention and displaced criticisms of its own conduct and culpability. As the *Report* focused attention on poverty, the riots became more and more spontaneous, irrational, and ephemeral. Dozens of books and hundreds of academic articles elaborated on the psychological roots of the disorders, while in 1968 the *Encyclopedia of Social Sciences* for the first time included an entry on violence to address riot studies. Many versions of this diagnosis of urban conflict adopted the influential thesis of cultural pathology and the breakdown in community, or to quote one author, "the spiraling interplay of unreciprocity . . . set in motion between mother and child" resulting in "homicidal offenders [who] have developed, then, in hostile, unreciprocating environments." In other words, by the 1970s many experts understood rioting as a symptom not only of economic deprivation but personal rage.

Perhaps no observer formulated a more intelligent version of social deprivation theory than Paul Ylvisaker, a white political scientist who combined an idealistic faith in the redemptive potential of the city with a career in public service. In 1966 Governor Hughes recruited Ylvisaker to head the newly created cabinet post of Community Relations Adviser, with responsibility for race relations and urban issues. Ylvisaker quickly gained a national reputation as an expert on urban problems of the stature of Kenneth Clark and Daniel Patrick Moynihan. In his communications and public lectures, Ylvisaker eloquently spoke of such effects as the "build up of human energy that was being dissipated in rage, blinding rage at society that couldn't deal with all the power that was there."[5] To alleviate suffering in the inner city, in an impassioned letter he urged "the President . . . [to] forge a grand national coalition to direct the Nation's resources at its city problems," particularly by designing programs for a massive redistribution of wealth through income taxes, income maintenance welfare, direct relief and health insurance, and job training.[6] Ylvisaker repeatedly cited the shortage of housing, writing that "20 million people live in 5,000,000 substandard and deteriorating slum dwellings throughout America," and boldly advocated the relocation of 500,000 residents of the inner city to the suburbs.[7] He wrote to Vice President Hubert Humphrey on the white "iron ring of suburbia," lobbying for a massive urban renewal project and a federal grants program.[8]

Only five days before the riots in Newark, Ylvisaker had written presciently to President Lyndon Johnson on the problem of the "growing apartheid of our urban populations" and warned him that severe segregation "presents this nation with an ugly fact and an ominous future—a possible threat to our security which may too soon overshadow that of Vietnam and proposed massive federal aid."[9] Yet Ylvisaker underestimated the level of political dissidence in the Central Ward, particularly the appeal of black nationalism.[10] In that regard, he reflected the flawed perspective of social scientists in which evidence of black radicalism was one more manifestation of pathology. Instead of studying and taking seriously more militant sentiments, sociologists asked the same questions assuming the same sort of psychological precipitants. If the Negro felt alienated, is that why he rioted? If the Negro anticipated improvement but became impatient, is that why he rioted? If the Negro experienced frustration because of slow progress or became jealous of white prosperity, is that why he rioted? In some cases, the scholarship tautologically characterized the poor as "riot-oriented" and more susceptible to or predisposed to "frustration politics." This frustration "gives rise to black nationalism," according one large volume published in 1968, and "the Negro's insecurity, demands, and frustrations pile on one another."[11]

If academic social science tended to reduce the variety and complexity of grassroots opposition to a state of black rage, the popular discourse that circulated outside the academy had totally objectified urban poverty. The average commentary on the problem of the ghetto assumed the response to segregation to be self-destructive despair. A series of pocket-size volumes, *Problems of American Society,* issued a new title in 1968 on *Riots,* a handy companion to the other social problem books, such as *The Consumer, Hunger, Prisons,* and *Racism,* that explained how an "incident occurred" that triggered an irrational outburst. One book featured a full-page photo of a decrepit toilet and warned that "this bathroom is not an extreme." Dilapidated housing in the ghetto, the authors suggested, accounted "for the fast developing 'burn-baby-burn' attitudes among young militant blacks."[12] But black migrants in the major cities had always suffered from economic hardship and impeded mobility, and few had engaged in rioting. Why did they eventually hit Newark, and not New Orleans? Black city dwellers had always lived in the poorest areas and tolerated worse housing conditions than whites. Why riot now? And what of the extraordinary expansion of the social welfare programs in the Great Society?

The impoverished conditions of the ghetto dominated the popular imagination in postwar America, but in reality black economic mobility had improved steadily from 1945 to 1970. In the prosperous 1960s, black male income increased from 59 to 65 percent of white incomes, in part because of improvements in black educational achievement.[13] Although social scientists and policy experts continued to write of a "grave crisis" caused by urban change, including a declining population, the transition from a white to a black population structure, and decreased per capita income, most studies failed to predict with specificity any of the disorderly consequences.[14] Deindustrialization caused higher unemployment rates and underutilization of full-time workers, with 30 percent of African Americans and 41 percent of white laborers reporting a drop in full-time hours.[15] Yet the structure of opportunity for black workers had steadily improved in the postwar era, and by the 1960s less than 4 percent divided blacks and whites in the lower echelon of average income categories. In Newark, for example, 12.2 percent of the black population were counted among the poor compared to 8.4 percent of whites. In the middle category, the black population outearned the white population, with 21.5 percent of blacks compared to 18.7 of whites sitting comfortably in the middle class. Only in the next higher income category did whites outearn blacks by 5 percent, and in the next category, by 8 percent, with 19.3 percent of whites reporting incomes between $10,000 and $15,000 compared to only 11.3 percent of African Americans.[16] On the other hand, one survey indicated that almost 30 percent fewer black workers found better-paying skilled jobs than whites.[17] But why would black workers protest the process of de-skilling now? The Labor Department data indicated that only 2 percent of African Americans found employment in the most prosperous industries, such as insurance and banking, and only 10 percent of whites had been able to secure these desirable positions. Yet working-class whites in the city undergoing the same structural transformations of deindustrialization as black workers had not chosen to riot.[18]

One statistic that may have been crucial to the deprivation theory was that the black unemployment rate was based on the theory that idleness led to frustration and despair, and to rioting. In the 1960s, the rate of unemployment for black men was almost double that for white men—an average of 10.6 percent compared to 5.37 percent—but this disparity was reflected in only one segment rather than throughout the black male population. For example, the rate of unemployment for white men in the age category 20–24 was 6.8 percent, compared to the slightly lower rate of 6.5 percent for black men. The problem was the comparison between black and white youth. Given the high percentage of youth in the black population, calculated at 42.7 percent, and comparatively lower percentage of elderly (8 percent compared to 31.2 percent white), the generally high unemployment rates for male youth skewed the overall rate of black employment.[19] Though black workers probably interpreted the gap as a matter of racial discrimination, they also recognized their remarkable gains in the past two decades. The median earnings for black men born in the era of World War I had doubled between 1936 and 1945 and again between 1956 and 1965.[20] Economic deprivation theory hardly explained the riots, at least not by assuming a declining income.[21]

The black population remained a community in flux, with a high percentage of recent migrants from the South pouring into the Central and South Wards of Newark. Although the vast majority of whites reported their birthplace as New Jersey, many African Americans reported being born in various southern states. While 49 percent of whites had always resided in Newark and another 17 percent had moved within the state, only 17 percent of African Americans were natives of the city, with 47 percent reporting Georgia, Alabama, North Carolina, South Carolina, and Florida as their places of birth.[22] Thus many of the arrested rioters were newcomers to the state but only 27 percent of the men and women arrested for all offenses in the riots identified themselves as unemployed.[23] By contrast, 73 percent reported that they worked regularly

—18 percent identified themselves as skilled, 23 percent as semiskilled, and 59 percent as unskilled labor.[24] Class or economics alone failed to explain the riots, but what if analysts combined their picture of retarded mobility with the demoralization of living in the ghetto?

The theory that ghettoization caused the disorders failed to account for the extraordinary progress in urban renewal and construction of housing units since 1950. From the recently established Housing and Urban Development (HUD) department came a wealth of new housing resources. From the Model Cities program, for which communities applied to demonstrate a renewal plan, came full-scale design and construction in a target area. From the Grant Law came funds to operate nonprofit organizations that constructed new moderate-income housing, as well as increased allocations for housing under traditional urban renewal.[25] Despite declining political support for renewal projects among whites, the NHA had planned to build ten new housing projects in as many years.[26] And the Great Society only promised more assistance to the inner-city poor. By the mid-1960s, a bevy of new federal programs poured some $7 million into education opportunities and Manpower Training Skills centers. Allocations for Aid to Dependent Children and old age assistance accounted for the single largest federal expenditure in Newark. Millions of dollar were transferred to the United Community Corporation (UCC) to coordinate grants and local services, which on the eve of the riots received twice its original federal allocation, more than $12 million.[27]

Some experts blamed the rioting on poor public schools and declining student performance on standardized exams.[28] By the opening of the 1960s, the drop-out rate for black high school students in Newark was at a record high. Many of them had been recent southern migrants and became unemployed. More than contributing to the problem of juvenile delinquency, this cohort threatened to become a permanent underclass of chronically poor and undisciplined residents, what the head of a community action program called "a volatile, unstable force in the Newark area labor market."[29] But again the Great Society had allocated massive spending on local education programs through Federal Title I, which established children-parent centers and community education and curriculum projects, such as the Camden Street School in Newark that carried a $300 per pupil allocation. Although test scores of poor black children showed an achievement gap, this hardly explained why their parents would riot. However, a closer examination of a particular convergence of anxieties in public education suggests the ways in which not only structural deficits, but political culture shaped the response of poor ghetto dwellers to upwardly mobile families to marginal nationalists, increasing the chances for a riot.[30]

By the beginning of 1967, the Newark school board had appointed an African American educator to serve as its chairman, but whites occupied all of the remaining seats. In a city that had just tipped to black majority—by 1965 the black population of Newark topped 50 percent—a growing number of parents challenged the board's legitimacy. When a vacancy opened, the debate over candidates raised not only the abstract question of political representation but of community control over the future of black children. Exacerbating parents' sense of powerlessness, Mayor Addonzio nominated one of his cronies, William Callaghan, to the vacancy. It was probably not an exaggeration when a speaker at the public hearings on the nomination (one of more than seventy speakers that night) "predicted that 'blood would run through the streets of Newark,' if Callaghan was named to the post at tonight's meeting."[31]

More parents and activists joined demonstrations against the mayor and demanded the appointment of Wilbur Parker, an experienced black educator. Within the month, Curvin and members of CORE and allied groups called for the Board of Education to issue reports on the employment of non-whites and whites in the public schools according to job category; to appoint three African Americans to the board to replace officers whose terms expired in June; and to hire an African American for the position of Director of Elementary Education. In the process, black parents joined the veteran activists in advancing a more radical agenda that not only called for racial balance in the appointments but also a new curriculum attuned to cultural diversity and teacher accountability. In the wake of the stalemate over electing only one more African American to the board, growing racial tensions compounded feelings of powerlessness in parents. Calls for curricular reform affirmed a more cultural nationalist agenda, leading otherwise moderate families to believe in the need for and efficacy of special courses to address the so-called special concerns of black students. Now, in response to intransigence at City Hall, not only the militants but the integrationists such as Curvin proposed diversity training for all school personnel, a "new history of the Negro," and Afrocentricism in "a special emphasis be placed on the history of the black man prior to the year 1619."[32] According to police surveillance records, Curvin also collaborated with the more radical

Fig. 5.1. Grassroots activists cooperated with African American residents in the Clinton Hill neighborhood to demand better housing and social services. Nationally recognized leader Tom Hayden was considered by some authorities to be a dangerous radical who led the protests. (Courtesy of Wisconsin Historical Society)

group known as the Black Man's Liberation Army in a three and a half hour public meeting about the nomination to the Board of Education.[33] Another report described a scene in which the board was forced to adjourn when "the foot stomping and heckling became so abusive and control of the meeting was lost."[34]

In the months before the disorders, African Americans in poor neighborhoods such as Clinton Hill actively demanded not only the end of discrimination but the redistribution of resources through the Great Society programs. In the process, like the parents who became involved in the school board controversy, local residents demonstrated a newfound sense of political agency that tested the limits of democracy. By summer 1965, both black and white activists in Clinton Hill and the Central Ward convened instructional forums on how to apply for various grants and entitlements, promising their neighbors in need that "all you have to do is go to the meeting."[35] The activists helped neighbors to receive federal funding for day-care centers, to receive tutoring services, and to learn "Negro History."[36] Many residents still needed to fight the bureaucracy—according to Hayden, fight for "everything . . . rules skirmishes within the War on Poverty."[37] Many of these campaigns attracted a large number of black women, according to NCUP activist Carol Glassman.[38] And according to the leading historian of the national New Left movement to organize the poor, Jennifer Frost, African American women "became the projects' first and largest community."[39] African American women actively participated in what were known as the Area Boards, each of which operated uniquely in relation to a particular neighborhood. At both public hearings and informal gatherings at the Area Boards, various groups applied for funding to the United Community Corporation, which in turn received allocations from the Office of Economic Opportunity in Washington. The boards strove for diversity and inclusion in the neighborhoods, exemplifying what Glassman called "maximum feasible participation in living color."[40]

The most voluminous and revealing extant sources pertain to Area Board Three in Clinton Hill, which experienced the politicization of local people.[41] The black activist Bessie Smith recalled that "it's hard for poor people at these meetings of the Area Board to express themselves and get their ideas across." In some ways, this critique of expertise implicitly questioned the legitimacy of white authorities and also followed in the New Left rejection of authoritarian government. The NCUP used terms like "poor," bracketing class as a critical category, and believed that the so-called "big ministers" from the African American leadership alienated the "poor" as much as the white experts from the agencies. And a black female volunteer, Billie Lassiter, questioned if anybody, including the leaders, cared "really about the people in the area, or how poor they are."[42] The intervention of NCUP and the building of interracial activism transformed their perceptions and enhanced a sense of efficacy. If the activists had originally rejected the Great Society, their local work produced a flyer that optimistically declared "it looks like they are beginning to see that the ones who know the most about poverty are the poor people themselves."[43] NCUP attempted to hold more informal, democratic meetings, and Bessie Smith testified that there was "no shame" and nobody was "outwitted." In 1966 Smith won election to the presidency of the Area Board but died before her term expired, lovingly remembered by Hayden in his memoir, and honored by residents of Clinton Hill with a community center in her name.[44] Although some observers criticized the white youth for creating a "puppet area board," which they presumably controlled, the record of this interracial activism demonstrated the ways in which volunteers expanded the politicization of the neighborhoods. Meetings with government, to quote another recruit to NCUP, Billie Lassiter, "make you feel like a fool for even thinking things," yet participating in the Area Board and helping out, reported Lucy Parker, "boosts your morale."[45]

Black women involved in the new community programs made plans for a new playground and recreation facilities, reviving a level of public engagement that harkened back to the days of Double V protest for the integration of swimming pools and beaches. A mother and activist, Joyce Wells proposed converting an abandoned factory into a recreation center. They justified the program in the name of gendered recreation—that "young girls, see, like to play hopscotch, and jump rope. And young boys, they like marbles and dodge ball. And my older girls, they like to sew and dance." The federal programs intersected with an ongoing female reform tradition in which women invoked maternal justice to persuade the government to implement particular programs, and in turn some female members in NCUP formed a presence in a citywide board of trustees. In neighborhoods, black women argued for safety and welfare, as they sought, in their words, to gain "power over the play streets," but a spokesman for the Newark Police Department opposed the program, saying it would not prevent future disturbances.[46] In fact, during that summer, when local black youth demanded but failed to receive additional community recreation services, they led the disorders in Plainfield, the most violent disturbances in the state outside of Newark.

If the dream of maximum feasible participation had effectively renewed the civic culture of black residents, two to three years into the implementation of the War on Poverty in Newark, more black residents experienced the realities of powerlessness and white domination at City Hall. Like those who protested against the white appointment to the Board of Education, black mothers felt a growing frustration after attending endless meetings with difficult city council members, and continued to face off against the police. By the time construction of the recreation center had resumed, Mayor Addonizio had managed to claim credit for the entire program.[47] Despite their percentage in the population, however, black city employees with substantial influence numbered a dozen, including Grace Malone, head of the city's welfare department; the head of the mayor's Human Rights Commission; and a few other

Fig. 5.2. The local Area Boards provided a point of engagement between the Great Society programs, such as the Office of Economic Opportunity, and poor minorities. Interracial activists facilitated greater deliberation among black residents of Clinton Hill, whose growing sense of efficacy raised expectations for representation at City Hall. (Courtesy of Wisconsin Historical Society)

administrators. The government failed to serve as a representative institution of the people.[48]

As the public sphere of the city proved increasingly unresponsive to black initiatives and requests for services, the black public sphere correspondingly increased by becoming more involved with radical black nationalists. To a great extent, of course, Martin Luther King, Jr., still dominated the leadership of the civil rights movement, and opinion surveys of African Americans showed mixed results on the question of popular support for nationalist organizations like the Nation of Islam. Approximately 40 percent approved teaching an African language to black children, but only 3 percent supported the nationalist proposal to establish a separate nation. Yet the same polls also showed cracks in the foundation of African American liberalism. An increasing number of African Americans described an intractable racism that many believed foreclosed opportunity and mobility.[49] To what extent was this dissatisfaction a breeding ground for black nationalism?[50]

Since the outbreak of civil disorders in Harlem and in several cities in New Jersey in 1964, and the massive riots in Watts in California in 1965, the Federal Bureau of Investigation (FBI) had investigated nationalists and other so-called subversives in Newark on suspicion of seditious activities and plotting of riots. In fact, only weeks before the Smith incident touched off the Newark disorders, the FBI produced a classified memo, "Racial Violence Potential in the United States," that reported on the allegedly suspicious activities of Martin Luther King, Jr., Stokely Carmichael (SNCC), and Floyd McKissick (Congress of Racial Equality, CORE). The reports accused civil rights leaders of "adopt[ing] the communist tactic of linking the civil rights movement with the Anti-Vietnam war protest," and advised the president to speak forcefully for public order and law.[51] Radicals read religiously the famous treatise *Wretched of the Earth* by Frantz Fanon published in 1963, which argued that "the naked truth" of decolonization is "searing bullets and bloodstained knives." "The development of violence," the Algerian psychoanalyst argued, "among the colonized people will be proportionate to the violence exercised by the threatened colonial regime."[52] Stokeley Carmichael, on his part, compared the "Negro community" in America with African decolonization, arguing that in both situations the black community members were "victim[s] of imperialism and colonial exploitation."[53] He was literally banned by several governments, including England and South Africa, and was facing dubious criminal charges in Washington, D.C., and at one point a member of the Newark Board of Education lobbied to prevent him from speaking. But Carmichael kept the invitation to address an audience of more than eight hundred high school students in the Central Ward, as well as a privileged, powerful student body at Princeton University, proclaiming in a speech there that "the masses can participate in making the decisions which govern their destiny." Carmichael told a crowd in Newark on Springfield Avenue (where the rioting erupted a year later) that black activists were "taking over" Lowndes County, Alabama, referring to the formation of a black political party there, and chastised the audience because "you should have taken Newark, N.J., over because it belongs to you." Carmichael openly challenged King's theory of nonviolent social change—he told the audience that he refused "to march and get hit on the head with rocks in order to be able to live next to savages."[54]

Black nationalist sentiment was rising in Newark not only because of frustration at City Hall, and Carmichael's public appearances, but also because of the black Muslims in the wake of the assassination of

Malcolm X. A half-century earlier, in 1913, Noble Drew Ali founded the Moorish Science Temple in the Central Ward, the progenitor of the black Muslim headquarters that had arisen in Detroit and then in Chicago to form the Nation of Islam (NOI) led by Elijah Muhammad. Throughout the 1950s, the black press printed stories on Elijah Muhammad and the growing operations of NOI in Detroit, and around 1961 the black Muslim activities in Newark appear with more frequency in the press. At one point, the Newark branch of the NOI drew crowds of more than a thousand and became so visible that the mayor authorized a secret police surveillance of their activities.

In the mid-1960s, black Muslims challenged the right of public schools to require students to recite the pledge of allegiance, and in a case involving the school board of nearby Elizabeth, the state supreme court excused the children from the civic ritual.[55] Although some black Newarkers converted to Islam and joined the NOI, the black Muslims rarely took public stands on the leading political issues. An activist in Newark recalled that "after the death of Malcolm X you really heard about the Muslims and their movement," but he also remembered that their organization was not overtly political or visibly involved in community organizing.[56] At one point, so much attention was focused on the Muslims that civil rights leaders exaggeratedly reported that "no Negro can make a speech anywhere now without some white person asking: 'Are you a Black Muslim?'"[57] To explain their growing appeal, radical black intellectuals such as Calvin Hernton blamed the intransigence of whites—that "they hated the NAACP and CORE" and pushed even moderate African Americans to the extremes of nationalism and the Nation of Islam.[58] Finally, only a week before the riots, Newark police made several highly controversial arrests of black Muslims in a nearby suburb, East Orange, in which police reported harassment, and observers reported excessive force in the arrest. Records indicated that the prisoners were variously treated for lacerations, a fractured skull, and abdominal pain after a black Muslim was "kicked in the balls."[59]

Black nationalism also gained new visibility in the public sphere because of Newark's location between two major cities with significant black nationalist movements. By the mid-1960s, a variety of black activists invested in nationalism frequently stopped in Newark and visited the Central Ward as well as Trenton, Camden, and Plainfield on railroad trips from Washington, D.C., to Philadelphia, and on to Harlem. (In fact, many locales along the Philadelphia–New York corridor later experienced significant riots or black-led disorders.) Also, Newark's reputation for volatility and black insurgency—according to one longtime activist, it "was already identified among those who knew as one of the potential hot spots in the country because of the shifting population"— attracted itinerant black radicals.[60] This was the case with the black communist revolutionary cadre known as Revolutionary Action Movement (RAM), founded by Alvin Oliver and Maxwell Curtis Stanford, Jr., in 1962 in Cleveland. RAM had mobilized a major branch in Philadelphia, and by 1966 the Newark Police Department's undercover investigations discovered RAM members at a number of CORE demonstrations. However, neither the interviews with members of RAM nor the Black Panthers who were active in the late 1960s and 1970s recall their presence in Newark.[61]

But the locally based, moderate black nationalist Nathan Wright enjoyed a great deal of influence. A popular writer with an established record of leadership, Wright had earned advanced degrees in social science and theology, published important books on black urban politics, and headed a nonprofit organization in Massachusetts before moving to New Jersey. In 1966 he was selected to serve as chairman of the 1967 National Conference on Black Power (with the meetings scheduled for mid-July in Newark). Wright melded a commitment to group uplift with the project of instilling the discipline of self-help, both time-tested strategies of conservative nationalism, but did not embrace the example of grassroots activism or militant rhetoric. If Black Power acolyte Carmichael called for revolution, Wright called for self-help. But like most Black Power advocates, Wright rejected the nonviolent theory of social change, largely for the pragmatic reason that such tactics proved ineffective. His book on Black Power and an unpublished manuscript criticized nonviolence because it lowered black self-esteem, and he argued that "sometimes when a man fails to engage in defense it may stem, at least in part, from feeling that what cries out for protection is not worth protecting."[62] This was a far cry from King's promulgation of nonviolence as the epitome of black moral superiority and courage. On the other hand, Wright rejected the strategy of rioting, and asked rhetorically if participating in civil disorders meant anything more than "black suicide before white men's bullets." "The crazed consequence of being a nobody boxed in on a dead-end street."[63]

Across the nation, in the aftermath of Watts, Wright and many black leaders joined white liberals in condemning the rioters as violent, irrational, and self-destructive. But the repudiation of rioters left a kind of vacuum in responsible leadership. The significant exception was a newcomer to the city, Colonel Ahmed Hassan of the Black Man's Volunteer Liberation Army (BMLA). Colonel Hassan was theatrical and spectacular as a commander of the BMLA in the tradition of Malcolm X, claiming that he knew the identity of Malcolm's assassins and vowing "at the right time they will take care of them."[64] According to extant police reports, the name Hassan was the alias of Tony Williams, who was convicted of several felonies and incarcerated in the South. After his release, he moved to Washington, D.C., and opened offices of the BMLA on Kennedy Street, N.W. To run his Newark operations, Hassan chose Clinton Bey (a friend of Phil Hutchings), who listed the telephone number of the Area Board in the Central Ward as his personal contact point. Hassan and Bey rented a building known in the Central Ward as the Black Liberation Center for $75 per month. It featured printed signs and a loudspeaker which, at one point, the police ordered them to turn off. After the premises were burned, they moved into a restaurant on South Orange operated by Clinton and Ozzie Bey. It served as a central meeting place that also attracted moderates such as Hutchings, Robert Fullilove, and Derek Winans. Hassan recruited rank-and-file members from the audiences at demonstrations, including both men and women, and "promised he [would] bring anything to Newark requested of him, men, guns (truck load)."[65] Probably exaggerating its size, Hassan estimated that his organization opened offices in fourteen cities.

Hassan had risen like a comet in part by employing a tactic that nationalists had used in cities across the nation, the so-called united or militant front. To gain leverage against the established civil rights bureaucratic structure and tap into their membership, nationalists to the left of the black public sphere established front organizations that accommodated different ideological positions, like the black Christian nationalist Rev. Albert Cleage in Detroit, and Ron Karenga's Black Congress in Los Angeles.[66] Hassan warned audiences that U.S. army bases would be used as concentration camps "in America for Negroes." He presided over meetings in full uniform—"Army shirt with green and red shoulder patch, red scarf and rank of Full Colonel)," according to police; or dressed completely in black, "a black berete [sic], black military boots, a black safari jacket . . . with red/black and green emblem sewn into his lapel." The colonel had supposedly received his rank from the Black Star Regiment, a group that invoked the black nationalist Marcus Garvey's Black Star Line, the famous "Back to Africa" scheme of the 1920s that attracted wide support from disillusioned African Americans. The BMLA projected a militant manhood not only to appeal to black women but to recruit them as well. They won over a few "fringe radical sisters" when appearing on college campuses. Hassan maintained visibility when "he got into the *Washington Post* talking about how he had an army of a thousand and more troops, each armed to the teeth and raised to defend black people where they were and all this stuff," recalled one skeptical activist from the era.[67]

If some were skeptical of Hassan, his disruptive tactics and spectacle had gathered a following in the Central Ward. In 1966, the Newark Housing Authority announced plans to build a new medical school on 150 acres of undeveloped land, and identified the Central Ward as a viable site. To the extent it is possible to characterize the sentiment of the community, survey data suggested continuing support in the neighborhood for renewal. A *Newark News* story reported that a clear majority of Central Ward residents supported the construction. The UCC conducted a more detailed survey that showed some declining support in the neighborhoods that were immediately impacted and whose residents would have to move. Although 76 percent of Central Ward residents supported building the new medical school somewhere in Newark, community opinion became evenly divided on the merits of the program. One poll showed that only 46 percent favored the school if they would be forced to relocate.[68] In the dailies a poll showed that "a large proportion of our respondents express a desire to move from where they currently live" and "77 percent of the tenants in the survey said they will move if they are given enough to pay for the cost of moving."[69]

In the spring of 1967, the NHA convened new blight hearings to air public opinion on the medical school project, which Hassan and the BMLA, and several other groups, adamantly opposed. Hassan reportedly "disrupted" a planning board meeting "with a noisy protest."[70] On the eve of the riots, to battle against the mayor's school board appointment and against urban renewal, a broad coalition of Newark politicos were joining the militant Hassan.[71] Even older white progressive activists such as Stanley Winters objected to a medical school in the name of community control, even if they shared little in the way of ideology or outlook with the nationalist militants.[72] When the police reported another disruption of a planning meeting, Hassan and several others in attendance were forcibly removed by the police. But Tom Hayden and other members from NCUP stayed on to demonstrate their support of the black nationalists. At a later date, attending a rally reportedly led by Hassan and the BMLA to demonstrate against the construction of the school were Newark political insider George Richardson, an unnamed minister from the Dutch Reformed Church, and the Central Ward Democratic chairman, among others. Police records also indicate that Hassan attempted to secure the support of Curvin and more mainstream politicians, particularly Kenneth Gibson (the black candidate for mayor in the 1966 elections). But Gibson remained at arm's length from much of the protests. Undercover police reports did place Curvin at additional meetings with Hassan.[73] But Curvin later denied lending the BMLA any support, and perhaps the police planted the report to undermine Curvin's credibility in his bid for a leadership role.

Perhaps attesting to the effectiveness of Hassan, liberals in the state government dismissed racial nationalism as little more than "old wine in new bottles."[74] In the larger scheme of things, the extremists like Hassan played a smaller role—they certainly participated in Newark politics for a shorter period of time, arriving in 1967 and leaving by October 1967 —than the mainstream, integrationists like Curvin, who later recalled that "if their presence had any real bearing on the city, it was to create a great deal more attention and unification on the Medical School issue." In retrospect, Curvin minimized "their strength—I don't think they ever had more than three or four people."[75] But clearly Hassan's style and disruptive tactics gained visibility, and the police considered both Curvin and Hassan to be threatening and a dangerous influence.[76]

To a far greater extent than the school board conflict or the planned medical school, the escalating protest against police brutality fostered what might be called the nationalization of the black public sphere, leading directly to rioting. The recurrence of police brutality constantly destabilized race relations in the city and fed into the rising influence of black militancy that rejected nonviolence in favor of armed self-defense. From another angle, police brutality was the result of worsening social conditions and poverty, particularly African American unemployment; that is, unemployed black men were more likely to gather in public spaces and in the streets where they could openly clash with police. Because the Newark Police Department was overwhelmingly white, like the Board of Education issue and the preponderance of white officials in charge of some of the poverty programs, the police confrontations

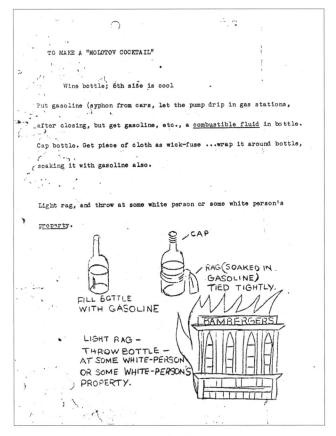

TO MAKE A "MOLOTOV COCKTAIL"

Wine bottle; 6th size is cool

Put gasoline (syphon from cars, let the pump drip in gas stations,

after closing, but get gasoline, etc., a combustible fluid in bottle.

Cap bottle. Get piece of cloth as wick-fuse ...wrap it around bottle,

soaking it with gasoline also.

Light rag, and throw at some white person or some white person's

property.

CAP

RAG (SOAKED IN GASOLINE) TIED TIGHTLY.

FILL BOTTLE WITH GASOLINE

BAMBERGERS

LIGHT RAG – THROW BOTTLE – AT SOME WHITE-PERSON OR SOME WHITE-PERSON'S PROPERTY.

Fig. 5.3. To make a "Molotov Cocktail."

racialized political conflicts between City Hall and the underrepresented African American population. Until the eruption of civil disobedience, of 1,512 men on the Newark police force only 145 were African American.[77]

While Curvin appeared at anti-police rallies and attempted to negotiate on issues of brutality with the mayor, Hassan and others organized self-defense groups and cadres of the BMLA in the Hayes Homes and Stella Wright Homes. In response to more incidents of wrongful arrest of young African American men and excessive force used against them, an anonymous activist or group distributed a flyer with instructions on how to assemble a "Molotov cocktail." The Molotov cocktail was an empty bottle, filled with gasoline and stopped with a rag, that was lit and thrown like a bomb. It could be detonated at riots.[78] In addition, a few extant sources document nationalist organizing in public housing, and activists recalled that the large towers represented a logistical obstacle to community organizing.[79] Meanwhile, Curvin pressed for reform within the nonviolent framework, including a board for police-community relations. Not only CORE and Curvin dared to challenge police brutality, for back in the 1950s the local NAACP members had already continually followed up on cases of police impropriety.[80] By the mid-1960s, a number of leaders lobbied for the creation of a civilian review board, and charged that the chief of police and the Newark Police Department (NPD) rejected black applicants for no reason.[81] They called on Harold Lett at the DAD to press enforcement of an antidiscrimination law in personnel of the NPD, and helped to organize publicity drives by posting flyers, printing newsletters, and picketing City Hall. Again, in concert with the more radical black organizations, Curvin filed a suit with the aid of the ACLU in federal court alleging that the NPD was "waging a class war against Negroes."[82] The remnants of the Essex County CORE led a campaign to force the resignation of the police chief and called for the defeat of Mayor Addonizio at the polls in May (though without supporting another candidate).[83]

Stories of Curvin's confrontations with chief of police, Dominick Spina, were splashed across the newspapers. Spina was born and raised in the Italian-American neighborhoods of north Newark and graduated from Barringer High School, the University of Newark, the Newark Law School, and later trained in the Federal Bureau of Investigation.[84] When Spina was quoted in the papers, it was frequently in anger at "minority pressure groups," either directly or euphemistically criticizing black leadership.[85] If Curvin, as a black leader, was the cream of the talented tenth, Spina was the civic hero of white ethnics, the president of the Kiwanis Club, who was named man of the year by the North Newark Lions Club at a ceremony in which speakers decried the decline of a strong police force. To boost the police's sagging image and restore moral order to the city, Spina orchestrated campaigns against liquor, nightclubs, and gambling, and spearheaded a youth group of junior crime fighters.[86] Since at least 1960, experts and policy analysts documented a long list of incidents that suggested "Negroes suffer from unfair treatment by police." The NPD was investigated for corruption and incurred half a dozen indictments annually, citing heavy involvement in gambling and loan sharking, and the police administration refused to respond to documented abuses. In 1962 Spina bowed to calls for reform by Curvin, and called for the promotion of black personnel, promising to "increase Negroes in the detective and plain clothes divisions." Yet the NPD failed to promote any black officers over the next five years.[87]

The fact was that the politicos of Newark, like most urban machines —for example, the notorious Mayor Richard Daley's reign over Chicago —typically refused to negotiate with protesters or even with civil rights leaders.[88] When Martin Luther King, Jr., marched in Chicago for open housing, Daley ignored or co-opted the movement by appearing to negotiate but refusing to concede anything on major stands. In Newark Addonizio and Spina refused to negotiate seriously with Curvin, indicating a level of government intransigence that signaled danger on the horizon, the breakdown of democratic deliberation. The national director of CORE, James Farmer, appeared on NBC radio and spoke at a major rally to publicize police brutality in Newark. But Addonizio and Spina refused to negotiate, not only pushing Curvin to mobilize more people in the community, but also pushing moderate groups to the more radical side of the black public sphere.[89]

In June 1967 Curvin and various activists from CORE led a major rally to commemorate the shooting death of Lester Long, Jr., a twenty-two-year-old African American man whom police shot to death two years before at the intersection of Oriental and Broadway while allegedly trying to escape an arrest for a traffic offense. In the process, peaceful, nonviolent activists inadvertently infused the public sphere with the drama of violence. They circulated an incendiary flyer that accused the police of murder, charging that "he was shot in the back of the head." Activists also recalled that less than three months later in 1965, an off-duty detective had shot and killed Walter Mathis, a seventeen-year-old black boy suspected of larceny and assault and battery. As Curvin led demonstrations protesting Long's death, the Police Benevolent Association, including Officer Henry Martinez, the man who shot Long, staged a counterprotest in front of City Hall.[90] If Curvin felt that the civic rituals protesting police corruption and brutality in the case of Long showed that "these people had all that kind of nonsense they could stand," other observers located urban violence in the context of southern lynching. A number of activists had recently returned from the South, and recalled the death of Emmet Till. "I think that the thing that really drove

it home was the lynching of Emmet Till. I remember vividly that day because my aunt came to me and said that if you don't straighten up this is
what's going to happen to you."[91] A generation of enraged black men
who turned militant in the mid-1960s, most famously Eldridge Cleaver
with his best-selling memoir, *Soul on Ice,* who "flew into a rage at myself, at America, at white women, at the history that had placed those
tension of lust and desire in my chest," rooted their violent backlash
in the murder of young black boys like Emmet Till and Lester Long.[92]
Violence against black men proved deeply divisive, stimulating separatism and the rejection of nonviolent tactics associated with interracial
activism. Yet after the death of Lester Long, NCUP coordinated a march
against the police and Officer Martinez that passed directly through the
middle of the Central Ward before arriving at City Hall.[93]

If the death of Lester Long haunted the Central Ward, the shooting
death of a white police officer in 1965 clouded the vision of many white
Newarkers. In December 1965 a highly publicized case of a thirty-seven-
year-old police sergeant, William Maver, who was injured by armed
bank robbers and permanently disabled only days before he was to be
promoted to the rank of lieutenant. The tragic story of his paralysis and
moving updates on his convalescence headlined the dailies. Based on
reports that the shooters were young black men, the police searched
the Central Ward, Orange, and even Harlem in New York City, and
attempted to link the police shooting to black Muslims. The employment of racial profiling dated back to the beginning of Chief Spina's
tenure, when on more than one occasion black leadership charged the
NPD with inflammatory remarks on the growing population of black
Muslims in Newark and East Orange. At one point, Spina was quoted
as characterizing all black Muslims as "misguided people who are in-
stigators of racial strife." Several months before the Maver shooting
Spina was again quoted in the dailies calling for the resignation of all
black Muslims from the police force. He disclosed that two black police
officers were under suspicion of practicing the "Muslim faith," and alleged that two officers, possibly the same suspects, were members of
CORE. "I am not too happy about CORE," Spina declared, although
he planned no action against the suspects on the police force. It was
charged that Spina's overzealous attacks in the context of sympathy for
the paralyzed police officer would trigger a white backlash.[94] Yet despite
intensification of black protest, Newark's police believed their relationship with black Newarkers to be one of "reasonable rapport." But as

late as 1967 no African American had been promoted to the rank of captain or sergeant (and only a handful had achieved that of lieutenant). Although white officials claimed they could not recruit qualified African Americans, few whites on the force possessed remarkable credentials. Worse, recruitment of African Americans had declined by more than 60 percent in five years, from twenty-four black recruits in 1962 to only nine in 1967.[95]

At the end of the day, word on the street was that the white police would not yield to reform or activism. And if some black residents retained a faith in democratic process, the home-grown black cultural nationalist, Amiri Baraka, disabused them of such illusions. Baraka was born Everett Leroi Jones in 1934 in a black hospital in the Central Ward, Kenney Memorial. He attended church regularly, presided over by the famous Reverend Hayes, whose namesake, the Hayes Homes, was the site of the riots.[96] Baraka had lived in public-housing apartments for a time, and the Jones family had climbed to the ranks of the middle class. His mother was a student at Tuskegee and Fisk, and his father was employed as an elevator operator at Bamberger's department store and later in the federal postal system. But Baraka never forgot the hardships of his family due to racial discrimination, such as the time his mother shopped at a Fannie Farmer candy store, and Baraka accompanied her: "The woman said she wanted, it was bout some peanuts, they called this things nigger toes and she said she wanted a pound of nigger toes and my mother told her those were Brazil nuts, lady."[97] After graduating from high school, he matriculated at Rutgers at Newark, and later transferred to Howard University.[98]

After the assassination of Malcolm X in 1965, Baraka essentially reconstructed himself, leading a life shaped decisively by the revival of black nationalism and local struggles for power. In the late 1950s, as a bohemian poet and dramatist, Baraka had thrived in an interracial milieu on the Lower East Side in Manhattan, marrying a white woman, Hettie Cohen, and fathering two biracial children. His avant-garde poetry and plays earned him an international reputation among white and black patrons of the arts, but in response to growing militancy in the wake of Malcolm's death, he divorced Hettie because, according to her, of his racial guilt, and he withdrew from the white art world. He changed his name to Amiri Baraka and converted to Sunni Muslim, marrying Sheila Robinson, who assumed the name Amina Baraka. Baraka interpreted Malcolm X to have declared the need for a black terri-

state, but he chose also to focus on consciousness and psychology rather than Pan-Africanism, and acted locally by shocking black audiences with cultural-nationalist plays that portrayed black psychological subjugation.[99] After his arrest in 1966 for weapons possession in Harlem, when police allegedly discovered a rifle range, bombs, and sawed-off shot gun, Baraka returned to Newark to live with his parents. He opened a drama workshop, The Spirit House, and directed its company, Spirit House Movers, which produced radical, nationalist-identified plays such as *The Slave* at a loft on Shipman Street, which, according to police investigations, Baraka had "turned into a makeshift theater and lecture hall." By 1966, artists associated with Baraka had founded the *Stirling Street News Paper,* a mimeographed compilation of community activities. While the undercover police investigations reported that "he was using this Newark location to spread Black Nationalist Aims," Baraka recalled Newark as home to the most racist police in the nation, which "magnified, actually blown-up, up and down the street. Killing niggers up and down the street," and believed that "there is a clearer feeling in Newark, than any other city I have ever been in, of Colonialism."[100]

Baraka radicalized a segment of the community that had not responded particularly to the civil rights and religious leadership. Mainstream veterans of the southern movement like Phil Hutchings felt comfortable with Baraka, spending evenings at Spirit House, even though he had also joined NCUP and worked closely with Hayden (whom he admired). As a kind of bridge between the end of civil rights and the resurgence of nationalism, Hutchings engaged the point of view of Stokely Carmichael and Baraka, both of whom had matriculated at Howard University.[101] A literary historian once described Baraka as a progenitor of populist modernism, perhaps because he focused on deploying tactics to mobilize the community. This impulse transformed Baraka's productions into what was referred to as street theater. He deliberately chose quite short dramas, in some cases so short that the written versions doubled as pamphlets, pioneering what one scholar terms "social protest performance." They were typified by an interactive process that stimulated a popular sense of efficacy, of being able to translate dissatisfaction into some kind of community action.[102] If a CORE demonstration provoked conservative whites by disrupting business as usual and by performing the spectacle of interracial sociability in places that still observed rituals of segregation, the Black Arts theater turned the tactics of

Fig. 5.4. Robert Curvin emerged as a major leader in the 1960s and helped to organize demonstrations against discrimination and police brutality. On the first night of the riots, Curvin addressed a crowd outside the police precinct, a moment captured in a photo that was reprinted in copies of the *Kerner Commission Report*. (*National Advisory Commission on Civil Disorders*, 1968)

spectacle on itself, staging protest not to shock whites but to mobilize African Americans. Baraka's radical street theater realistically reported on the day-to-day victimization of African Americans in Newark.

When the civil society of Newark expanded dynamically in rhythm to the development of an interracial public sphere that became more aligned with black nationalism, the louder and more insistent voices served to raise expectations—perhaps too high or too soon, but certainly raised expectations beyond the control of Curvin, Hayden, or Hassan. At this point, civil disobedience became almost inevitable. Curvin's Princeton University dissertation, finished years after the riots, argued that "in a deeper sense it [the riot] was the result of a breakdown in the city's political system; a system that represented a minority white population and was virtually closed to the Black majority," giving us a glimpse of how democracy sustains its own guardians.[103] On the first night of the riots in July 1967, Curvin, the most visible nonviolent activist in the city, took the bullhorn offered to him by the police, stood on top of a parked automobile, and theatrically yelled that the police had declared war on the black community. He probably did not intend to lead the crowd of demonstrators into a riot, but then an activist does not so directly lead—he amplifies the voice of the people, like a bullhorn. Curvin, without knowing what would happen but certain that injustice had fallen not only on John Smith but on the entire black community, watched as black Newarkers sustained one of the most violent black-led riots in U.S. history.

PART II

Uprising

6

Testimonies of Violation and Violence

Between July 12 and 17, 1967, twenty-four African Americans and two whites died in law enforcement maneuvers, from stray bullets and motor vehicle accidents, in lethal skirmishes of defiance and retribution. More than 1,100 sustained injuries; approximately 1,400 were arrested; some 350 arsons damaged private and public buildings; millions of dollars of merchandise was destroyed or stolen; and law enforcement expended 13,326 rounds of ammunition.[1] Tellingly, official investigation proceeded without inquiring into the culpability of the government: "The incident of Smith's arrest was . . . spontaneously brought about by the hot humid weather together with the climate that had been created in the city by dissidents, racists, and subversives."[2] In reality, the brutal arrest of Smith had incited a combustible anger in the black community, and Governor Hughes deployed overwhelmingly white troops to occupy the Central Ward. In less than seventy-two hours, using the military capacity at its disposal, the state defeated what some were calling a black revolutionary insurrection that had captured the attention of the world.

In the wake of a succession of riots in Newark, Detroit, and Milwaukee, President Lyndon Johnson enlisted the sympathies of the nation, appropriating some of the thunder from the political right in his early calls of law and order. In a televised address, he declared: "My Fellow Americans: we have endured a week such as no nation should live through," and then inaugurated the largest investigation into urban problems in U.S. history with the National Advisory Commission on Civil Disorders. Authorized by the Federal Disaster Relief Act, he instructed his appointees to present him with a full report on the events in the three major, and dozens of smaller, disorders.[3] Had the summer riots signified the effects of social isolation—in the liberal Ylvisaker's words, "the overriding problem of . . . segregation by race and income?" Or, in the famous phrasing in the *Report of the National Advisory Commission on Civil Disorders,* had the riots demonstrated the depth of division in America? "Because our Nation is moving toward two societies, one black, one white—separate and unequal." Or because, as the New Jersey Governor's Commission concluded, "attitudinally, whites and Negroes are in two almost separate worlds."[4]

Respondents to surveys on the summer of rioting diverged by race on almost every important issue.[5] Whites blamed crime and pathological behavior; blacks blamed excessive police brutality. Black respondents cited "bad housing, unemployment, breaking of official promises, lack of job opportunities; overcrowding of Negro areas; police brutality," and whites blamed "none of the above items . . . as a cause of the riots." The white respondents doubted that the disorders sprang from legitimate black political agency and credited "outside trouble makers, criminals and hoodlums, the search for excitement."[6] Black nationalists articulated the opposite view, attributing to the rioters an ideological coherence and purpose that few had demonstrated. One week later, Nathan Wright convened the National Black Power conference but its agenda curiously ignored what had just happened. The radical faction in attendance—Amiri Baraka, Ron Karenga, Floyd McKissick, and Stokely Carmichael—broke away and called a press conference to speak out. They ejected a white journalist to demonstrate their anger at the bias in reporting on the riots, while posing for the cameras in the Black Power style (black beret, sunglasses, white shirt and dark suits), and raising their fists in the famous salute. If whites watched the rioting in a state of anxiety and incomprehension, the black militants moved quickly to fill a vacuum of confusion—what Baraka described as a vacuum in the leadership of the "establishment Negroes, Toms"—by declaring that the rebellion ushered in the next stage of the revolutionary uprising.[7]

The most powerful vision of the riots, the *Kerner Report* (named for the head of the President's commission, Governor Otto Kerner of Illinois) was both famous and controversial for explaining the disorders as the result of white racism. In contrast to the series of riot studies issued by the states, it addressed a much broader and more complex society of an unprecedented scale, reporting on the "Magnitude of Poverty" and the "Magnitude of the Migration" in an analysis that never really settled on one comprehensive or concise explanation.[8] Perhaps because of its length—the small-typeface Bantam edition exceeded seven hundred pages—it complicated more than clarified understanding of urban disorders. As an administrator in the federal government who specialized in urban policy argued at the time, "it failed to have any priorities."[9]

A historical reconstruction that moves beyond the conclusions of the *Kerner Report* needs to examine the full documentary record—the hundreds of official and unpublished printed and archival documents—but perhaps more importantly also develop a critical analysis. This involves creating a narrative order that balances the official version of events with the statistical record of destruction and death, and the level of military escalation. If the historian may favor the story of law enforcement, then the government prevails over its very definition and sets the agenda of research. If the historian chooses to favor the role of black resistance, then black nationalists and radicals take precedence in the chronology and causes. To my mind, the best formulation of chronological order was articulated shortly after the riots by the white radical Eric Mann, an occasional member of NCUP and a public-school teacher who had been recently fired for espousing revolutionary ideas in the classroom. He argued that "essentially there were two riots in Newark. One was started by black people and one by the State Police. The first riot was over in two days. It took very few lives but a hell of a lot of property. The second riot was pure retribution on the part of the National Guard and State police."[10] By contrast, the commander of the National Guard, General James Cantwell, identified a decisive moment when Newark "had blown." His chronology justified military intervention: "The riot, the real riot in Newark happened before we moved in or the State Police moved in. So we had to put the lid on what had already blown."[11]

Around 8:00 P.M. on July 12, a resident in the Hayes Homes located just across the street called Robert Curvin to the scene outside the Fourth Precinct, where the police were holding the injured John Smith. Curvin recalled: "It was a kind of hysterical, anxious call that unfortunately is frequently received by me and members of our organization in the city of Newark on many occasions."[12] More community leaders were contacted, and the crowd grew spontaneously. Around the city, black cab drivers radioed news of Smith's injuries and arrest, organized shuttles of activists, and proved to be reliable sources of mobilization. A leading scholar of ethnic rioting, David Horowitz, has argued that hundreds of riots around the world were ethnically based when the rumor of a murder was a major precipitant of conflict. But in Newark the crowd outside the precinct disbelieved such a rumor, with some having seen Smith alive.[13]

When the crowd asked about Smith's injuries, several police officers apparently repeated the official explanation that he assaulted an officer and injured him in the mouth. This only provoked more disbelief and anger. When someone saw that the man who had assaulted Smith had no signs of physical injury, "there was a kind of an outburst of disgust and people were saying, 'Oh, bully' and 'You are crazy' and stuff like that. It was very obvious that the temperament was beginning to boil." The crowd apparently was speaking to itself, inciting itself. Curvin recalled: "They were saying things like, 'We are tired of this shit. It happens all the time.' "[14] In the early stages of the gathering, African American women figured prominently, from the first attempts to reach Curvin to the comments later reported by observers, but their presence or influence gradually declined during the riots, and never really returned to the same level of community leadership.

As the assembly continued to deliberate, the police admitted Curvin to the holding cell where Smith "was lying on the bench with his eyes closed and his feet up." He had never met Smith, asked him to explain the situation, and also asked, "What happened to you?" Smith said, "They hit me on the head." "For what?" " 'Well, are you hurt?' He really looked like he was hurt. He was moaning in fact. 'What hurts you?' " According to Curvin, he said, " 'My side hurts me." A longtime Newark resident born in the South, an amateur jazz musician down on his luck, Smith was a loner whose injuries touched a nerve, perhaps because he really did symbolize everyman.[15] Curvin asked if anyone had summoned a physician, and the police claimed that Smith never requested medical attention, though he testified to the contrary. Outside the precinct, a girl was keeping the crowd informed, and Curvin reported that "I don't recall if it was the young girl who said she had followed him up the steps, but she began describing the way that she had seen Smith dragged across the street and kicked."[16] A voice of conscience in the crowd reminded them that Smith was not the only problem—rather it was that what "we see here is happening every day."[17]

Curvin was drawn into the civic or crowd interpretation of the police assault, and he recalled that when a member of the crowd asked about Smith, he "was interrupted by a woman who . . . might have been about forty years old who said, 'Wait, we don't just want to talk about this; we want to talk about what we see here happening every day time and time again.' "[18] Cynical and lacking confidence in their political agency, some black people in the crowd doubted if "two people today in the whole

Hill district . . . could even tell you the name of the cab driver which started this." In fact, Smith later expressed "the deepest sympathy" for the casualties in the riots that were started in his name, but the people were reframing the incident in ways that mobilized a larger group around politically relevant, explosive issues.[19]

When an anonymous voice skeptically pronounced that this was "just someone looking" for a reason to cause trouble, another voice reminded them of the long history of police brutality.[20] From approximately 8:00 P.M. to 10:00 P.M., the number of the waiting crowd increased from about twenty-five to more than two hundred, forming a kind of vigil for the taxi driver. As the crowd's advocate, Curvin conferred with Sergeant Kenneth Melchior, the highest-ranking officer at the precinct.[21] No one appeared before the crowd to address its protest against police brutality. In fact, that night and again the next day, Mayor Addonizio refused to discuss a political solution to the demands of the rioters, which one observer called a "tragic mistake."[22] But silence was the official response. By this time, a range of local activists, representing community programs such as the Newark Legal Services Project and United Community Corporation, had joined the crowd, as well as several black members of NCUP, including Jesse Allen and Derek Winans. According to Curvin, "It was very obvious that the crowd was getting quite large at that time." "I got on top of a car right in front of the precinct this time and asked the crowd to assemble together."[23]

A photograph of Curvin, published in newspapers and reprinted in *The Report of the National Advisory Commission,* carried the caption: "Tries to calm crowd," speaking to the incapacity of the ideology of nonviolence to contain the popular anger of the people.[24] Curvin later testified that he believed it was a "bad idea" to disperse before some kind of venting of the crowd's anger and wanted to "allow them to express their dissatisfaction with what had happened." But he denied responsibility for civil disobedience: "The police have the guns. The police have the weapons and everything, and you can't win," exhorted Curvin.[25] But his political nemesis, the chief of police Dominick Spina, charged that "Curvin did not once try to disperse the crowd but told them, 'we're tired of being beaten, we're tired of being dragged, and we ain't going to take it any more.'"[26] Intentionally or not, the *Kerner Report* recognized genuine dissent in the community when they attempted to praise leaders for channeling "the energies of the people into a nonviolent protest."[27]

When several other speakers addressed the crowd from the top of an

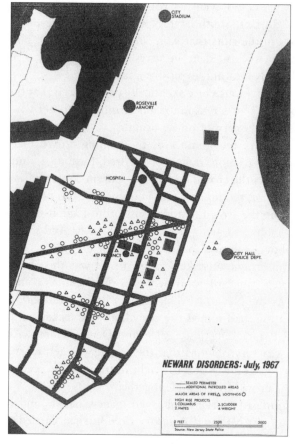

Fig. 6.1. Newark disorders: July 1967. Δ = fires; ○ = lootings.

automobile bumper, either that vehicle or another one was set on fire, alerting the fire department as well as raising about fifteen officers. A Molotov cocktail was thrown at the precinct wall. Then, testified Curvin, "at that point everything just broke up. People started running. Then the police moved out toward the projects."[28] From the perspective of the police, the incident required a response, and the highest-ranking officer at the Fourth Precinct, Sergeant John Redden, issued orders to begin mixing plain-clothes and uniformed officers around the crowd, to patrol the major commercial areas of Broad and Springfield, and to "observe the conduct of the people."[29] Reliable independent witnesses of what happened next were scarce.

The governor's aide, Paul Ylvisaker, arrived from his home in Cranbury at 9:00 P.M., and remembered that "all hell had broken loose." (*The Report for Action* listed the official start of the rioting at just before midnight.) But this was the starting point of the narrative of the events—for establishing a beginning depended upon the perspective of the various interested groups. For Ylvisaker, the onset of the disorders was signified by "looting in various parts of the city," on the one hand, and by mobilized law enforcement, on the other, which he recalled "was out in force and as I drove through there was very little I could do other than get out of the way of the people who were running carrying items or articles and the police who, in some instances were shooting, and other instances chasing people with articles."[30] The police identified the start with looting in retail establishments and setting fires, which served expressive rather than instrumental grassroots protest.

That is, political arson destroyed abandoned structures, such as warehouses, closed stores, and homes, but the arsonists had set fires at a distance from the residences and general population, resulting in few injuries and no casualties in the Central Ward. From the perspective of the government, the riots started with arson, because of injuries to white fire fighters. At least thirty-five firefighters were "injured due to rocks and other items thrown at them while fighting fires or responding to alarms," according to unpublished records. The Newark Fire Department's report to Governor Hughes indicated that unknown gunfire repeatedly was directed at rescue squads, particularly at the thoroughfares such as Hunterdon Street, Springfield Avenue, and South Broome Street in Orange, as well as at fire stations in the area. Firefighters responded to an estimated 364 real and false alarms and rescues, and at least fifteen firefighting vehicles were damaged by vandalism that resulted in broken windshields, blown tires, bullet holes, and dents. In the end, all of the arsons were contained, and none spread beyond its original point of origin.[31] And the firefighters reduced the rate of arson steadily over the next five days.[32]

It was the increase in looting on Springfield Avenue, and disorderly crowds throughout the Central Ward, alarmingly, that continued. As the NPD dispatched more police officers, a number of black residents deliberately disobeyed routine orders to return home, risking physical harm, arrest, and jail. Police brutality had incited the crowd to riot on Wednesday, so, not surprisingly, subsequent attempts to impose police control over small acts of disobedience spiraled into racialized confrontation.

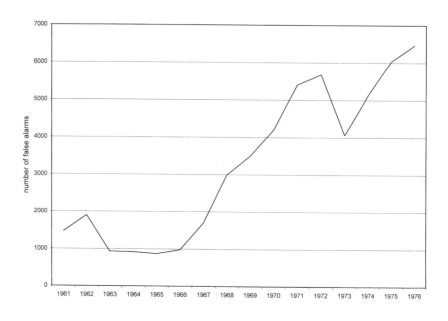

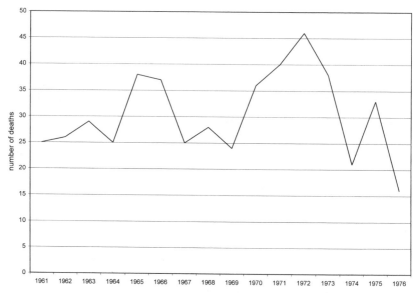

Fig. 6.2. (*top*) Annual false fires alarms in Newark.
Fig. 6.3. (*bottom*) Annual fire deaths in Newark.

Not only were virtually all of the officers white but Italian American, and the NPD had instinctively tried to protect the two officers against accusations of assault on Smith. According to the testimony of two officers, Smith had "opened up his car door striking De Simone in the chest," and "struck Patrolman De Simone in the face with his fist . . . [and] then attempted to assault both policemen and was subdued and placed in the rear seat of Radio Car #42." The officer also testified that he *believed* "he struck my partner in the car because before you know it they were arguing."[33] But their version of the incident defied common sense: why would a black man with no record of violent crime, and at most guilty of a traffic violation, resist arrest and risk a felony charge? Officer De Simone reported that Smith ripped his pants during the struggle, and yet when police Sergeant Melchior "asked him [De Simone] to show me where they had been torn . . . he could come up with nothing."[34]

In the confusion of looting, a number of black leaders demanded greater representation on the police force and a permanent board to review complaints. Some time later, Mayor Addonizio offered to appoint a blue ribbon commission to investigate the allegation of police brutality —but only in the Smith case and nothing else. For many, this was a matter of too little, too late, and observers later testified that a second night of rioting, looting, and arson seemed almost inevitable.[35] According to the assistant to the mayor, they erroneously adopted the strategy of "project[ing] an image of a return to normal." The next day more leaders called for civilian review and the promotion of police officer Eddie Williams to captain (before four qualified white lieutenants) but the mayor spoke of resolution and dissipation of protest.[36] Not only local observers blamed the mayor's poor political response. A memo to the Vice President Humphrey charged that Addonizio was "extremely complacent about rising community tensions before the riots," and lost the opportunity to "head off further trouble" by not responding to the demands for more black police, "remaining in city hall."[37] As a black witness later testified, "To say it was an isolated incident I think was the most tragic mistake that was made following Wednesday night."[38] By Friday morning, thirty-six hours had passed without evidence of a substantial government concession, and the riots escalated.

Contrary to the certainties conveyed to the public by the official documentation in the *Report for Action,* the fact was that the coordinates of disorder varied by perspective, situations, and idiosyncratic experiences.

For the president and the national audience he addressed, the worsening riots signified a crisis, an apocalyptic rupture from the past, a threatening disorder that departed from anything that the city of Newark had ever experienced. Yet, to many residents of the Central Ward the riots signified a kind of acceleration, intensification, and politicization of experience, but not wholly imperceptible as an extension of daily political conflict. Urban theorists argue that at moments of extreme disorder, residents of cities reflexively search for continuities and stability. When the entrance of white law enforcement undermined that sense of continuity, or the structure of urban form and function, the destruction of civility became apparent on many levels.[39] Anonymous activists continued to organize during the riots, blending public assembly with civil disobedience, and law enforcement invoked public safety to justify a curfew and to prohibit gatherings in some areas. The police never recognized the disorders as a First Amendment act of civil disobedience, but characterized the riots simply as criminal activity. Therefore, all public assembly was deemed and prosecuted as criminal. In regulating the public sphere, the enforcement of a curfew helped to cauterize more organized dissent. (The word "curfew" derived from the medieval French *cuevre,* in which peasants cover a fire at a fixed time to prevent a larger spread.) Now the curfew laws confined black residents to their homes, prohibited vehicle traffic, and interrupted businesses. All liquor stores and bars were ordered closed, and mail delivery was stopped. Arrests for minor violations of conduct ranged from 935 in Detroit to only 95 in Newark, which perhaps reflects the fact that the city did not declare a curfew until relatively late in the process of bringing the disorders to an end.[40]

With the increase of police repression in the name of social control, black opposition in the public sphere gathered force, drawing from continuities with a prefigurative interracial and black activism. At some point, seasoned activists posted a flyer that appropriated the police command heard by black rioters everywhere—"Halt" or "Stop"—only re-signified its meaning: "Stop! Police Brutality."[41] Despite official representation of the riots as an emergency, it is possible to see the riots rather as an acceleration of crises and violations of everyday life. In the daily conflicts between police on the beat and informal groups of idle men, street life had not really changed. In the riot areas, law enforcement disaggregated crowds and disciplined individual men by demanding that they obey orders, halt, and submit to arrest. They restrained and searched black men randomly. In turn, civil disobedience reflected

Fig. 6.4. From 1955 to 1965, the mainstream media portrayed black demonstrators in the Jim Crow South as sympathetic victims of vicious white police, but the coverage of the riots in the northern cities always seemed to justify ever-increasing levels of white police force against black protesters. (Courtesy of New Jersey News Service and Newark Public Library)

the new black male confrontational attitude toward the police. A flyer asked, "Black Policemen—where do you stand?" As during the decade before July 12, 1967, the street life of the Central Ward involved black residents fighting with white police.[42]

If the random police harassment, arrest at gunpoint, search, and detention without legitimate criminal charges felt more like acceleration than a disjuncture, black resistance to police authority now changed in intensity and consequence. It was more of the same, only physically harder and more dangerous. In the continuity column, consider the insurance claims filed by New Jersey Bell. In the riots the public utility suffered the destruction of 262 outdoor telephone booths, nine telephone cables, and other property, but recall the direct action protest against the telephone company's practice of racial discrimination initiated by CORE several years earlier.[43] Black participants were performing the same acts of defiance as before the official declaration of the crisis, and the police arrested more than 1,400 residents. Prisoners were temporarily housed in the armory, Caldwell Penitentiary, and Newark Street Jail.[44] Bail for disorderly persons had been set at about $1,000 for curfew violations,

$1,500 for misdemeanors, and $2,500 for serious offenses (possession of deadly weapons) ranging up to $50,000, all designed to keep rioters off the streets. To prevent the return of violent black rioters to the crowds, a notoriously conservative municipal judge set bail at $50,000 for serious offenses, the majority of which were weapons-related charges.[45] To secure their release, volunteers prepared a "Release on Recognizance" form based on international protocol for processing civil disobedience, which volunteers duplicated at the offices of the Newark Legal Service Project and distributed to detainees.[46] Some 85.4 percent of those arrested in the riots were black males, 9.4 percent were black women, and 5 percent were white men.[47] Though the large number of arrests caused logistical problems, the Newark total of 1,510 paled in comparison to that in Watts, with 3,852 arrests, and a staggering 7,231 in Detroit.[48]

The typical arrest was of a male, black, and unmarried, ages 15 to 24.[49] The most significant information available in the archival materials about the background of them is that the majority were born in the South. A minority also matched the stereotype of rioters as criminals: about 20 percent listed prior convictions for criminal offenses, and more than 40 percent had records of some kind. That a fifth of the arrested in the riots carried criminal records could indicate that they endured a higher rate of poverty, or economic disadvantage, rather than support an interpretation of criminality. A majority of those arrested declared they were employed. Within this group, a majority identified themselves as unskilled labor, a pool weighted toward poor workers, a characteristic of recent immigrant populations. The police arrested these rioters for larceny, breaking and entering, and other offenses related to looting. Perhaps their behavior signified an immigrant's impatience with the slow pace of mobility, but economic need fails to explain the particular profile of the average black male rioter. According to a survey, a large percentage chose to identify as "black" rather than Negro, and supported the study of black studies in public education. They were more likely to say that they "hated whitey," and were less concerned with "Negro rights."[50] Again, race and class inextricably defined the political culture of the black public sphere.

A young graduate student at the University of Michigan, Jeffrey Paige, conducted interviews with residents in the Central Ward for about a year after the riots to create a profile both of the participants and the bystanders. He had conducted investigations for the Kerner Commission while completing his dissertation, but his methods were

State	Number of Arrests
Alabama	70
California	2
Florida	59
Georgia	147
Mississippi	10
New Jersey	122
North Carolina	200
Pennsylvania	21
South Carolina	128
Virginia	101
Puerto Rico	32
Unknown	55

Fig. 6.5. Places of birth of persons arrested—July 18, 1967. *Source*: Box 1, Hughes Commission on Civil Disorders, New Jersey State Archives.

criticized, especially for mistaking the addresses of the respondents (some of whom lied about living in the target area to protect their real residences).[51] Paige sampled residents in the core area of the riots, accounting for 70,243 of a total of 138,035 black population based on the 1960 census.[52] Paige found no correlation between economic status and rate of participation in the riots. When asked to reflect on their state of mind before the riots, many residents of the target area reported feelings of frustration with economic opportunity, but these respondents were no more likely to riot than those who were not economically frustrated. In fact, a higher percentage of nonrioters believed the gap between white and black wealth had increased than those who chose to riot. Thus, Paige concluded that "rioting, then, is not a consequence of acute feelings of deprivation relative to whites."[53]

Paige's final survey indicated that looting, including breaking and entering stores, stealing goods, and shattering windows, accounted for 40–50 percent of criminal offenses. By contrast, only 6 percent of interviewees later admitted to constructing fire bombs, and only 4 percent later admitted to throwing fire bombs (a distribution similar to that in Detroit). Despite the focus on consumer goods, evidence indicated that racial nationalist or separatist sentiments had also sharpened. Paige found that racial consciousness and the issue of substantive political power had shaped the behavior and rebelliousness of the rioters rather than class or economic motives. His research indicated that the greater the preference for residential integration, the less likely to engage in rioting.

Those who recalled a kind of identification with the riots or actually participated in them clearly identified with the newest configurations of racial identity in the Black Power movement, and some of those also identified with the Afrocentric cultural turn led by Baraka and other nationalists.[54] In the same vein, participants in the riots were more likely than nonparticipants to believe that the civil rights movement would be "better off" without whites (58 percent to 42 percent). This percentage of black respondents who said they sometimes hated whites had increased in Newark since a 1949 survey, when only 28 percent admitted such feelings. A year after the riots, 44 percent felt something they identified as hate toward whites.[55] Of the black men who identified with militancy, many did so because they felt alienated from the current political system at City Hall. Although the truly radical rioter never trusted the political system, many others searched for alternatives within the democracy of the nation.[56] The NAACP, Urban League, and experts such as Kenneth Clark declared the riots lawless, criminal, and wrong, and Martin Luther King, Jr., rejected all violent protest and pleaded with rioters to return to their homes.[57] Several months later, King criticized the response of the government to the riots, and charged that "Congress has revealed that it loves rats more than it does people" after it voted down federal allocation for sanitation (including a measure for pest and rodent control) in the inner cities.[58]

But the fact was that these black men felt increasingly hopeless about the efficacy of the old methods used in the civil rights movement. At the same time, more than four hundred arrests correlated with resistance to the imposition of order by law enforcement rather than economic deprivation and materialism. Arrests for so-called disorderly conduct often occurred in direct confrontations between police and residents who challenged the authority of police rather than from looting.[59] In a study of black male attitudes toward the law in Newark, a majority of 130 interviewees proclaimed their impatience with the legal methods of civil rights, and cited employment discrimination as a leading problem. But they doubted the efficacy of the Division Against Discrimination (DAD) because "they take too long" or because "they passed the law just to make it look good." Although black men approved of the NAACP or the National Urban League, they believed the best way for "Negroes to get their civil rights" was through education and "strength." In this sense, black nationalist criticism of integration—impatience with civil rights as usual—animated the rioting.[60]

Fig. 6.6. Law enforcement arrested thousands of black residents for curfew violations, looting, and weapons possession. The vast majority of news reports featured armed white law enforcement officers equipped with impressive military gear, but few if any photos showed black rioters wielding weapons of any type. (Courtesy of New Jersey News Service and Newark Public Library)

As the civil rights movement's association with impersonal bureau-cracy and the failures of integration disillusioned black men, the escala-tion of police brutality dealt the final blow to whatever remained of their commitment to nonviolent methods of protest. In the riots, black witnesses had clearly recalled not only the local police but the National Guard as, in the words of one black rioter, "full of Klan and Birchite el-ements."[61] As black rioters recalled the beatings they suffered from po-lice for minor infractions—for example, for using the term Black Power or hesitating to obey orders to halt on command—they testified to the ways in which the viability of nonviolent protest had evaporated. White law enforcement pursued Phil Hutchings, the head of SNCC who after the riots proposed a merger with the violent Black Panthers, for raising his fist in a Black Power salute, detained him and his friend, and beat both of them. Police released the two, but his friend was badly bruised (Hutchings had learned how to protect himself from the police baton in the southern civil rights demos). Another emergent black leader, Dennis Westbrooks (who would win election to the City Council representing the Central Ward), testified that police "threw a stick, threw a couple of rocks" at him. When Westbrooks responded by picking up a stick, the police yelled, " 'Hey, he has got a gun. Let's go get him.' " In the course of questioning African American bystanders and enforcing curfews, according to Westbrooks, "they were pushing and shoving, the best thing I had to do was escape the blows of the clubs and protect myself from being hurt." Similar to Hutchings, Westbrooks "outran them so they didn't chase after me any further."[62]

Rather than accepting responsibility for the escalation, the police again engaged a memory that justified their action. They argued that before the arrival of law enforcement, black anger was "simmering throughout the community" in the morning of July 13, and this was one reason why law enforcement believed in and advised military escalation. "You could feel the tension in the air," said General James Cantwell from the Department of Defense and commander of the New Jersey National Guard. By the third night of rioting, Governor Hughes had mobilized additional state police and the National Guard, the vast majority of whom were white. In escalating military force, the state escalated racial conflict. Of 17,529 New Jersey Guardsmen, only 303 were African American.[63] In 1967 African Americans accounted for only 1.7 percent of all state units of the National Guard.[64] Founded as a civic association in the post–Civil War era to protect capital against labor during the Great Upheaval, the role of the National Guard in controlling civil disturbances had increased since the 1940s.[65] In World War II the Congress had voted to give the army command over reserves and militias, and the president summoned the Guard to assist with civil disturbances approximately one hundred times in thirty-three states, and eighteen times alone in the summer of 1967 in response to racial disorders. Black rioting precipitated activation rates of 60 percent in Watts; 80 percent in Detroit; and 31 percent in New Jersey. Despite constant pressure from national and local black legislators for the integration of the Guard, southern units resisted, and de facto segregation prevailed elsewhere.[66] The timing of the deployment of law enforcement at first reflected the interest of the government in protecting private commercial establishments, but the subsequent military decision to implement a policy of random shooting raised the question of motivation. The fact was that none of the testimony before the Governor's Commission corroborated the claims by law enforcement of imminent danger of defeat due to gunfire from African Americans.[67]

Fig. 6.7. (*top*) The governor of New Jersey ordered the deployment of the National Guard and state police by the third day of the riots, sharply escalating the level of violence as well as the number of injuries and fatalities. (Courtesy of New Jersey New Service and Newark Public Library)

Fig. 6.8. (*bottom*) The fear of continuing disorder and violence led the governor to authorize the mobilization of jeeps and armored tanks, which were maintained at a makeshift headquarters in a high school athletic stadium. (Courtesy of New Jersey News Service and Newark Public Library)

When police were summoned to respond to a disorder, including what they claimed was sniper fire, the units nearest to the origins of the gunshots were dispatched to that house or apartment, and divided into ten-man squads commanded by a sergeant, with one lieutenant assigned to every three squads. The local and state police and the National Guard were equipped with M-1 rifles and carbines, but not with automatic machine guns (though machine guns were mounted on some jeeps borrowed from the U.S. Department of Defense). The head of the state police in New Jersey, Colonel Kelly, reported that "The reason for the jeeps is for the all around vision and the cars, of course, we don't have the open top thing. The rifles were needed for the . . . high rise."[68] By the time the Guard arrived, the standing orders were to shoot if fired upon, because of reports of shifting sniper points from different floors in the buildings. Again, these reports proved impossible to corroborate with independent witnesses or evidence, and no law enforcement personnel were reported as wounded by the fire from public housing.[69] Despite the lack of verifiable reports, central command sent patrols into the stairwells of public housing complexes, armed with rifles. When traces of sniper activity were allegedly discovered in several residences, this justified further militarization. To corroborate these sightings of snipers, Colonel Kelly said that ammunition "casings" were found in the stairwells of the Hayes Homes.[70]

The Newark police, state police, and National Guard largely operated in tandem but disagreed over the strategy of firing on public housing buildings. The police were adamant: "We would meet force with force," testified Colonel Kelly.[71] Although the vast majority of injuries to police were incurred through physical contact rather than weapons, Colonel Kelly painted a scenario of combat: "Be they firing at you or be they not firing at you, no one wants to see anybody get hurt." "If fire was not returned, how long would this man continue to fire at them?"[72] But General Cantwell questioned the state police strategy. "If you got a sniper in a high rise apartment you might as well back off. There is no sense in shooting up the apartment building," he testified. Although the Guard cooperated, they obeyed orders only from other guardsmen, despite the strategy of deploying mixed contingents into the riot areas. "The tendency of most people involved was to return fire against the location where the firing was coming from." But Cantwell could not lay blame—"Who followed shooting at times like that I honestly don't know."[73] In the days after the rioting, authorities would challenge law enforcement's strategy as well as their conduct. Rather than planning to "saturate the area with manpower," it was argued that command erred "with firepower." This strategy was blamed for the death toll.[74]

To witness the riots from the perspective of the people in the community, Ylvisaker decided to move into Hayes Homes, and he recalled that one night the police "went away and [an unidentified black man] came out a second time. That time he shot right over my house. He didn't shoot anybody but had shot his rifle." In response to the Commission's questioning on the "use of any firepower to quell snipers," Ylvisaker testified that the "police opened fire on a lone fellow and killed him on the corner of 18th Street." He refused to identify the victim as a sniper or testify that the victim was in possession of firearms.[75] One of the few positive identifications of snipers was given in the testimony of Bud Shauvisian, an aide in the Addonizio administration, who told the commission that he observed snipers emerging from a building and that the National Guard was literally firing up and down the front of the building.[76] The only black witness of a sniper summoned to testify before the Commission observed a man wearing a "peculiar looking uniform—and had a rifle." Perhaps he was affiliated with Hassan's Black Man's Liberation Army, though it never claimed responsibility, nor did any official investigation identify the BMLA as a proponent of sniping.[77]

Whether or not law enforcement really faced lethal danger, the event that sealed the fate of military escalation, and the policy of firing without provocation, was the death of Detective Frederick Toto on the third day of rioting at approximately 3:00 P.M., only ten hours after military personnel had arrived to suppress the riots. Needless to say, if the strategy of the governor was to activate military reinforcement to prevent more violence, it failed badly. According to journalist Ron Porambo, police had shot at a crowd near the Scudder Housing Projects located near the center of rioting on Springfield Avenue, and "killed a seventy-year-old man and wounded his son, killed another man, and a little girl on the upper floor of the projects lost an eye." "At least three angry men returned the fire with handguns from the upper stories and Toto was hit." The assailants in the murder of Toto were never apprehended, and the national media, particularly the authoritative *New York Times*, reiterated uncritically the sniper scenario. Rather than admitting the possibility of stray fire, they recounted as fact "snipers hiding on roofs even opened fire on firehouses." This scenario in the death of the white officer was never corroborated.[78]

In response, the national press characterized the riots as a tragedy, in which violent and criminal black residents wantonly attacked heroic law enforcement. In a study comparing news coverage of the Newark riots in the United States and Russia, the researcher found favorable "coverage given to white victims—their injuries or funerals and the like—African-Americans received second class treatment . . . at best perfunctorily mentioned" in the American press.[79] By contrast, the foreign press depicted the riots as a military conspiracy to quash repression. To impress their readers, descriptions of riots in the foreign press were accompanied by graphic photographs, usually depicting black Newarkers under attack from law enforcement. One Russian reporter described a scene in which "soldiers walk with their rifles at ready along the street of the city of Newark . . . [to patrol] violent actions of the Negro population for civil rights and against police tyranny and racial discrimination."[80]

When law enforcement officers were injured or died, the dominant national media responded by portraying only African Americans in the riots, and their public protest as little more than criminal activity. Contrary to the media and the conservative efforts to criticize the riots and civil disobedience, black reporters treated the disorders as a form of black resistance arising from a long history of urban conflicts, especially the nineteenth century-working-class strikes for wages.[81] The major national news establishment fed the public with extraordinarily racially biased journalism, a fact that would prompt the National Advisory Commission on Civil Disorders to devote a section of its report to the problem of under-representation of minorities in the media. Thus in the wake of the deaths of white officers in Newark, the *New York Times* easily assigned guilt and innocence in the urban tragedy, and identified "Frederick Toto, 34 years old, white, slain by a sniper," and "Fire Captain Michael Moran, 44, white, slain by a sniper," followed by a list of fourteen African American dead. They listed the addresses of each black victim and his race, "Negro," but the editors stated that the whites were "slain by snipers"; while the "Negroes" died generically from a "gunshot wound," implying an accident or shots from black participants in the disorder.

The public would need to think critically to detect the ways in which the media manipulated race, gender, and age. The *New York Times* quoted the governor's characterization of the events as "criminal insurrection," and routinely used the term "terrorists" to refer to "Negroes" in the riots.[82] Some local liberal reporters expressed resentment in the mainstream stories criticizing black actions in the disorders that blamed them for the damage to the city.[83] Both the *Los Angeles Times* and the *New York Times* printed stories of rising death tolls and injuries of non-participants, and photos that supposedly showed "mob scorn" for the police, which in turn justified the police's policy of escalation. At one point one of a handful of critical reporters asked the president for his opinion about police shooting at looters, but the question was referred to a memorandum issued by the White House and summarily brushed off.[84]

In the climate of a national backlash, the number of black fatalities quickly increased. By the end of the day on Friday, July 14, there were sixteen dead—fifteen black Newarkers and one white policeman. But law enforcement escalated again after the death of Michael Moran, a fire captain.[85] Witnesses alleged that two African American men in a vehicle had fired at Moran, one of whom, a man from Staten Island, the police later apprehended. The national media circulated a version of the incident that alleged a black motorist killed Moran, but police eventually released the suspect. "In one story we are told the police believe this unknown, wounded Negro to be the killer," while in another story police admitted that "we couldn't see where the bullets were coming from." Tom Hayden's analysis raised a valid question of stray fire, an estimation with which Porambo agreed: "Does this incredible maze of statements seem more believable than the idea that police were firing on themselves and could very well have killed Captain Moran?"[86] By Sunday, the government account of the incident mapped the scene of the riot moving from random confrontations between police and unarmed crowds, "to the battle between snipers and the police and National Guardsmen." But the figure of the terrorist sniper was only a media image and an official explanation, not a real military target.[87]

From another perspective, most black participants later testified that the white law enforcement officers were blatantly racist and excessively violent. A nonparticipant bystander, Olivia McRimmon, admitted, on the one hand, her dislike for "those damned Black Nationalists," and identified black nationalists in Newark with "them Mau Mau from Harlem and them Muslims up there." On the other hand, McRimmon firmly believed that the National Guard were more guilty of violence, because they fired upon the innocent and destroyed African American commercial property. "The only one that shot those windows were those National Guard," she testified. Though she did not approve of black nationalist rhetoric—"get whitey" and the insulting of police with the epithet "pig"—the woman vividly remembered that the Guardsmen were really "the only [ones] I heard any filth from."[88]

Another witness, Willie Odom, believed that the main intention of law enforcement was to revenge the deaths of Moran and Toto. "They said [referring to whomever it was that killed the white officers], 'You tell that black nigger we are going to kill him.'" "That was the State Troopers." Odom also alleged that law enforcement capriciously damaged his store as an act of retribution, and testified that when he attempted to copy the license plate number of the police car driven by the officers responsible for the destruction, he was threatened with arrest and his note to himself was confiscated. "He took the pad that I had away from me and tore the numbers of the police car that I had off the pad, but of course, I remembered them. I just jotted them back down on the pad, so I have the number of police cars and everything." Black Newarkers remained critical of excessive force and discriminatory arrest: "They are worse, because they are supposed to be protecting the law, and they are going around shooting up the shops."[89] Recalling years of abuse from white officers, the more daring in the crowds yelled out the name of police officer Martinez, the officer responsible in the shooting of the martyred Lester Long. They recalled that Martinez's "name is a sort of pretty famous name in the Negro community."[90]

In the maelstrom of the escalation, the riot was described as a crime, as a pathological or suicidal outburst, and as the result of black rage. In taking up arms, injuring law enforcement, and destroying government property, some rioters undoubtedly viewed the struggle as a revolutionary moment—a war against the white man. Amiri Baraka was probably the most astute critic of the police, and he became the most famous black rioter. Random police patrol and automobile searches of suspect vehicles, particularly those of black drivers, caught up with Baraka on July 14, at approximately 2:20 A.M., when a "Police Alarm was broadcast alerting all police to be on the lookout for a 1966 Green Volkswagen containing three colored males." Baraka's car was going west on Springfield Avenue, and it was alleged in the police report that three men were shooting guns from the moving vehicle. At approximately 2:45 A.M., Patrolmen Scarpone and McCormick stopped this car at South Orange Avenue and South 7th Street and found "three colored males," two revolvers, and fifty-eight bullets. With Baraka were Charles McCray and Barry Wynn, all of whom were charged with weapons possession and arrested. By the time Baraka arrived with the police at the Fourth Precinct, he suffered from serious injuries to the body and head—at the least a laceration that remained bandaged for some time afterwards— and was brought through a crowd of black onlookers who spread word of Baraka's arrest and condition, before he was transported to Essex County Penitentiary and kept in isolation until posting bail of $25,000.[91]

The police accused him of continuing to incite his followers, but Baraka insisted that it was police brutality that had caused a crisis of recognition in the black community. The middle class had "deluded themselves" with a faith in assimilation and harmony with whites. But now "a great many of the middle class Negroes found out when bayonets were thrust into their cars and their cars were stopped and the abusive language and abusive attitudes were put upon their heads as upon the black man walking in the street you saw the nature of the regard America has for the black citizen in general." Was Baraka correct that "the police functioned pretty much the way they function all the time. It is just during the rebellion it was exaggerated"?[92] He rejected police statements that they faced black sniping, pointedly asking observers—"if black snipers really threatened police, why weren't there more dead policemen? . . . Where are the snipers? Has anybody caught a sniper? Has anybody brought any snipers to light?"[93] In the more violent Detroit riots, only one so-called sniper materialized. Was this really the cause for massive military mobilization in Newark?[94]

The conceptual challenge of plotting a conclusion to the disorders involves evaluating several maps of evidence, not only the powerful narrative deployed by the government, comprised of official witnesses such as Ylvisaker and municipal workers and law enforcement. In this narrative, the riot stemmed from the socioeconomic distress of African Americans, resulted in property damage and violence, and was over on Monday, July 17, when the Governor declared the city of Newark returned to control. Each day from July 12 to July 17, the level of violence increased or decreased, and can be viewed on a graph, such as that published in the official federal history, *The National Advisory Commission on Civil Disorders Report*. Almost twice as many died in Detroit as in Newark, thirty of whom were slain by law enforcement.[95] If plotted in the declining number of police injuries, a narrative signifies the seriousness of black challengers and the successful imposition of military control. At least seventy-five police officers were treated for gunshot wounds, abrasions, contusions, lacerations, and sprains of the limbs and back, injuries that suggested in some cases significant physical resistance on the part of black Newarkers.[96] At the peak of black insurgence, the number of police injuries steadily rose from nineteen on July 13 to thirty-six on July 14. Then military troops arrived. When the National Guard mobilized in Newark on the morning of July 15, the number of police injuries at the end of the day was six and dropped below four for the next two days, at which point the injuries were now sustained only by black rioters as well as black spectators or bystanders caught away from home during curfew or in the crossfire in their homes.[97]

Neither the state nor the nation acknowledged the participants' belief that escalation of military force was retribution for the death of a white police officer. But the official liberal response eventually reprimanded law enforcement for excess and recklessness, steering a course between outraged black nationalists and complacent white conservatives who later would blindly support police in law and order campaigns.[98] The evidence seriously questions the credibility of witnesses who defended the conduct of law enforcement. Of more than six thousand law enforcement personnel deployed over the five days of rioting (and into the following week of cleanup and reconstruction), only five policemen were wounded by gunfire—at least one of them by accidental friendly fire—and two (a police officer and a firefighter) were killed. Witnesses testified that police promised that the black community would pay for the death of one of their own.[99] As both extraordinary acts of violence and a familiar violation, the deaths in the riots appeared to put down rebellion and impose order. But in retrospect, official maneuvers against both real and imagined threats dispersed racial conflict across the terrain.

7

The Reconstruction of
Black Womanhood

In the aftermath of a major conflict or war, scholars theorize that the traumatized society must undergo a process of reconstruction. Governments not only reconstruct the infrastructure but also sponsor cultural programs that help the survivors to make sense of the aftermath, a process involving gender as a "contested political issue." After the Civil War, for example, northern leaders reconstructed the nation by not only amending the Constitution but also implementing new policies that enlarged the role of women in society. After World War I in Europe and to a lesser extent in the United States, the popular construct of the New Woman in fashion and film served to help citizens adjust to social change.[1] In Newark, a range of voices debated the role of black women in the public sphere during post-riot reconstruction. Of course, observers at the time and in more recent scholarship almost reflexively explained the riots as a matter of gender—in this case, it was an assertion of black manhood. What more thoroughly destroyed the myth of black man's emasculation than his armed confrontation with white law enforcement? Though it has been rarely studied, a growing discourse over the conduct of law enforcement and the criminality of civil disobedience both denied and valorized the experience of black women.

By the time the rioting had spread from Newark to Detroit, President Johnson had invoked black women and the black family to distinguish the friends from the foes of the nation, aligning law and order with the obedience of all to white law enforcement and, conversely, sedition and criminality with the assertive black male. Operating in an unpredictable political climate, when the White House worried over how voters perceived their response to the riots (and the president's approval ratings on civil rights had dropped from 50 percent to only 32 percent favorable), the use of gendered discourse served to deflect the criticism that social programs—"pouring in federal aid"—in effect rewarded the rioters. The same administration that won the struggle for civil rights in the South more comfortably announced its condemnation of the black rioters by distinguishing them from those heroic demonstrators. Reportedly thrown by the riots into a "mood of deep despair," President Johnson implored the nation: "Let us condemn the violent few." Yet in defending the recipients of aid as deserving, he pleaded: "But let us remember that it is law-abiding Negro families who have really suffered most at the hands of the rioters."[2]

On the local level, the *Report for Action* deployed powerful gendered images of poor African Americans to justify both ameliorative and punitive actions. To comfort the anxious white observer, the editorial strategy was to select photographs of elderly women and children situated in squalid homes, dilapidated bedrooms, and decrepit kitchens. Such images of young, innocent black boys and earnest older men served to counteract the media's propaganda of photographs of threatening black men in militant poses or under arrest by white uniformed (often read as chivalrous) law enforcement, deservingly bloodied or at least reassuringly disarmed. The one exception to the editorial erasure of black adult men in *The Report for Action* was a photo of several high school students, four black and two white, working together on an automobile engine in an industrial education classroom, harkening back to an era of industrial progress and interracial cooperation.

The government's deployment of gender discourses, which was further amplified by the media, diverted attention from law enforcement's excessive violence against black women. During the riots, every level of military force in the state had been deployed to capture black male snipers who were supposedly occupying public housing complexes. The irony was that despite calls for help from residents in the housing projects, most of the time only the guards employed by the Newark Housing Authority, not the local or state police, responded. In more than a few cases, in the pursuit of what the state denoted as public safety, law enforcement violated the rights to domestic safety of black women in public housing. In response, some black cultural nationalists such as Amiri Baraka attempted to expose the state as criminal while deploying new definitions of the role of black womanhood and the family. In turn, the government—Governor Hughes, Vice President Hubert Humphrey, and the presidential aide on the disorders, Joseph Califano—spoke of "doing all they can to help restore the city," while evading the question of the homicide of black women.[3]

In the state's attempt to justify and reconstruct the polity, they published statistical tables and data in ways that concealed the fate of women. A published table entitled "Exhibit C-117, Homicides—Newark Riot, 7-14–7-17" displayed some of the relevant information on the death of the rioters in separate columns, along with an "Autopsy Report/Ballistic Report" that indicated a majority of bullets fired in the riots passed through the bodies and escaped police investigation or autopsy. In classifying the fatalities, the table listed the ages and races but not their gender. Only by reading the first names of African American fatalities does the category of women materialize. The report listed their ages as 45, 68, 29, 40, 31, 41, and 53. Of course, as mostly middle-aged women, the victims were not likely to be suspects or girlfriends or collaborators of the men who allegedly posed a threat to public safety. If law enforcement claimed they shot black men for looting, none of the women's deaths involved any criminal charges.[4] Like the state's failure to produce compelling evidence of a black sniper to justify its use of lethal force, the state also failed to establish justifiable cause in the deaths of black women.[5]

The African American press held up the example of Eloise Spellman, perhaps the most famous of the female fatalities, to mobilize a critique of and investigation into the conduct of law enforcement. A 41-year-old mother of eleven, Spellman was sitting in the living room of her Hayes Homes apartment, with her children in the kitchen. She went to the living room couch, and glanced out the window. She was then fatally injured, and later cried out, "Oh, God." According to the testimony of one of her sons, when a family member came to the living room and discovered their injured mother, they attempted to signal the police to end the firing, and hung a white sheet in their window to signify surrender. "When they put the sheet out, some of the bullets stopped coming in," the son testified. At that point the Newark police entered their apartment in the Hayes Homes, and confronted the Spellman family. The son testified under oath that a police man angrily said, "You damned niggers don't need to be in this hallway anyway."[6] The graphic description of the innocent death of Spellman served to buttress criticism against the State of New Jersey and to defend the community from one-sided accounts that stressed black violence. (Spellman's younger children were placed in foster care and each only received the paltry benefit payment of $298.) "The victim was seated with her back to the window . . . on a couch soaked with blood and the curtains spattered red," reported the *New Jersey Afro-American* on its front page, describing how "two shots pierced Mrs. Spellman's neck and back." A relative of Spellman permitted more reporters to tour the premises, showing them slugs pulled from the walls and furniture.[7] Shortly after the women's deaths, a movement to indict white police officers gathered force, and a grand jury was convened. In the end, jurors found no cause for indictment.[8]

In the wake of unjustified female fatalities, the government and media deployed a negative image of black women that was drawn in equal parts from ongoing discourse of black cultural pathology and new inventions of racism. Some of the official discourse recalled the debates around the so-called Moynihan thesis, a theoretical paper written in 1965 by a high-ranking assistant in the White House dealing with the supposedly pathological state of the black family. Daniel Patrick Moynihan had argued that the inner-city African American suffered from a tangle of pathology caused by the absence of fathers and husbands, which in turn injured the development of manhood, and that this explained black poverty and social distress. The report had touched off a storm of protest, including the gathering forces of the Black Power movement, because of its allegedly racist assumptions. Moynihan assumed that a history of slavery ruined the family structure and the proper development of boys into men. Members of CORE and new converts to Black Power denounced the report because Moynihan had centered the distress of the victims and distracted attention from the "sickness of American society."[9] Although black women were three times more likely to head a household than white women, liberal social science depicted them as failures and deviants.[10] On some level, the disorders inspired some black female heads of household to reject the received stereotypes, like a woman who, according to a housing manager, had refused to pay rent, "demanding some things that I know that her attitude prior" to the riots was different.[11]

The second strain of the official discourse was derived from the publication of photographs of the riots that depicted men as dangerous and women as greedy looters. Since the rise of photojournalism in the 1940s, around the time of the publication of *Life* magazine (and then *Look*), the national media redefined the public's perception of violence and conflict, manipulating photographic images in ways that celebrated patriotism.[12] In the Detroit race riots of 1943, which caused as many deaths of African Americans as in Newark in 1967, *Life* had run a series of twenty photographs with captions that depicted a kind of social drama of white violence and black vicitimization, in ways that elicited the sympathy of a white liberal audience. Their point of view affirmed the American creed of equality and fair treatment for all regardless of race, as well as faith in the government's capacity to protect and redeem blacks in the city. In the July 28, 1967, issue of *Life,* writer Dale Wittner and photographer Bud Lee contributed a front-page story on "Newark: The Predictable Insurrection," which featured a stunning cover photo of Joe Bass, a 12-year-old boy, lying on blackened cement on his side, his elbow raised distortedly over his head. Bass was apparently unconscious as the result of injuries from stray bullets from law enforcement, and his appearance on the cover of the mainstream weekly magazine elicited public sympathy for the innocent youth.[13] But the majority of published photos demonized black men as violent perpetrators. Inside the riot issue of *Life,* under the headline, "In a Grim City, A Secret Meeting With Snipers," the editors ran two quarter-page photos of the faces of two dark-skinned men who look defiantly into the cameras. Though their faces and heads were wounded, scarred, and one man had sutures, their facial expressions conveyed a kind of righteousness and satisfied triumph. The photographic subjects served as spokesmen and claimed a certain representative voice, testifying that "insurrection was supported by the vast majority of black people."[14]

In this way, the photographs corroborated the official reconstruction of the post-riot terrain by reinforcing a perceptual dichotomy of innocent victim and dangerous threat.[15] If black men were figured as lethal and dangerous, the media depicted black women as criminal and culpable for their participation in looting. Some law enforcement agents distinguished between looting of provisions because of shortages in the disorders and acts of criminal theft of articles like furniture, appliances, or liquor. A high-ranking police officer wondered aloud: "Do you shoot a woman loading up in a grocery store with a load of groceries? Do you shoot some kid who has gone in a day or two after this thing and is walking out with some property which is really trifling?"[16] Perhaps the dominant sentiment was that of the infamous chief of police, Spina, who characterized looting as "crimes . . . committed by Negroes on whites, especially merchants."[17] In this vision, effective use of military strategy to put an end to the disorders necessitated the mass arrest of looters—if necessary by lethal force—particularly after the deaths of white law enforcement officers. By Thursday, Tom Hayden characterized the new strategy: "Murdering looters was now possible."[18]

The spectacle of the black female looter was bathed in the negative ideological light of the undeserving poor. In a series of philosophical essays on civil disobedience, Hannah Arendt had argued that the looting deserved to be seen as legitimate rather than criminal because of the publicity of the action. "There is all the difference in the world between the criminal's avoiding the public eye and the civil disobedient taking the law into his own hands in open defiance. This distinction between an open violation of the law, performed in public, and a clandestine one is so glaringly obvious that it can be neglected only by prejudice or will."[19] Yet in recent memory, this conflation of the civil with the criminal characterized a popular portrayal of the riots, *American Pastoral* by the Newark-born novelist, Philip Roth. At the scene, while the protagonist's mistress pleads with a National Guardsman to "think before you shoot . . . this is their home," Swede Levov chooses to see greed among the rioters rather than protest or the violation of innocent women by the police. Swede describes the greedy female looter: "Springfield Avenue in flames, South Orange Avenue in flames, Bergen Street under attack. . . . The shattering of the glass was intoxicating. Women pushing baby carriages heavily loaded with cartons of liquor and cases of beer . . . stealing sofas, cribs, kitchen tables. This is shoplifting. The American appetite for ownership is dazzling to behold."[20]

Contrary to the white liberalism of Roth and more like Arendt, many black nationalists valorized the looting as an extension of the black rebellion. Baraka wrote a poem entitled "Black People" that became famous when Essex County trial judge Leon Kapp read it out loud from a copy in the *Evergreen Review* before sentencing him to serve three to seven years in prison for weapons possession. Asserting his point of view in black urban vernacular, Baraka asked: "What about that bad shirt you saw last week on Frelinghuysen, or those stoves and refrigerators/record players, in Sears, Bamberger's, Klein's, Hahne's, Chase, and the smaller joosh enterprises?" If Baraka typically criticized Jews in his writings on the urban political machine, here he referred to the "joosh" as retailers and bearers of social status. Yet he also claimed that consumer culture and striving for white social status instilled self-hate in women: "What about that bad jewelry . . . on Springfield? You know how to get it, you can get it, no money down, no money never, money

Fig. 7.1. A major objective of the deployment of law enforcement was to protect commercial areas from looters, with
armed officers guarding the entrances to stores and shops in
the Central Ward. (Courtesy of New Jersey and Newark Public Library)

don't grow on trees no way, only whitey's got it." Rather than a variant
of materialism, Baraka defined looting as a deliberate racial act against
the white people, the enemy.[21] Many years later, Baraka wrote a second
poem on the riots that revised his original insistence on the primacy of
race and anti-white feelings, and valorization of female looting; he instead called for a worker's socialist revolution.[22]

If some black women stole goods to cope with temporary shortages,
they also looted stores selling luxuries. Here black women became tar-
gets of law enforcement, and took on the ubiquitous image of the criminal black male. In figure 7.1, white law enforcement guards the storefronts; the installation of military personnel in the storefronts established

Fig. 7.2. The news coverage rarely showed the extent of police brutality against female protesters. Although black
women participated in the civil disobedience and represented
approximately 10 percent of arrests, including looting and
curfew violations, much of law enforcement conduct proved
to be unjustified and excessive. (Courtesy of New Jersey News
Service and Newark Public Library)

the contested terrain and the defeat of looters. In figure 7.2, two white
law enforcement officers carry away a heavy-set black woman, looking
down at her in contempt. With the head and feet cut off from the view,
the serious, angry faces of the officers show their determination to command, take possession of, and take away this older black woman. This
was a kind of violent consumption. In figure 7.3, two older black
women and a young boy stand on the sidewalk, gazing into the broken
window of a department store. In a *Life* photo, a severely wounded

black man lies prostrate in a department store window, with pieces of mannequins strewn about the scene. In figure 7.4, a similar photographic image recorded traces of black women's political agency. Again in front of a department store, here eight to ten female mannequins pour

Fig. 7.3. (*top*) The destruction of familiar urban landmarks affected all residents of the Central Ward, whether or not they supported the civil disobedience. Perhaps the majority of black Newarkers, like this woman and young boy, had sought shelter from the violence. (Courtesy of New Jersey News Service and Newark Public Library)

Fig. 7.4. (*bottom*) Newark's local department stores, such as Klein's and Bamberger's, had been sites of protest since the Double V campaigns. The looting of shop windows and disrobing of mannequins represented a form of political demonstration by black women against racial and economic inequality. (Courtesy of New Jersey News Service and Newark Public Library)

out of the display window, in different states of damage, with several lying entirely on the sidewalk. All of the mannequins were naked and tan, signifying the racial figure of a white woman. But the viewer wonders if what had happened off camera, before the photographer shot the scene, was more than an act of looting—an act not only of disobedience but retribution, in which any number of women quite literally attacked the mannequins. Black women removed the clothing (which appeared fashionable behind the glass but probably prohibitively expensive) from the signifier of white privilege and left them lying on the sidewalk. It seems reasonable to suggest that black women attacking mannequins flowed from currents of mounting resentment against status inequality and the envy of white womanhood.

In this sense, apparently random and spontaneous actions were manifestations of long-term social contests. Figure 7.5 supplements the other shots of riot-time consumption by depicting two shoppers. Here two black women carry away a load of clothing; some of it in boxes, but most of it apparently not purchased. Their participation in looting powerfully registered their dissent from the consumer's republic and resistance to their mishandling by law enforcement. Reported after-riot losses for retailers was $1,734,925, of which $1,412,375 was in stock (and the remainder in property damage).[23] By the end of the riots, 85 percent of the storefronts suffered broken window glass, and the total number of businesses destroyed was 1,029, leaving 4,492 employees at least temporarily out of work. The estimate for building damage was $2 million. The auditors submitted a total loss estimate of $10,251,200, more than half of which they classified as "light damage," the consequence of smaller acts of defiance by men and women.[24]

In the post-riot reconstruction period, the State of New Jersey deployed a political narrative that marginalized any space for political agency for black women.[25] They represented looting as a series of statistics—of loss of property and damages—ignoring the political implications. By contrast, Tom Hayden's brief history had depicted looting as an expression of populist democracy, for the looters represented "people [who] voted with their feet to expropriate property to which they felt entitled. They were tearing up the stores with trick contracts and installment plans, the second-hand television sets going for top-quality prices, the phone scales, the inferior meat and vegetables."[26] Many participants in the riots who were summoned to testify emphasized anti-white sentiments not only economic activism. They recalled that many consciously

Fig. 7.5. The specter of looting sparked a public outcry against the riots, in turn fueling negative publicity. Much of the looting involved household goods or apparel from department stores, rather than, as was often assumed, thefts from liquor stores. (Courtesy of New Jersey News Service and Newark Public Library)

distinguished between white-owned stores and those owned by the black community, and that local proprietors protected their businesses by spray painting the word "soul" on their windows, indicating which side they were on.[27] The point is that many black female looters acted not only as nationalist dissenters but as agitated consumers. As mothers, they routinely assumed responsibility for family shopping, and as shoppers absorbed the alluring advertisements, replete with photographs of white affluence and standards of beauty. Without enough income, for the average black woman the dream of consumption faded into frustration. In 1964 the Social Security Administration had invented a so-called poverty index that measured income, excluding noncash benefits such as food stamps, Medicaid, or public housing, in accordance with the Consumer Price Index.[28] The release of a federal census study in 1968 optimistically announced that the number of people living beneath the poverty level had gradually decreased since 1959. At that time, more than 31 million Americans lived in poverty, but in 1968 the poor population had dropped to 23 million. In 1859, 8 million African Americans had lived in poverty, but the number had declined to 7,350,000 in 1968. The startling trend, however, was that in the same span of time, the rate of poverty for African American women had steadily increased. The number of black women living beneath the poverty line increased from 2,609,000 in 1959 to 3,323,000 in 1969.[29]

As the poorest consumers in the nation, black women had organized small, informal actions against recalcitrant retailers before the riots.[30] In the mid-1960s, black women led several demonstrations against the retailers on Springfield Avenue, including a major action in which the police arrested nineteen protesters. The demonstrators eventually convinced the "frightened merchants [to] clean up their stores." Shards of information indicate pickets and other demonstrations against food stores in the South Ward before the riots.[31] By the 1960s, with the increase in credit cards and purchasing accounts for shoppers, African American women in cities across the nation protested discrimination in lending, inflated interest and terms, price gouging in the poor neighborhoods, and inferior merchandise. Despite several decades of concerted effort by angry consumers, white proprietors continued to gouge black customers, and, when their accounts fell into delinquency, attempted to garnish their wages. A federal study of retailers that specialized in the sale of furniture and appliances to low-income consumers found that they "resorted to court action once for every 2,200 of sales," equaling an average of legal collections for every eleven customers. By contrast, department stores in white suburbs entered into legal collection only once for every 14,500 customers.[32] The aggressive collections tightened the screws on an already vulnerable group of African American women, one reason that they had protested racism in retail since the days of Double V.

In the wake of property destruction and personal injury, many black women experienced emotional trauma and sought withdrawal from the front lines of activism. Others were ideologically forced to the side lines. Although they joined grassroots campaigns against white-owned stores, now primarily black men planned and headed these actions. To disrupt the return to business as usual, in a number of cities after the riots in 1967 and the massive disorders that erupted after the assassination of Martin Luther King, Jr., black activists advocated "filling shopping carts and taking the full grocery sacks unpaid for at the checkout counters." A second maneuver was to shift goods around within the stores, "cross-filing merchandise from one shelf to another among the departments."[33] In Newark, nationalists pressed white retailers to reform unpopular practices, such as price gouging or overcharging for credit, and some solicited so-called donations to support community ventures by placing canisters in taverns and stores. In one case, the police investigated charges that "Dominic Palma, owner of the Colonade Meat Market," allowed a black nationalist organization (self-identified as the Black Star, possibly associated with Black Man's Liberation Army) to set up a canister for donations because they "told him if they placed a canister in his store it would help his business with people in the area." On another occasion, the Newark police reported that when "a Negro male" was approached by one of the Black Star people and he refused to place the canister, "a fight almost initiated."[34] The owner of the Marcellino Bakery, which had been "there for over fifty years," stated that he "has not been bothered by the foundation." Across the nation and in Newark, the nationalist retail campaigns involved many more men than women, a significant reversal of retail politics before the rioting.[35]

The leading black nationalist groups such as the Black Panther Party (BPP) and the Nation of Islam (NOI) proposed economic self-help programs and advanced what some were calling black capitalism. They called for the establishment of black businesses and, in the words of a directive from the leadership of NOI, "separatist investment plans and operation advice."[36] Baraka proselytized for his personal philosophy of Kawaida, a religious-like nationalist cult, because he felt that "we had to have a different set of values to bring about national liberation" in Newark. But Kawaida also called for a renewed commitment to economic self-sufficiency, particularly the concept of Ujama, or economic communalism. Their public organization, Committee for a Unified Newark (CFUN), constructed a nationalist print culture that called for the rejection of both black bourgeois, or "Uncle Tom," middle-class conventions and white economic control in the neighborhoods, to help the community avoid "being lost in various white controlled negative employment situations."[37] To support what Kawaida called "the cadre-life" in the "bitter struggle for National Liberation, PanAfrikanism, and World Socialism," the CFUN advocated black capitalism. Baraka's strategies dovetailed with the more conservative post-riot policy initiatives by the new federal administration, specifically the Small Business Administration (SBA) under President Nixon, which requested approval for mobilization under the federal disaster provisions of the president and dispatched advisers to Newark to administer commercial loans and offer managerial assistance for qualified applicants.[38] In response to the riots, the SBA also initiated a program aimed at minority businesses by providing loans and education. From 1968 to 1978, the number of loans distributed to minorities steadily increased. Deliberately or not, the calls by black nationalists for black capitalism conceded ideological ground to white conservatives and in the 1968 campaign for the presidency, Richard Nixon promoted federal funding for minority enterprises as the antidote to the urban crisis. If Nixon proclaimed that the most fundamental civil right is "the right to be safe from violence," he appropriated black nationalist rhetoric by calling for independence, dignity, and an end to dependency on whites. Even nationalist leaders like Floyd McKissick applauded the conservative emphasis on self-help, showing less affinity with the War on Poverty than the Republican ethos of upward mobility through individual success.[39]

According to my survey of licenses granted to private entrepreneurs at the office of the city clerk, by the 1970s, more African Americans than ever before applied for licenses and started up new businesses in Newark. The data suggest the extent to which white shop owners moved away after the riots, marking a final round of ethnic succession, from Irish to Jewish and Italian at midcentury, and from white ethnic to African American at late-century.[40] According to the city clerk, as early as 1971 a business woman applied for a license to open "Africanus" and another to open "the African Room," new enterprises suggesting the influence of Kawaida or other kinds of Afrocentric cultural nationalism. From the 1970s to the 1980s, the following establishments are listed in the business indexes: The Afro-Con International, African Shippers Transport, Afrika-Newark Festival Committee, African Spectators, African Roots Grocery and Produce, African Hair Braiding. In the period of post-riot reconstruction, black community nationalists operated in storefronts and sponsored retail, health, and educational operations, as well as Ujama boutiques that sold goods for the promotion of African heritage in opposition to Western values.[41] The new black capitalism, with

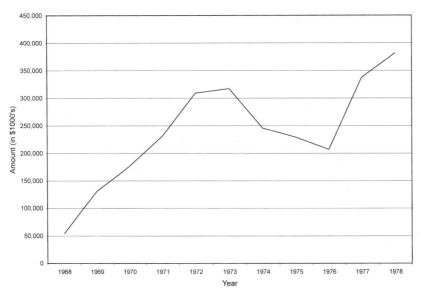

Fig. 7.6. Total dollar amount for loans granted to minority businesses.

its focus not only on entrepreneurial uplift but on consumption as a practice for realizing a new racial identity, particularly affected African American women. When the daughter of Malcolm X and Betty Shabazz appeared at a rally in Newark, local black cultural nationalists could point to several blocks of South Orange with a Shabazz Restaurant and Bakery, the Shabazz Superette, and the B & S Sunoco Auto service station, all of which were black owned.[42] The Newark Nation of Islam (NOI) also opened more Shake-N-Steak restaurants in the Central Ward and in several other areas, as well as marketed fish and sold bean pies in new local bakeries.[43] According to their own theory, the Kawaida nationalists advanced the "creation of small business by revolutionary nationalists" in the project of constructing a new black public sphere of "book stores, printing presses, food stores, clothing factories, cooperative food buying."[44] They also linked this construction of blackness to consumption for the home, promoting the adoption of an authentic African-style interior. Their pamphlets advised that "the house décor is organized to reflect a Black ethos . . . i.e. the arranging of pictures, colors, furniture, artifacts." At home the mother prepared the proper food for her family, and outside the black woman should "try to work with neighborhood schools on their breakfast and lunch programs . . .

substituting beef for pork, avoiding sugar coated cereals and pastries, serving more fresh fruits and juices."[45]

Black women responded both positively and negatively to the rise of this brand of racial consumerism, reflecting their contradictory place in the maelstrom of post-riot politics more generally. This contradiction reflected the fact that many women, especially black women, felt subordinated and endangered by the rioting and the increase armed conflict between men in their neighborhoods. (At the same time, a percentage of those arrested on weapons charges were women.) Yet, as black people opposed to white domination, many black women took pride in the uprising against the police. Though many scholars emphasize this racial struggle over the more subtle gendered anxiety, a series of early 1970s oral histories with black women who had migrated from the South and spent varying periods of time in Newark before the riots contradicted the nationalist image of unity against whites. Rather than recalling race as the main issue, one black woman said that "the only difference that there is, is in the skin. . . . I wonder why the whole can't join together." Some African American women did not understand the emergent politics of nationalism, referring to the new radicalism as "something that I don't know."[46]

Another woman who arrived in Newark during World War II and lived in public housing recalled that "I were living right here when the riots started." She too disapproved of black militants, and claimed to witness so-called "snipers . . . all up on top of that building over there." The riots had immobilized the woman, frightening her into turning off her lights and withdrawing from the line of fire. Later, when she took the chance to look, she witnessed police beating people on the streets, "making em all blood" with a "stick."[47] Perhaps out of fear and resentment at the danger they faced, many African American women were disaffected with the disorders and feared for the future of the city. "Now Newark is gonna soon be a ghost town. They're tearin it up and burning it."[48] Some located the riots as an event of a personal nature. A woman recalled that "the time of the riot we had just left on vacation," but she did not attach a political message to the event. "I didn't know what it meant by riot. We was visiting my daughter in Florida . . . and hear that they raising the devil in Newark."[49] Although African American old-timers believed they understood the problem of racism as well as the militant black nationalists, many rejected the strategy of separatism and supported accommodation with whites. "I don't know what white people think. I think it's ridiculous. Why should we burn up our homes, the only places we have to live?" What was striking was that African American women in the community had formed a powerful critique of the riots that blamed radicals for endangering them, and referred to them as "a gang of hoodlums." "Burnin' the house down—they don't care if your in there asleep."[50]

Yet the rise of militant nationalism undeniably fulfilled the desire of black female activists and women in relationships with radicals for a sense of security. A historian of the Nation of Islam, Ula Taylor, has argued that many sought refuge in alternative communities, subcultures, or religious sects, and she illustrates the ways in which "nationalist precepts of gender promoted a conservative agenda where patriarchy took center stage."[51] Although various schools of nationalism constructed very conservative roles for women, the cultural activists around Baraka opened a small space for political engagement. Many female converts to NOI, including former activists, deliberately withdrew from protest and activism, and in retrospect attributed their conversion to the need for a "safe home."[52]

Both strains of black nationalist ideology emphasized a politics of respectability, a demand for recognition of the sanctity and defense of black women, which women spoke of in terms of "respect." One female member of NOI recalled that "women on the other hand were looking for the respect of being a woman,"[53] and one black male nationalist reported that "in the sixties in Newark, New Jersey, you could not disrespect a Muslim woman, oh no, you'd better be walking a straight line when you walked past a sister, or some brother would snatch you up."[54] If the NOI believed in the fusion of nation and family, and in the submersion of women within both, many black women felt thankful for the protection. "It was right after the riots, and our city was in turmoil. The streets we lived on, and the community in which we lived was all torn down." Other women felt more ambivalent, questioning the cost in marginalization and political subordination for their protection. "The brothers just don't see that the sisters should be involved in the public sector . . . I want for my brother what I want for myself." Yet, as one historian of black nationalist women has argued, "black Muslim women were agents of change in the Black community of Newark."[55]

Black Muslims joined several organizations that Baraka helped to build, including the United Brothers and CFUN, in defiance of the strictures issued by the NOI that members refrain from political activities.

Baraka had recast his own black sexual politics from a fairly traditional investment in rebellious transgression of the taboo of miscegenation—recall that he had defiantly married across the color line and fathered two interracial children—and now repudiated interracialism, advocating anti-whiteness and racial separatism.[56] Rather than a radical provocateur who took the prized possession of white society, the white women, Baraka now denounced the victimization of black women by recasting the miscegenation story—that "the [ex-slave] freedmen came out of sexual meetings between the slave master and slave woman," in which the progeny, the so-called "mulattoes," were figured as the betrayers of the black community.[57] By the late 1960s, Baraka frequently repudiated the sexual revolution—which he characterized as "wild sexual excesses"—distinguishing the ascetic discipline of Kawaida nationalism from the decadence of white youth. In an interview in 1970 Baraka once distinguished his nationalist radicalism from the counterculture by proclaiming that the black nationalists "don't believe fighting in the community for the right to smoke marijuana or being homosexual." Instead of moral laxity, their prescription for revolution demanded of women the attainment of a kind of sexual rigor, to be achieved first, at least in ideology if not in practice, through the strict subordination of black women to black men (with their relation to white men left largely unremarked). As if any stylistic similarity between men and women threatened male dominance, the new nationalist ideology prescribed gender asymmetry. Black women ought not to wear pants or jeans, for example. The new ideologues never explained how their grooming recommendations would bring on the revolution, but they justified everything because of the race: "We must aspire to not only talk Black but look Black."[58]

The implication was that carrying the revolution forward required women to pledge themselves to a kind of gendered regime, in which the permissible expression of black female sexuality was service to the nation. By 1968, the United Brothers sponsored Soul Sessions every Sunday evening and invited single men in the community to dance and socialize with a group of black women who had converted to Kawaida. An interview by a man whose name appeared as NGUVU in the documents recalled such a soul session, where he heard Baraka deliver a particularly moving lecture. NGUVU had just returned from serving in the armed forces in Vietnam, and "came in the door and it was the first time I was in a gathering of black people like that since I had left the army."

Fig. 7.7. United Brothers of Newark.

Most important was a feeling of belonging with black women. "To come back and see all these pretty sisters in the bubas . . . the 'fros, [at] the Soul Session" helped convert him and other younger black men. For several men interviewed in the 1980s, joining the United Brothers meant "dealing with morality, like cleaning up your lifestyle—drinking and smoking" and "the new man, an alternative system." Black men felt converted, not simply persuaded by black nationalism. "When I walked out from the Soul Session because I was smoking cigarettes at that time. I remember that I got a block away from the place I through (*sic*) cigarettes away, I never smoked again. That was the impact it had on me."[59]

The pamphlets and literature that were sold at the growing number of Black Power bookstores further spelled out the reconstruction of womanhood, which was necessary to correct the community's "unnatural situation among unnatural people." Because of the permissiveness of the West, a society which one text equated with the enslavement of blacks, "the black woman was dehumanized" and therefore "the African woman has a natural and necessary role to play in the building of our nation." Once reconstructed, the black women served the men and the nation. Privileged as "the inner spirit of the nation," the nationalist women "should support their men in whatever they do in Nationalism." Baraka coordinated the activities of United Brothers, Black Community Defense and Development, and the community center, the Spirit House, and only men enjoyed leadership positions in the groups. Black women performed women's work, including education, and pitched in with the "necessary skills" of stenographer and note-taker so that she "takes dictation as well as record notes, minutes, resolutions from meetings, conferences, etc." Additional skills included typing, telephone, switchboard, desk board—but not leadership.[60] Over the next several years, the all-male United Brothers served as a powerful center for the training and promotion of future political leaders, a number of whom entered city government as head of Newark Manpower, superintendent of schools, head of urban renewal programs, head of Model Cities, and other community-oriented programs that bridged neighborhood organizations and black empowerment in municipal government. But the nationalists never promoted a woman into politics in Newark, and not until 1996 was a black woman elected to the City Council. Into the early 1970s, even when Baraka supposedly repudiated the culturally conservative program of Kawaida for a new socialist Pan-Africanism, he retained the same conservative gender definitions and asymmetry, at least in theory.[61] As late as 1974, for example, the Congress of African People (CAP) position papers spoke simultaneously of a "unified ideological base" and of "revolutionary Kawaida," but a cadre of women in CAP formed a Black Women's United Front that convened planning sessions to challenge patriarchy but evidently did not gain more visibility or power.[62]

In the aftermath of the riots, the rise of the Kawaida message attempted to stress a strong black masculinity that exemplified traditional attributes of power and control, as well as discipline and asceticism, that many had admired in Malcolm X. When converts to Kawaida had first encountered Baraka, he represented for them the liberating potential of such a black masculinity. A visitor to the Spirit House recalled that "he still had patches on his head at the time from the rebellion," but Baraka defiantly returned to lead the nationalist movement against the government and racist whites. His opposition to whiteness, what might be called the post-riot construction of anti-whiteness discussed in the next chapter, at first sprang from his assertion of an oppositional masculinity. Now the white youth from SDS who had volunteered to mobilize black residents and whom Baraka once recognized as "dissidents," were now cast as enemies, and he now criticized them as less than manly.[63] If Baraka depicted white culture as comparatively effeminate, he also deftly wielded homophobia against political enemies. Although he believed that racial consciousness was derived from race, it is not clear if Baraka embraced its biological-determinism. But he seemed to accept a biological theory of gender that presupposed homosexuals were effeminate, which he melded to a political theory that assumed that only whites or the white-identified were homosexual.[64] Baraka had written of homosexuality for years—"a subject I have always been very serious about," and also once admitted to admiring the gay poet Alan Ginsburg's flamboyantly homosexual ode, "Howl." But at the height of post-riot reconstruction, Baraka repudiated homosexuality along with bohemians and interracial relationships, and viewed homosexuality as a disease of Western culture, noting the role of homosexuals in cultural institutions such as museums, theaters, and literature.[65] Like the morally corrupt white ethnic, according to Kawaida theory, the white left—"The bush-smoking, wine drinking, homo-superhetero sexual, bellbottomed life of the hippy"—suffered from a state of degeneracy and emasculation.[66] In advancing black masculinity and reconstructing womanhood, the black nationalists recuperated the riots as a victory over the weakness of white culture.

In the next phase of the aftermath of the riots, however, the struggle intensified not in the realm of cultural reconstruction—which had powerfully invoked the symbol of black womanhood—but in a sphere constituted both as masculine and as potentially violent as the riots. In this next stage, a new movement to defend white neighborhoods was organized to demobilize the black nationalists, and in the process black and white men battled one another in law and politics.

8

Baraka v. Imperiale
The Excesses of Racial Nationalism

Like a bombshell in the public sphere, the disorders closed off avenues of cooperation between black and white activists, divided neighbors, and mobilized extremists. In response to massive property destruction and unexplained riot-related deaths, two new charismatic leaders—Amiri Baraka of the Black Arts and Kawaida movements, and a white neo-populist, Anthony Imperiale of the conservative campaigns for law and order—reconstructed the parameters of racial discourse in the post–civil rights metropolitan landscape. In tandem as much as in opposition, they created a powerful dialogic spectacle and invented a new urban nationalism that organized ethnic-based groups into vigilantes that furthered the popular acceptance of racism. Both sides repudiated the civic consensus, and attacked the assumptions of liberalism. The new politics attempted to discredit previous social movements (if from varied but not totally unrelated ideological vantages), foreclosing prospects for future racial integration. In the local and national elections in 1968, the far right in the Republican Party benefited from the likes of Newark's culture wars, catalyzing realignment in the party system from the liberal, urban, multiethnic coalition of the New Deal to the white-identified, suburban, southern-based conservatism of the New Right.[1]

Recall that back in the 1950s, an admittedly conservative but still optimistic generation of whites had fled the crowded cities, and some had rejected racial integration of the suburbs. But a majority of the Levittowners on Long Island or near Camden still adhered to basic liberal values. At the very least, most urban whites and recent converts to the suburbs still voted Democratic in the 1960s. By contrast, the post-sixties suburbanites were moving fairly far to the racial right, founding a new white conservativism that originated not so much in the flight from cities—after all, not only whites but blacks wanted to move into suburbs—but in the ruins of the riots, specifically in the deliberative breakdown and the increasingly combative tenor of the public sphere. White nationalism was not only more visible than before the riots, but also more legitimate and acceptable. By 1967 a broad spectrum of the public lauded the nonviolent passivity of black bodies in southern demonstrations against Jim Crow but denounced black resistance to the police in the rebellions of the north.

A lion's share of the civil rights establishment, from King, Roy Wilkins of the NAACP, and Whitney Young of the National Urban League to the social psychologist Kenneth Clark, also publicly rejected the rioting. In 1965 the NAACP had responded to the Watts riots by opening a local branch to assist some 1,500 homeless victims, but they repudiated the nationalists for defending violence, and even publicly warned the federal government that some black radicals were training in a secret, subversive camp "to create a riot."[2] Robert Curvin, perhaps the most significant black voice before the riots, felt ambivalent about the destruction and violence, even as he acknowledged his own as well as the community's rage at police brutality. The few remaining members of Newark's CORE had disbanded by 1968, at a time when the national body amended its constitution to eliminate the "multiracial requirement" for the branches, an imprimatur for racial separatism. As we shall see, Curvin briefly realigned with Baraka and the cultural nationalists to help with the building of a political party that would elect black candidates into office. But he never supported Baraka's black nationalist program, nor accepted racial separatism, and around 1968–1969 retired to his study to complete a doctorate in political science from Princeton University.[3]

Nathan Wright, who was somewhere to the nationalist left of Curvin and the moderate right of Baraka, also remained ambivalent on the question of the riots. Wright had gained visibility in Newark because of his leadership as well as his writings, receiving offers of publishing contracts, speaking engagements, and teaching positions after the riots. Although his political analysis stressed the need for cultural self-determination and the distrust of whites, he rarely agreed with the radicals like Malcolm X or Stokely Carmichael in advocating civil disobedience. Wright held up an old-fashioned faith in self-help but was silent on the question of armed resistance at the Black Power convention, which he convened shortly after the riots.[4]

As leader after leader in Newark renounced the violence and destruction of the disorders, Amiri Baraka's experience as a victim of the police improved his level of identification with residents in the Central Ward. Baraka used his charisma and publications to bring black men who were recuperating from the riots into his Spirit House, combining Black Arts display with grassroots organizing in the United Brothers. These new departures in community politics absorbed or eliminated competing organizations in the Central Ward. The Black Man's Liberation Army disbanded after its premises burned down, and Colonel Hassan, the most visible radical nationalist up to that point, reportedly left town around August (and does not resurface in the archival or historical records). A number of black Muslims from East Orange who had clashed with white Newark police officers only a week before the riots were arraigned, and at least two defendants were convicted. Others chose to leave for Detroit in October 1967. A fledgling branch of SNCC persisted under the leadership of Phil Hutchings but did not exert significant influence over Baraka or his growing nationalist following, and Hutchings (and Fullilove, Winans, Allen) and others who had bridged black and white activism in the tense years of the earlier movement quietly withdrew from the front lines.[5]

Tom Hayden and the white radicals had long recognized the legitimacy of civil disobedience, and joined black dissidents against militarized law enforcement during the riots. For many whites, the injustices of the disorders seared a connection in the political imagination between the violence of racist America and protest against the war and the colonial domination of Vietnam—between, as Hayden put it, "burning villages and burning cities." But few whites continued to attend meetings or enter the new dialogue on the question of black liberation. At one point, Hayden wondered aloud why whites felt welcome in liberation movements for peasants in Vietnam: "Why didn't they hate us? If we were among American blacks, we would be resented and made to feel guilty for our whiteness, for our lack of sufficient understanding, for our comfortable privilege, and we would find it hard to disagree." He later recalled that "the trend toward black power made it impossible to work effectively in Newark after July 1967."[6] Within a year after the rioting, most of the white youth had departed Clinton Hill, joining new causes of Second Wave feminism, the counterculture, or the antiwar movement. Hayden moved back to Berkeley, California, while a diminished NCUP stayed on in community action programs.[7]

When activists uprooted themselves, and as others withered under the pressures of separatism, the fate of interracial progressivism in the cities came into question.[8] By 1967 most moderate liberals had already lost patience with the unpredictable outbursts of black radicals, and resented their sometimes indecipherable demands of the government. As leaders of the Democratic Party, both President Johnson and Governor Hughes had publicly condemned the riots, a strategy to prevent future groups from threatening to riot as a form of "blackmail." Though the Kerner Commission had strongly condemned racism as a fundamental cause of the riots while downplaying the favorite diatribes of conservatives, such as black criminality and rage or irrationality, liberals viewed the document with skepticism. Their responses also signaled the extent of white withdrawal from public discourse on race.

When Paul Ylvisaker arrived in Washington to help draft the introduction to the *Kerner Report,* he resented the fact that the commission members and especially President Johnson had ignored his earlier reports on ghettoization. Ylvisaker recalled that "when Newark blew, you can imagine how angry we were . . . the final report is the report that we in effect handed in that weekend." Though he had already predicted much of what was finally published, Ylvisaker criticized the ways in which race appeared to substitute for a concrete policy initiative, and in a 1970 interview he blamed Mayor John Lindsay for forcing the language of a "divided America" upon them in exchange for agreeing to sign the document after he had threatened to stall."[9] In New Jersey, Governor Richard Hughes announced his support for the Kerner Commission, agreeing with the argument that "if you take too hard a line here you're not punishing rioters, you are just not responding constructively in many cases to legitimate community demands."[10] But softening the law and ordering attacks on rioters had failed to bring peace or a return to the civic deliberations of before.[11] Instead Ylvisaker movingly remembered he "faced white crowds who accused him of communism and insulted him as a nigger lover," only to travel the urban landscape and discover a political context where "a philosophic revolution [was] going on in the [black] household, almost a denial of our culture."[12] The growing popularity of black nationalism among youth, he recalled, "scared me, because nothing is relevant that we have to offer to that mood and climate."[13]

Ylvisaker's influence had risen with the fortunes of the Great Society, but now his professional options and, by extension his ideological viewpoint, were declining. When he was a rising star of the Democratic Party, he wrote to Hubert Humphrey and pushed for a new national policy on the cities that, in his words, "mix[ed] idealism with solving urgent problems."[14] After the Republican victory in the White House, Ylvisaker received a letter from President-elect Richard Nixon, informing him that he had been recommended for a federal appointment, but the administration never followed up.[15] At one point, they wrote to Ylvisaker with the news that his policy recommendations would not be included in the forthcoming report from the Task Force on Housing and Urban Renewal, and to a great extent his vision of a major reconstruction for the poor died in the ruins of Newark.[16] In 1970, Ylvisaker was ousted from his cabinet post when Governor Hughes lost his bid for reelection to Republican Thomas Cahill in what appeared to be a white backlash against the inner cities. In the following years, Ylvisaker returned to his teaching position at Princeton University, and later left the state for Cambridge, Massachusetts, to serve as dean of the School of Education at Harvard University.

In this aftermath of white liberal loss and withdrawal, a kind of tolerance or acceptance of discourse of racial bigotry and insult reconfigured the margins and moved into the center of the political terrain. Here the urban nationalist ideologies—what was dispensed in the vogue of Afrocentrism as a justification for anti-whiteness and in Imperiale's denouncements of civil rights as reverse racism—encouraged the acceptability of racial prejudice. Although historians study the rise of ethnic revivalism of the 1970s, when the generations of white immigrants celebrated its foreign heritage, few acknowledge the extent to which these white groups utilized ideas and tactics invented by people of African descent. Even fewer recognize this politicization of white ethnic revivalism as a form of racial nationalism. In turn, few scholars question the extent of manifest racial essentialism in the revival of black nationalism, deploying blackness as unchanging, nondeliberative, and most significantly, as noninterracial. By examining historical convergences between certain conservative strands of black political ideology and white conservative racial movements, an analysis of post-riot Newark suggests a shared dynamics of racial nationalism.[17]

According to leading political theorists, in Western democracies liberal governments have always promoted nationalism for their institutions and the population, in part to instill political identities of social order and loyalty during the rise of industrialization. In light of recent upsurges of interminable ethnic conflict around the globe, a number political philosophers and social theorists have examined the ways in which nationalism produced categories and modes of imagination and viewpoints centered on the fictive entity, the nation-state, by emphasizing group destiny and feelings of belonging that flowed from ethnic heritage or religious sectarianism.[18] The philosopher of the public sphere, Jürgen Habermas, explored the ways in which ethnic nationalism divided "liberation movements in multicultural societies" into different categories based on their political intentions and strategies, and identifies "groups . . . of a common historical fate . . . [that] want to protect their identity not only as an ethnic community but as a people forming a nation with the capacity for political action."[19] If the white ethnic did not really seek to build a nation, the mobilized factions had glimpsed their deteriorating racial position in America from a new vantage. For the first time, Italian Americans perceived whiteness in contradictory terms rather than as a natural entitlement that secured a certain kind of superiority and status over people of color. Because of challenges by black nationalists, some Italian Americans experienced whiteness in much the same way as their forefathers in the First Ward, as a potential social liability and sign of political vulnerability. Despite their long-standing political hegemony in city government, they now faced what was fast becoming a black majority in Newark, and therefore felt compelled to embrace white nationalism as the only viable political defense.

Both in response to and as an expression of their growing feeling of vulnerability, whites adopted the tactics and rhetoric of African Americans. The first example of this crossover was—not surprisingly, given the immediate context of the riots—the appropriation of the rhetoric of civil disobedience. In more and more cities, whites combined a resurgent cultural awareness of, or pride in, their particular foreign heritage with the tactics of "by any means necessary." It was in the context of rioting that Newark law enforcement first reported resistance and disobedience among whites, when they "had to ride in various areas of the city . . . to allay the fears of whites, to talk to groups of whites who were armed." The chief and other officers found that "whites refused to disperse for . . . white radio policemen and stoned them [police]."[20] But this proved to be only a temporary lapse in an ongoing partnership with the Newark Police Department.

Despite the heavy black casualties at the hands of police, many whites felt they were endangered by black militants and were left vulnerable by an inattentive police force, a very popular sentiment circulating before the riots. Because they were neglected by the government,

Imperiale and others called on young men in their neighborhoods to join vigilante groups to defend themselves against their black neighbors, but quickly realized their power lay in mutual cooperation with law enforcement. In effect, the ethnic group in Newark that was once widely considered impossible to assimilate because of its innate criminality and Mafia connections loudly proclaimed its allegiance to the cant of law and order.

While old-fashioned white liberals felt ambivalent about the riots, the new white conservative hawks were embarking on military escalation. In 1968 the political historian and critic Gary Wills conducted hundreds of interviews in police precincts in a dozen major cities for his book, *The Second Civil War: Arming for Armageddon*, which reported on the popular sentiment for more force, "blanket it, instantly, with blue; just pour the men in." If my historical reconstruction of the daily events in the riots demonstrated that military escalation caused more black fatalities, the police had concluded instead that violent force proved more effective than negotiations or political solutions. "Once the violence starts, there should be no negotiating with ghetto leaders," was the perspective that Wills found.[21] Many white ethnic conservatives pressed city councils and city halls to allocate hundreds of thousands of dollars for requisitions of sophisticated arms and state-of-the-art anti-riot technology. Conservative whites enthusiastically approved of large budgets for plastic super-teargas grenades, new defense uniforms, and fifteen-ton tanks designed especially for riots that dispersed massive doses of tear gas, and even special fire extinguishers specifically designed to diffuse Molotov cocktails. For law-and-order whites, the new militarism not only promised to prevent crime and defend against black subversives, but fortified their political control over the cities. For African Americans in the post–civil rights era, law and order signaled dangerous escalation of violence against the community, for as one black writer queried, if "last summer, using only old-fashioned weapons, the National Guardsmen managed to shoot hundreds of demonstrators . . . and women and children in the safety of their homes," "can you imagine what they could do with ultra-modern guns?"[22]

Growing white support for authoritarian city government was matched only by the maligning of black activists. White mothers, wives, and conservative pundits wrote to Newark Police Chief Dominick Spina to congratulate the NPD on its performance. "Isn't it about time that the niggers started to help themselves?" one correspondent asked rhetorically. If liberal indulgence and laxity of the Great Society permitted or even encouraged the riots, the correspondents called for defeating those liberals—"Johnson, Kennedy, and Dopey Warren" (the last a reference to liberal Supreme Court decisions), and for "stiffen[ing] your back to these and other bums like the rioters."[23] In an effort to control political terrain, white ethnics made donations to and rallied for the Policemen's Benevolent Association, the New Jersey Narcotic Enforcement Officers Association, the State Fraternal Order of Police, and the Firemen's Benevolent Association.[24] More whites joined the Ku Klux Klan in the state, as they had in Los Angeles after the Watts riots (where historian Gerald Horne discovered connections between the Los Angeles Police Department and John Birch Society).[25] Across the nation, the John Birch Society, the ultra right anticommunist organization that accused civil rights activists of plotting a communist revolution, grew by an estimated two hundred new chapters, including two thousand to three thousand dues-paying members in New Jersey, along with new chapters of Americans for Law and Order.[26]

If the riots had set in motion the first wave of law and order movements, the increasing economic vulnerability of whites fueled further white nationalist organizing and racist outlook. For the white working-class ethnics, every new sign of decline in their social or economic status appeared to accrue to their rivals, the supposedly aggrieved African Americans. Recent sociological data indicated that a large cohort of Italians in Newark now ranked "relatively low on wealth, prestige, reputation, education," according to researchers at Rutgers University.[27] For these left-behind whites who were clustered in transitional neighborhoods, the continuing process of integration through public housing felt like a racial attack on their autonomy. Now even the Ironbound district, a white ethnic stronghold that eventually formed a major base of support for Imperiale, experienced racial integration with the arrival of two thousand African Americans into the projects. With the out-migration of the white middle class and rise of black poor, according to one study, "It was no longer simple for Newark whites to define themselves as better off, at least, than the blacks."[28]

In contrast to the 1940s urban geography, when white neighborhoods always signified higher per capita income, by the late-1960s some black-majority census tracts out-earned white census tracts. In the upper brackets, black median income promised to close the racial gap, and in three tracts of East Orange more black families reported a median income between $11,000 and $12,000, while comparable white tracts had declined such that only three produced income equal to that of black families in the same census. For the first time, the average income for three Essex County tracts with a majority of black families surpassed median family income in every census tract in Newark. By the 1960s, more than half of the workers in the Italian American North Ward fell into the category of blue collar, few reported managerial or administrative employment, and prospects for mobility diminished as white education declined. In six census tracts that included nearby suburban Orange and Montclair, African Americans had attained a higher median graduation rate than any area in Newark, including any white tract.[29]

The intensity of white status anxiety under deindustrialization operationalized the racialization of Italian Americans. Fear of social and economic decline informed every dimension of the new construction of whiteness, which ironically in some ways produced a mirror image of the black nationalist type. Some observers of the Italians and other whites compared their status to the black ghetto dwellers, and referred to the whites who rebelled against their decline as "the invisible of the Newark Rebellion."[30] The popular Italian American leader Stephen Abudato coined the term "white nigger" to express white frustration with downward mobility, an appropriation testifying to the love-hate relationship between the two unmeltable ethnics.[31]

The phenomenon of the "white nigger," which reflected some identification with black oppression, complicated the pluralistic tone of white ethnic movements.[32] To a greater extent than they admitted, Italian Americans shared cultural characteristics with emergent African Americans. Social scientists pointed to the prevalence of hyper-masculinity in both groups that resulted from failure in the economy and political powerlessness. Academic studies distinguished working from middle-class concepts and uses of manhood, feeding stereotypes of the masculine Italian-American man as a bearer of the provincial "expressive order in which they express their solidarity by disregarding the clothing fads, novel language, and new dances of the wider society . . . more than any other ethnic group." Like African Americans, according to one ethnographic account, Italian Americans engaged in a "code-switch"— that is, they supposedly "assume proper patterns of speech and gesture while in the presence of alien authority figures," and then revert to a familiar stance when safe in their own territory. The upwardly mobile whites referred to these Italians as "Nicky and Natalie Newark" to denote their provincial working-class background, such that "even an attempt at hippie fashion only earns them the appellation of 'hip greaser.' "[33] Opinion surveys showed that the average lower-class white felt "disrespected" at a time when, as one author reported, "an important thing for the son of an immigrant was to be respected." If the Black Power movement attempted to increase the pride and facilitate state recognition for the culture of the group, some white ethnics felt cultureless, without their own working-class novelist or public intellectual to represent their heritage, resulting in "the son of the disillusioned white worker [who] finds himself out of step."[34]

White ethnic nationalism gave rise also to the articulation of what might be called negative ethnic identities. Not only Italian Americans but other white groups crafted an image of themselves as victims of society, in which they had been victimized by the media attention and political promises showered on civil rights demonstrators and black rioters. The silent majority felt they had to scream to be heard, to act spectacularly and rebelliously to receive a piece of the pie. In this post-riot culture, a highly publicized, spectacular duel pitted the white ethnic everyman Anthony Imperiale against black radical Amiri Baraka, in ways that polarized the very expression of ethnic identity.[35] Before this, in the history of Newark's infamous machine, white ethnics deployed their group culture through social networks that in turn served to gain power in the political system, including control over major issues, city services, and employment opportunities. It was in the battle for elected office and control at City Hall that the racial nationalists pushed ethnic politics as usual to new heights of group conflict and personal bitterness.[36]

In 1968, after reportedly more than ten attempts to join the police force, Anthony Imperiale decided to toss his hat in the ring and run for councilman at-large. His campaign would prove as momentous as the riots that inspired it. Imperiale was born and raised in Newark and attended working-class Barringer High School, but did not graduate. Unlike Baraka, who enrolled in several universities and excelled at literary studies at Howard University and the arts scene in Manhattan, Imperiale barely earned his high school diploma later, and only intermittently attended a local community college. By far more provincial than Baraka, Imperiale had married young, raised four sons and one daughter, and served in the U.S. Marines in the Mediterranean in the late 1940s (and received a dishonorable discharge). He also joined the National Guard (but was not activated in the rioting). At the height of his visibility as a white nationalist maverick, he was vilified by liberals as an extremist, but Imperiale was cut from the same fabric of mainstream America. He was as civic minded as any white husband and father: a scoutmaster, fund-raiser for charity, member of the National Rifle Association, and president of the local karate club.[37]

Less experienced and sophisticated than Baraka, Imperiale nonetheless recognized the utility of grassroots organizing as the first step toward regaining control for white men like himself in the halls of power in the city. Imperiale had created a new organizational vehicle, the Citizens' Council, the first meetings of which were convened during the riots to defend the North Ward neighborhoods from the real and imagined dangers of black snipers. Imperiale's vigilantism received criticism as well as gathered recruits, and whites who were more mainstream considered Imperiale to be nothing more than a thug. Governor Hughes once likened his group to Hitler's Brown Shirts. Yet he quickly attracted several hundred dues-paying members and an estimated several thousand genuine sympathizers, despite the fact that the ACLU had filed for an injunction to restrain Imperiale from even organizing.[38] The racism of the councils, not unlike the White Citizens' Councils in the South that had terrorized Martin Luther King, Jr., and civil rights demonstrators, appealed to a core of "angry militants within the white community," according to news reports. On the face of it, the members espoused no particular ideology except violent confrontation and were united primarily by their ability to operate firearms, patrol neighborhoods, and skill in the martial arts.[39] Beyond physical defense, the ethos of the Citizens' Council appealed to the outlook and psychology of men like Imperiale. Clearly part of the local working class, Imperiale never spoke of economic policy or unions. He was a white ethnic, and he was anti-black. A newspaper informant once said that Imperiale "developed a familiarity with the term 'nigger' and 'coon' that did wonders for his popularity."[40]

In response to the rise of Imperiale in the aftermath of the riots, Amiri Baraka increased his commitment to armed self-defense as well as engaged the more practical work of aiding electoral campaigns, applying for grants, and educating the community. Working with a group not totally unlike the Citizens' Council, the United Brothers, he helped to organize Black Community Defense and Development (BCD), with membership of about one hundred men, including teachers, clerks, laborers, and "a hard core of rugged young men called Simbas," a Swahili term for lion.[41] Baraka's leadership of CFUN prepared volunteers to take on Imperiale, and the group shared offices with the BCD in a building on High Street, about a block down from the Black Arts theater.[42] Like Imperiale, Baraka employed a certain ethnic construction of race that served to mobilize and unify these diverse voices in the local community.[43] From the time he called for black people to "revenge" the assassination of Malcolm X at a memorial service, to a highly publicized appearance with Revolutionary Action Movement (RAM), a group that advocated terrorism against the government, Baraka also called for armed struggle to build a nation against white domination. In an in-depth essay in a black journal, Newark was hailed as the city where "Italian Power must be second only to that in the Vatican," and in response black nationalists felt challenged to advance their own cultural regime to repudiate Western Culture. As Baraka told an audience, "If you internalize the white boy's system, you will come to his same conclusions about the world."[44]

In turn, from the dying civil rights movement, Imperiale had appropriated the tactics of direct action and used the force of his personal charisma in face-to-face encounters to build a white movement. He fused this sort of appealing personalism with his own toxic brand of white ethnic aggrandizement. By 1968 he had steadily expanded his base of support beyond the North Ward and the Portuguese Ironbound district, appealing to young white ethnic men in the suburbs of Essex County even if they did not vote in the city elections. (Imperiale later won a seat in the state assembly with the support of these voters in the suburbs of the county.) By 1969 the Citizens' Council claimed chapters in Nutley, Belleville, Point Pleasant, the racially integrated suburbs of East Orange and Orange, and three chapters in Newark.[45] With support for Imperiale peaking among radical right whites, the FBI launched an investigation and characterized him as "the most belligerent of the whites toward the Negroes." They continued to conduct surveillance on Baraka, whom investigators characterized as the "person who will probably emerge as the leader of the Pan-African movement in the United States."[46]

Imperiale took as much inspiration from white supremacists in the South as from northern right-wing groups, when a conflict broke out between United Brothers and the Citizens' Council over the so-called "K9 program" as "groups of young Negroes and whites rushed at each other," according to an FBI "racial matters" investigation.[47] The unsuccessful city council proposal to use police dogs recalled southern attacks on the civil rights workers—an ironic memorial to the days of Birmingham, Bull Connor, and George Wallace—just as Imperiale's network of vigilantes had drawn inspiration, and their name, from the murderous southern White Citizens' Councils.[48] As a moral conservative, Imperiale attacked sex education, real estate agents, and busing to achieve integration, and vowed to "fight crime in the streets, narcotics, and 'judges with lace on their pants.' " As such, Imperiale's bread-and-butter issue was law and order for young white ethnic men, but he also attempted to cross over to mainstream white voters and accepted invitations to address the Lions Club, American Legion, and police fraternal organizations.[49]

From every side, the silent majority of Americans called for resolution of racial conflict and obeisance to law and order. In these times of anxiety and anger, both Imperiale and Baraka tested the limits of law and order by taking the law into their own hands. As a black militant radical, Baraka appeared on the criminal side of the law and order divide, a challenger of the legitimacy of the legal order, while Imperiale championed the police and their racist patrolling of the public sphere. After his arrest in the riots, Baraka and two companions, Barry Wynn and Charlie McCray, were convicted in Newark district court, in what some observers called a show trial that the government staged in the name of retribution for the riots. The defendants were hardly habitual criminals. McCray was a former accountant turned activist, who volunteered his expertise at the Area One Board.[50] He and Baraka were found guilty of possessing two unlicensed revolvers, and Baraka was sentenced to two and a half to three years in state prison, but eventually released on $25,000 bail.[51] Later, at the second trial, Baraka basked in the spotlight of publicity, flouted the legal authority, and mocked the trial, while his defense team attempted to demonstrate that doctors treated Baraka for scalp lacerations resulting from unprovoked police attacks.

In his performance of the law and order discourse, Baraka recalled the unjustified violence against black people in the disorders of 1967. In this scenario, Baraka, indeed every black man, was a John Smith. The trial testified to the inconsistencies in the police record, suggesting the corruption of the arresting officers, and Baraka emphasized key symbols of African cultural nationalism and white racism.[52] The police had discovered Baraka's weapon after it had fallen from beneath his African tunic. On another occasion, his African tunic was the object of stares and insults by the police, and the white newspaper reported on his "bushy" haircut. But Baraka's self-conscious ethnic pride found a positive reception in the black community. In oral history, black observers testified that "it really woke up a lot of white people."[53]

The great public trial not only replayed the dramatic racial confrontations of the riots, but kept alive a black nationalist critique of racist police. In courtroom testimony, Baraka accused the arresting officer of assault and brutality. He testified that he was "pulled" from the seat of a car, thrown to the ground, and assaulted with the butts of police firearms while one of his companions yelled, "Why are you doing this to me?" At one point the lawyer suggested that the police planted the gun in the vehicle, accusing the officer of corrupting the legal process. Then, inappropriately, the judge, citing Baraka's visibility as a black nationalist and his reputation for radical rhetoric, denied appeals by his lawyers for reasonable bail. "The preaching of hate and his call to arms is a well-known philosophy of this man," the judge charged.[54] Later, in controversial instructions, he told the jury that the defense's charges that police gave false testimony and planted evidence was only a diversion.[55] Baraka was found guilty and sentenced to serve three years in prison, and was released on bail to await his appeal. In 1969 the state supreme court of New Jersey would overturn the conviction in part because of improper instruction to the jury.[56]

In November 1968, at the height of Imperiale's popularity and the Citizens' Council's rising influence, Baraka again challenged the legitimacy of the Newark Police Department. While conducting personal business at his bank in his neighborhood on Springfield Avenue (the site of the riots), Baraka allegedly picked a fight with a white police guard. Baraka said that he resented the presence of the officer, whom he recognized from demonstrations and rallies, and later testified that he was trapped into an argument with him.[57] Baraka was tried before a local judge on charges of using profanity with a police officer and resisting arrest. But his defense attorney argued for "animosity towards Jones on the part of the policeman," and that police "attempted to ridicule, embarrass, and needle Mr. Jones." Why didn't Baraka control himself? At the trial the police testified that Baraka used the epithets "faggot" and "punk" to ridicule the officer, as well as berated the officer for bearing arms in a black community institution. Still out on bail and pending an appeal in the riots conviction, Baraka was convicted, and sentenced to sixty days and $100 fine.[58]

Fig. 8.1. The cultural nationalist Amiri Baraka rose to prominence in the aftermath of the rioting, engaging in ethnic battles with Anthony Imperiale and the Newark Police Department. Baraka is escorted outside Essex County Court House by his wife, Amina Baraka, with their child after sentencing for one of several convictions involving police. (Courtesy of the Schomburg Library for Research in Black Culture)

But in a second trial on the profanity charges, the defense lined up an array of witnesses that totally denied police charges that Baraka had been abusive, and in fact alleged that the police had actively harassed Baraka.[59] One witness testified that an officer spoke of the election of George Wallace, the governor of Alabama, which would "get rid of all your kind."[60] Then the police officer testified that Baraka used anti-white insults—and called the officer "white trash" and a "white faggot."[61] The defense testified that the police badgered him by asking if he "was going downtown to see Mr. (George) Wallace." And Baraka replied, "Who? Your white father? All you white people look like Wallace to me." He attacked the manliness of the police: "If you didn't have that shotgun, you'd be nothing but a fag and a punk." Another witness blamed the white officer for taunting Baraka with references to Imperiale: "How's your friend, Mr. Imperiale?"[62] In the end, Baraka won a reversal of the conviction in part because the judge was not satisfied with any of the evidence, and he felt the arrest had smacked of Italian strongarming.[63]

Although Imperiale and Baraka positioned themselves on different sides of the law and order divide, they similarly manipulated pro-police or anti-police imagery to mobilize larger and larger constituencies. Although it is difficult to estimate the number of whites who endorsed tactical violence, Imperiale's supporters lauded police conduct in the riots that had caused so many black fatalities. In New Jersey, white nationalism and the police mutually shaped each other for several years. Even before the riots, numerous reports linked New Jersey police to rightwing fringe groups. For example, a publication charged that a Jersey City policeman used official police pouches to distribute John Birch Society literature, and a report from the police chief in Trenton quoted the Birchite monthly bulletins in a department memo. A New Jersey state trooper, George Demetry, resigned from the force to take a full-time job as a Birch organizer, and in Newark a policeman received a three-month leave of absence so he could devote himself full time to recruiting for the Birch Society.[64] Now, Italian candidates publicly celebrated their relations with the police, and white candidates in the city council races received campaign contributions from the so-called Toto-Moran Fund, a trust established in honor of the two white officers killed in the riots.[65]

In response to the heightened tensions between police and residents, the Essex County grand jury investigating violence summoned Imperiale to answer allegations of race hate. He attempted to defend the group by claiming that their maneuvers had secured two-thirds of the city, and publicly took credit for making the streets safe to walk again. His idea of a defensive militia paled in comparison to the violence perpetrated by black rioters, and he quietly conceded that "my fight is strictly with black radicals who want to stomp, burn, and bang."[66] If he was forced to disarm the Citizens' Council, Imperiale demanded that "Negro militants" in the city discontinue their patrols.[67] Meanwhile, the state passed a bill to prohibit paramilitary organizations.[68] But Baraka, who had been arrested in 1965 in his Harlem loft with a cache of weapons, including shotguns, continued to practice armed resistance. And Imperiale's militia never disarmed.[69] By spring 1968 the FBI, in a report for the Department of Justice, classified Imperiale under multiple categories of "subversive, ultra rightist, racist, and fascist" and upgraded surveillance after they suspected his group of trading in firearms. Following newspaper reports and a meeting between the assistant district attorney and civic leaders, it was rumored that black and white militants had stolen weapons from the Port Authority in Newark, as well as that "Imperiale, head of the North Ward Citizens Committee, is selling weapons including machine guns, for $85 each."[70]

As the fanning of racial antagonism polarized supporters of the candidates, Imperiale's enemies carried out a series of actions to neutralize his campaign. Like Baraka in the riots, Imperiale claimed that his safety was threatened.[71] In August police reported the detonation of at least three bombs outside the North Ward Citizens Committee headquarters, causing fairly extensive damage—"two automobiles were damaged, windows of some sixteen houses broken, clay tile pipe and curbing broken, and exterior damage to one of the homes," according to FBI files.[72] The city dailies later reported on several fires in a black neighborhood "within hours after the explosions," speculating that they were set in retaliation for the bombs.[73] However, neither of the attacks resulted in deaths or injuries. Then, in October 1968, a month before the elections in which Imperiale was running for City Council, two unnamed assailants that Imperiale identified as black men allegedly fired a shotgun from a moving vehicle but missed the political candidate. Police recovered "bird shot" from a nearby storefront close to where Imperiale was walking. Neither the press nor the FBI apparently suspected Baraka, however. Although the press reported the incident, there were also suspicions that Imperiale planted the evidence of the shooting in order to gain white voter sympathy, as no witnesses or other evidence corroborated his allegations.[74]

By exchanging spectacular tactical maneuvers, black and white nationalism dialectically evolved, with Imperiale and Baraka an unflattering mirror image of each other. Both Baraka and Imperiale had repudiated the civil rights movement, though employing different nationalist ideologies of differing levels of complexity, and for different reasons. In the summer of 1967, while Baraka rejected integration, Imperiale staged an incredible spectacle at an appearance by Martin Luther King, Jr. He requested a meeting with the civil rights leader, who declined, and he accused King and his colleagues of perpetrating a "big hoax." "Every time a big leader comes to Newark he goes to the Negro districts." In theory, a genuine pluralist would visit every neighborhood, without regard to race. For Imperiale, even the most important leader in the black struggle for freedom was false—virtually a racist—when he was not acting on the basis of what Imperiale termed color blindness, that is, blindness toward civil rights and the continuing problems of racial discrimination. Just when it seemed that the riots were firmly anchored, Imperiale uprooted the issue of violence to undermine King—the global symbol of nonviolence—and publicly chided black leaders for tolerating violence around the time of his visit. "They tell how to make Molotov cocktails and preach hate but they don't put out leaflets telling how to get a job."[75]

Imperiale claimed that he rejected the civil rights movement because of its betrayal of the ideal of color blindness, and accused black leaders of reverse racism. Why did King speak of black empowerment and not white empowerment? Perhaps Imperiale was right to see King as more racial and less integrationist now than in the days of "I Have a Dream" at the March on Washington. On a highly publicized trip to Newark in 1968, only a month before his assassination, King scheduled an informal meeting with Baraka at the Spirit House, and in a photo opportunity shook hands with the radical nationalist and his family. Baraka remembered that "King was talking about a national leadership, a community movement," and was attempting to ignite the movement again in the North. He recalled that he encountered a less transcendent, God-like King—according to him, unshaved, unpolished, "not that Atlanta look."[76] But in April 1968, during the national funeral for the slain civil rights leader, rather than joining processions of citizens in mourning, Imperiale waved a rifle in front of his headquarters, shouting in front of a television camera: he was infuriated because Mayor Addonizio had sent his condolences to the black community.[77]

At one point in the dialogic spectacle, Baraka and Imperiale agreed to install an official telephone "hot line" between the two warring factions in a program overseen by Police Chief Dominick Spina. When Imperiale complained that "I don't like the ways Jones' people have been campaigning in the streets," he announced that he would unplug the hotline from his North Ward offices.[78] In this new dialogic nationalism, both Imperiale and Baraka decided to publicize their cause to youth. Back in late 1967 Imperiale appeared at one of Newark's predominantly white high schools, Barringer, and sometime later Baraka "spoke to black students" who comprised a minority at the school. The two leaders exchanged allegations of misconduct, and Baraka particularly criticized the suspension of black students. As nationalist representatives of polarized constituencies, both Imperiale and Baraka met with the governor during separate sessions.[79] Despite the legal troubles that followed Baraka, the school district elected him to the Title I Board of Education, an advisory board to the City of Newark school system.[80] Baraka's wife, Amina Baraka, who had transferred their children from the public school to a nationalist, Kawaida-approved school, and led efforts to reform the curriculum. Not surprisingly, at some point a conservative member of the school board announced there would be an inquiry into the appointment, and Baraka was denounced as a radical supporter of the riots because he had distributed a flyer, "Riot for Black Revolution."[81] Although his appointment actually was legal, white opponents alleged impropriety and procedural malfeasance.[82]

But the standoff between black and white nationalists went to the public in the fall, and the returns showed a white nationalist landslide. Both Imperiale and Anthony Giuliano, the president of the Police Benevolent Association, won city council seats in the November elections. All of the black candidates, some of whom were helped by Baraka-led workers, finished far back in the field. For his part, having topped the list of candidates in the at-large races, Imperiale emerged as the early frontrunner for the mayoral races in 1970, and the white nationalists dealt another blow of revenge for the riots.[83] When Imperiale opened his North Ward city council offices, he chose to use Citizens' Council headquarters on Seventh Street, the original armed militia from the riots.[84] He had campaigned on a law and order platform—"to support the police, right or wrong"—and he promised to uphold the values of the white nationalism that distinguished his candidacy from those who had shown leniency toward the rioters. His first order of business was to attack the machine and Addonizio, and he promised his supporters the same vigilance with the mayor as with policing the neighborhoods against black invaders, proclaiming that "If he [Mayor Addonizio] continued to bend to the will of radicals, he's in trouble."[85]

In cities around the nation, from Boston to Sacramento, from Brooklyn to Atlanta, conservative whites of the lower middle class drew on the direct-action tradition of left and black activists, but frequently without a reasonable reference to its original political dynamics and moral purpose. Conservative whites staged protest rallies, marched on City Hall, and chanted slogans to advance antiliberal policies, and in the process helped to sustain a national political realignment from the Great Society to the New Right.[86] Just as black nationalists withdrew from interracial alliances, white conservatives disavowed their liberalism. By the end of the 1960s, in the political sphere, black nationalism operated dialectically with white nationalism. When Baraka fanned the flames of post-riot Newark by training and arming young black men in the Central Ward, Imperiale recruited young white men. When Baraka clashed with the police in symbolic conflicts that touched the heart of his community, Imperiale actively embraced the police and their families in the Italian neighborhoods. When black militants allegedly detonated a bomb in Imperiale territory, several bombs destroyed homes in black neighborhoods. When the Italian Americans utilized long-standing civic groups to organize and mobilize for city elections, Baraka organized his "brothers" to mobilize, register voters, and plan for the elections in 1970.

Wop for wop, nigger for nigger, both factions polluted the public sphere with epithets, and never apologized. Neither group nor its leadership—and this is especially troubling for an intellectual of the caliber of Baraka—questioned the righteousness of its cause. The irony for Baraka was that this urban political dialectic circumscribed the development of nationalism into a sophisticated ideology and organization. Most obviously, fighting with Imperiale on his own terms prevented the attainment of what political scientist Michael Dawson considers a critical objective of black nationalism, namely self-determination.[87] In Newark in the struggle for Black Power, Baraka was very much determined by Imperiale, and he by Baraka. With the force of hate and the tools of violence, the racial nationalists created rigidly opposed, yet dialogically constrained, identities of ethnocitizenship.

Most historians of that famous moment around the world—1968—assumed that the broad fabric of the national political culture was divided by issues, between support or criticism of the Great Society and growing dissent from U.S. involvement in Vietnam, not by fundamentally different racial ideologies. Yet Imperiale's rise exposed dogged ideological commitments and dangerously divided cultural values. These raging nationalist conflicts mobilized extremism on both sides, exposing the interconnection between white racism and party politics, not only in Newark but in the nation. As the governor of New Jersey entreated liberals to search for ways in which to "keep the racial peace," this very conjunction largely determined the outcome of the 1968 New Hampshire primaries.[88] Presidential candidate Richard Nixon adamantly denounced the Kerner Commission for even mentioning "white racism" and for blaming "everybody for the riots except the perpetrators of the riots," and on the campaign trail he urged "retaliation against the perpetrators of violence" that was "swift and sure." The New Jersey electorate responded to the rhetoric with a victory for the Republican Party, when only four years earlier Lyndon Johnson had received twice the vote cast for Republican candidate Barry Goldwater in the state. This racial fallout from the riots foreshadowed a similar realignment in Michigan (the Detroit disorders) and Wisconsin (the Milwaukee disorders), both of which gave first- or second-place finishes to ultraright segregationist presidential candidate George Wallace in 1972, and eventually witnessed party realignment by the 1970s. Although the ascendance of the Republican Party inaugurated what some historians dubbed the "southernization of American politics," in which the old southern racism of the Dixiecrats resurged in the 1968 elections and increasingly shaped electoral behavior across the nation, the roots of the right in the North hailed from white ethnics in cities that were under the pressure of racial conflict.[89] What one historian characterized as "Blue-collar ethnic neighborhoods" polled 259,000 votes for Republicans in New Jersey (and a similar number in Michigan of 317,000) in 1968. In little over a year, the wrongful police beating of John Smith, a black Newark taxi driver, had finally ended with the defeat of the Great Society.[90]

9

Black Power in Newark

By the end of the 1960s, the civil rights movement had won a major commitment from the federal government to protect citizenship, and then gradually collapsed under various social pressures from within and without. Some veterans of the movement were fatigued by the repression and violence, and others had grown resentful of overbearing whites who were supposed to instill confidence in rural black folk. Some radical whites became alienated from black nationalists who refused to see a difference between them and the enemy, and black activists accused whites of bankrupting the organizations when they left in anger. In the northern cities, Malcolm X and other radicals insistently questioned the cost of passive demonstrations for the well-being of the larger community. Further exacerbating deterioration of interracial trust were several consecutive summers of urban disorders pitting the ghetto against predominantly white police forces. Just as the March on Washington signified the dream of pluralism and nonviolent democracy, the assassination of King in 1968 meant that more black activists than ever before took up arms and echoed the urban rage voiced by Malcolm X.[1] As for white liberals, the very same intransigence that precipitated civil disobedience—ignoring reasonable grievances and refusing to negotiate —continued to characterize the response of the federal government. President Johnson tapped two extreme black conservatives—Senator Edward Brooke of Massachusetts and Roy Wilkins of the NAACP—to represent the black interest in the Kerner Commission hearings. When asked specifically by a reporter if the president had considered appointing an "advocate of Black Power," Johnson spoke in generalities about high qualifications and experience, and rejected considering a member from the "standpoint of militancy or nonmilitancy." Although after the summer of civil disobedience the government admitted the existence of white racism, and the need for federal aid, Johnson's civil rights-as-usual approach failed to recognize the revolutionary change in the ideological climate of U.S. cities.[2] Left unacknowledged by the state, many dissatisfied activists gravitated toward the radicals who promoted Black Power, particularly the anti-white, Afrocentric impulses, like the Kawaida program of Maulana Karenga and Amiri Baraka.

From the moment in 1966 that Stokely Carmichael, the chairman of the Student Nonviolent Coordinating Committee (SNCC), invoked the term "Black Power" in anger at the shooting injury of James Meredith in Mississippi, his words captured the imagination of many but the understanding of few. Precursors to Black Power surfaced around direct action demonstrators in CORE, and the most radical branches of the NAACP. As early as 1963 Malcolm X called for a United Front of militant and mainstream civil rights leaders—including King, Adam Clayton Powell, Whitney Young, and James Forman—to deal with what he called the "destructive ingredients" that "may soon erupt into an uncontrollable explosion."[3] Black Power, if defined as the expression of this impatient, outraged militancy, can be found in Pan-African organizations in New York City and in the deeds of black southerners who took arms against the Ku Klux Klan in the early 1960s.[4] But clearly the public visibility of the slogan and its identification with a particular expression of blackness increased around 1967. The national media and the white press often confused Black Power with the outbreak of violence in cities, as if every black man in a riot or under arrest for a crime defined the movement and everyone else was an "Uncle Tom." Similarly, more conservative black leaders identified it with stereotypes of ghettoization and social pathology, criticizing various iterations of militancy in the same breath as citing statistics of black infant mortality, drug addiction, and venereal disease. Another group of traditional civil rights leaders strategically supported Black Power at a calculated distance from radical nationalists like Baraka, but continued to disavow even legitimate grievances expressed in the riots.[5] Even the out-of-touch strategist of the nonviolent movement, Bayard Rustin, gave speeches and wrote essays on Black Power, hailing the movement as a crossroads of new directions and agendas.

A range of periodicals in the black public sphere—from *Sepia, Black World, Negro Digest* to the radical *Muhammad Speaks* and *Freedomways*—ran stories on Black Power to take stock of the gains in civil rights and to contemplate future directions. If the frequent contributor to *Ebony*, Lerone Bennett, was correct that "the lessons of Newark and Detroit were that a large number of black people are totally alienated from a society which has done everything to bring about the worst in them," then did Black Power signify the end of the dream of integration? If the black Muslim newspaper, *Muhammad Speaks,* called the rioting an act of white genocide against the black community, then was Black Power a backward-looking ideology rooted in racial vengeance? Even if a few nationalist militants anticipated the spirit of self-determination that sprang from the radicalization of civil rights activism, to talk about Black Power as far back as the 1950s remains anachronistic. Precisely by locating its moment of political viability—in this case, the years between 1967 and 1969 when the terminology of Black Power had mobilized people and noticeably entered the public sphere—historians serve the cause of accurate scholarship. In Newark, the broad swath of Black Power was characterized by black-led coalitions and strategic pragmatism, rather than by ideology and revolution. If Black Power signified the withdrawal of political workers into a separate, perhaps still overlapping, black public sphere, the movement also overcame sectarian rituals and doctrinaire leaders in the pursuit of practical gains. Not unlike King's struggle for integration, black empowerment activists believed in democratic values of community and (both physical and political) representation.[6]

Yet, as the struggle for civil rights wound down, its leaders searched for new ways to overcome feelings of inferiority and resentment that afflicted the veterans. Just as the fight for integration and equal treatment spawned theories of race psychology, such as the argument that Jim Crow damaged the psyche of black children, so too the rise of Black Power required new psychological models of identity. The African American press suggested that the mind of the black man was injured or depressed merely by association with whites. A leading black psychologist, Alvin Poussaint, explained the growing popularity of Black Power as a response to internalized inferiority and "increased feelings by Negroes of alienation from whites."[7] Stories examined the revitalization of African American interest in their heritage and the culture of Africa; many identified this trend as a kind of compensatory psychology. Thus Poussaint argued that the Black Arts movement served as a kind of compensation for the "shame remaining in the Afro-American hearts about their blackness."[8]

Although the Black Power movement believed in psychological separation from whites as a necessary stage in the development of a healthy personality, it also emphasized the attainment of political independence.

Black Power writings cast the Newark disorders both as a manifestation of rage and, more profoundly, as the coming revolution. When you "take a city composed of almost 60 percent black people and rule them by white people who . . . are unresponsive," "you have a fully-clothed riot," a long political story concluded.[9] Although the rituals of Black Power—the compulsory Afro hairstyle, the soul handshake between black men, and the popularization of black vernacular—provided vital therapy in a racist world, this cultural signification was not the goal of the movement. In a major book, *Black Power,* the radical that had first raised his fist, Stokely Carmichael, and a political scientist, Charles Hamilton, constructed a long history of empowerment going back to 1940s dialogues on civil rights and nonviolence that rejected integration as unworkable because the process of inclusion always required assimilation. Like the cultural nationalists, they argued that the white members of organizations always assumed that "white is automatically superior and black by definition is inferior." And if Carmichael and Hamilton wrote that cultivating black cultural pride was "so obvious that it seems almost simple-minded to spell things out at this length," they nonetheless refused to foreclose the option of future interracial cooperation. But rather than create an alternative cultural regime so elaborate that following its rituals became an objective, Carmichael and Hamilton envisioned Black Power as a concrete and realistic movement for group advancement.[10]

Black Power ideology called for temporary racial separatism to create an autonomous deliberative sphere, as well as for the ousting of conservative black leadership. Commentators from around the globe had claimed that the riots signified both an uprising against whites and a search for black leaders who, in the words of Hamilton, would become "fully cognizant of our needs and aspirations."[11] In the Newark elections in 1968 and over the next two years leading to the crucial mayoral races in 1970, the Black Power movement attempted to promote their own hand-picked organic or local people over traditional leadership. Among the first to fall was the legendary councilman Irvine Turner, who had frequently clashed with cultural nationalists. Turner had called for white involvement in the affairs of the "Negro in America," and asserted the essential sameness of blacks and whites as a justification for equal treatment. He "asserted that Negro teachers, doctors, lawyers and preachers of the present generation do not speak . . . in the vernacular of the stupid Amos nor in the overbearingly presumptuous Andy," referring to the demeaning radio and television program that integrationists had fought against since the 1940s. Like the stereotypical black bourgeoisie going back to the accommodationists, Turner identified himself as a New Negro and assured audiences that the black middle class wished to talk and act just like the white middle class.[12] To his nationalist left, Turner took aim at the Nation of Islam because it repudiated direct political activities, quipping that "Malcolm X has had another seizure of grandeur." Turner lambasted his nationalist supporters as deluded for "thinking that the American people are weak enough to even honor anything he says or advocates," and characterized racial separatism as "a farce."[13]

Turner dismissed other formidable opponents as unrealistic and irrelevant whether or not they really were. He once criticized the former director of CORE, James Farmer, still popular in more moderate interracial circles, for pointing out that "Newark was no longer a white city," disregarding him as a "little leaguer attempting to play with the major leaguers."[14] No sooner had Turner attacked direct action protests as a gimmick to "use their lung power" than he recorded a speech on television to air his own populist message in which he proclaimed his loyalty to the Central Ward: "When those people are sick, I get sick. When they're happy, I get happy. When they are without bread and water and food, I'm without bread, water and food."[15] In Turner the most famous nationalist, Amiri Baraka, could not have found a better foil. Baraka charged that rather than a man of the people Turner actually represented "the self-importance and incompetence . . . of Negro leadership."[16] If Baraka believed that Newark was analogous to a colonized Third World nation, then Turner symbolized its petite bourgeoisie, a black servant that showed more loyalty to whites in the government than to his own people, a clique Baraka categorized as "the nigger-o ministers" and "Toms on the planet."[17]

Under attack and in failing health, Turner continued to pursue the interests and concerns of the Central Ward, appealing for more housing, jobs, and Great Society programs.[18] But Turner went down to defeat to a Black Power candidate in 1970, and died four years later. He was buried at the Metropolitan Baptist Church in a ceremony in which Calvin West, the first African American to win an at-large seat on the city council in 1966, elegantly eulogized him as a figure that "changed the face of Newark." While the papers reported that Turner had been under investigation by a federal agency, none of the investigators apparently had uncovered evidence of corruption.[19] Even if Turner had delivered various rewards and benefits to his very needy constituency in the Central Ward, he had not brought them full and adequate representation at City Hall.

From time to time, Baraka had reflected on the tendency of the Black Power ideology to interfere with the "real" issues of governance and community control. But his leadership of the movement raised vexing issues of cultural identity—which were reflected in his public theater, education programs, and book stores. He effectively challenged the validity of a model of pluralism that excluded black Newarkers, but the pro-black and anti-white discourses tapped and stimulated emotional impulses rather than constructive political action. Baraka envisioned a nationalist revolutionary overthrow, while head of the Nation of Islam, Louis Farrakhan, had prohibited members' participation in political institutions. Although the Nation of Islam clashed sharply with Baraka and United Brothers, the two shared the zero-sum game of anti-whiteness. Invited by Baraka to a conference to inaugurate a major Pan-African socialist organization, in a vitriolic speech Farakhan railed against cooperation with whites: "Now you want alliance with sissies. Let me tell you something. Black man, if you are caught up in that sick freakish bag, when you know the glory of being a man, how could you dare want to be a woman?"[20] But where was the agenda—what was the next step? Carmichael and Hamilton affirmed that Black Power meant "genuinely independent action."[21] At the same time, there is little convincing evidence that black Newarkers embraced the Kawaida identity movement without first demanding concrete political objectives, and soon Baraka spent more time in building a coalition of black activists and moderate integrationists, to practice the art of politics.[22]

Not since the era of Reconstruction when the enfranchisement of former slaves resulted in black majority governments in several southern states had such a strategy seemed viable. In both epics of citizenship, despite the problems of economic underdevelopment, African Americans gained crucial experience. From 1921 to 2000, in Essex County thirty-one African Americans had served in elected office, ranging from a few months to twenty-seven years, but all except four of them served after the electoral revolution in 1970.[23] As Komozi Woodard has demonstrated, like the convention movement in Reconstruction, in 1968 Baraka and the United Brothers helped to build a new political network in which much of the day-to-day work harkened back to a long tradition of mobilization.[24] Since at least 1962, both the radical and more mainstream black organizations coordinated major voter registration drives, including a campaign to register two thousand black voters in the Branch Brook Park area, adding an average of 260 new registrants to their lists each day. As a result of these campaigns in the early 1960s, in just two years registration numbers in the Central Ward increased from 21,417 to 28,208, and a total increase of more than 27,000 city-wide. Although nationalists helped to bring the idea of a political party to fruition, they built upon the foundation laid by the old civic integra-tionists—the NAACP, Urban League, United Essex Civic Association, and League of Women Voters.[25]

But, more effectively than traditional civic organizations and their an-nual drives, the Black Power–identified organizers responded to defeat in the 1968 elections by urgently forming a community-based political party, registering voters, and running candidates. Although some clearly voiced nationalist rhetoric, they made an alliance with Puerto Rican na-tionalists, the Young Lords, in what came to be named the Community Choice Party. If the everyday workers claimed an allegiance to Baraka, on some level they followed a political vision created by Robert Curvin, who claimed to have invented the concept of a community party and later served as its chairman. The rules of the convention gave three votes to all recognized organizations and neighborhood-based groups, such as block clubs, the Parent-Teacher's Association, or any group grounded in the public sphere; they forbade these pledges or groups from running on another ticket if defeated here. The thinking was that if the losers in the community convention still ran, the resulting factionalism would divide the black and Puerto Rican vote, destroying their chances for victory. Not all black leaders with ambitions for office joined the Community Choice Party, and in one particularly heated race for an at-large seat, the incumbent Calvin West blasted his opponents as "advocates of racial separatism," joining a ticket under the incumbent white mayor, the so-called Peace and Progress Party.[26] But a number of the early picks for office wisely acceded to the rules of the Community Choice Party con-vention, both to expand their base of support and to help legitimize the candidacies of other community-oriented people of color.[27]

In the end, neither the radical Baraka nor the experienced Curvin led the convention. That title went to a young, modest engineer, Kenneth Gibson, who became the black forerunner in the mayoral contest after finishing a surprising third in the 1966 races (taking away votes from

Mayor Addonizio). Gibson had arrived in the Central Ward from Enter-prise, Alabama, at the age of 8, and was raised by a religious mother, who always upheld what he referred to as conservative values. As a young man growing up in the ghetto, Gibson had experienced the full brunt of racial discrimination, recalling that his family "could not move into an apartment" reserved for whites, and that a major company re-fused to hire him as a permanent employee.[28] As a man of the people who had suffered their hardships, Gibson appealed to the average voter in ways that Baraka, and even Curvin, rarely approached. Gibson later recalled numerous popular calls to run for office, which he originally de-clined. "But six weeks before the elections, I changed my mind. Because the five candidates were not addressing the issues. I ran a civil rights type of campaign, and forced a run-off," recalled Gibson. Both in 1966 and more so four years later, Gibson sold himself as a simple and gen-uine leader. Thus, even if Curvin was more articulate and Baraka more inspirational, Gibson exuded authenticity that appealed to the populist sensibility in the black community that Turner had originally sparked. The leading candidates of the convention movement represented a wide spectrum of black leadership—from the militant grassroots was Den-nis Westbrooks, from the moderate tradition was Reverend Sharp, and from the Great Society liberalism came Earl Harris. A number of ob-servers attributed the success of Gibson to his effective espousal of core values of work, community, and upward mobility through education, but he identified education as his most passionate cause.[29]

While some black candidates were divided between Black Power (and orientation toward the community) and continuing in traditional alle-giance to the political machine, the racial divide between black and white proved more decisive in the following months. Sooner than later the campaigns of the two white candidates predictably devolved into false accusations and race baiting, despite the fact that Addonizio pro-moted himself as an alternative to the right-wing chauvinism of Imperi-ale. Addonizio was a tested veteran of New Jersey politics (who won his first race in a contest for a seat in the state assembly in 1948) but trailed Imperiale in some polls. On the larger national political scene in the 1970s, according to political scientist Tali Mendelberg, the major "par-ties were aligned on race, but that alignment was constrained by a norm of racial equality."[30] In other words, race mattered in political prefer-ences, but most people were wont to adopt full-scale racist political

views of the sort that characterized the supporters of Imperiale. Addonizio had campaigned with a message of unity, and promised to "keep
Newark together" and to represent the politics "of progress and peace,"
the name of his political party.[31] But under pressure he played the so-
called race card, sent both crude and more subtle "implicit" racial messages, and accused black candidates of causing divisiveness in the city.
The Black Power candidates ran a spectacular campaign, hosting black
celebrities like Dick Gregory and Carl Stokes, the black mayor of Cleveland, which claimed unprecedented visibility for black politicians. In
theory, Mendelberg believes that whites with high levels of resentment
are particularly responsive to these kinds of racial messages, but racial
liberals, particularly the economically successful voters, feel personally
uncomfortable with racial feelings.[32]

In May, Gibson overcame the politics of polarization, as well as criticism that he had excluded whites from his campaign, by outpacing
seven candidates and winning a plurality of the votes. But since nobody
had gained a majority, Gibson and Addonzio faced off in a final race. In
June, Gibson defeated Addonizio by 55,097 to 43,086 votes, capturing
56 percent of the ballots. The Community Choice Party prevailed in two
ward races, and their at-large candidate, a coordinator of the poverty
program, Earl Harris, posted a surprise victory over the more conservative black incumbent, Calvin West. Like other victorious black candidates in tight elections, Gibson earned a crucial margin of white votes
(15 percent), specifically Democratic and Jewish (even as black candidates in several races directly challenged Jewish opponents).[33] Gibson
put together overwhelming wins in the ghetto—19,927 in the South
Ward and 11,286 in Central Ward—with strong showings in the West
and East Wards.[34] Across the nation, Americans had elected black mayors in sixty-seven cities with populations of more than 50,000 from the
1960s to the early 1990s, and by 1972 the state of New Jersey alone had
four black mayors.[35] To a greater extent than the spectacle of Baraka defiantly attacking Imperiale, the rise of municipal empowerment proved
to be the legacy of Black Power in the post–civil rights era. Eloquent testimony by Larry Hamm, a black member of United Brothers, suggested
the extent to which integrationist and nationalist alike celebrated the
electoral victory in the wake of the riots. "Black people [were] losing
their homes . . . then after the riots it was the election of Ken Gibson,
you know; which virtually called a euphoria in Newark, everybody, I

believe really believed that by the election of Ken Gibson that the face of Newark was going to be changed like some advocates used to say, 'we are going to turn the slave ship into a New Ark.' "[36]

Riding the wave of Black Power enthusiasm for elections and gaining influence at City Hall, Gibson nonetheless refused to lead only in terms of black and white. Although the mayor appointed African Americans as a reward for their support in the campaign, he firmly believed in merit, the civil service system, and interracial cooperation. Although the major Black Power mayors credited positive emphasis on black heritage for their margin of victory, they still attempted to govern like any mayor. Richard Hatcher, the first black candidate elected to mayor in Gary, Indiana, had proclaimed, "My blackness had been the dominant fact of life's experience as it is the dominant fact in the life of every Black man." Despite the moderate stances of Hatcher and Gibson, commentators on the races such as nationally renowned leader Jesse Jackson attributed Gibson's win to the help of Baraka and, he argued, not "just with his poetry but his politics."[37] Baraka himself claimed credit for the election of Gibson, and in a 1970 interview pronounced that "there was no black mayor until the nationalists." According to Baraka, "We created that consciousness."[38] But Mayor Gibson always positioned himself halfway between traditional and nationalist. "On the one hand," wrote Gibson, "I recognize my election as mayor as relatively conventional," and "on the other hand, I recognize my election . . . as an extension of the revolt of slaves aboard a slave ship."[39] As a moderate, Gibson enjoyed appearing at a civic awards dinner sponsored by the corporate giant, Johnson & Johnson, and received honors from the Black Fathers Association, a "shining example to the kids that the system can work."[40] Yet the fact was that black politicians secured the loyalty of the community by adopting the rhetoric and symbols of Black Power, according to several polls conducted in the early 1970s.[41] (Only 21 percent of white elected officials reported a favorable response to the slogan of Black Power, but 61 percent of black officials approved.)[42]

Gibson combined a commitment to his bread-and-butter black constituency with the broader obligations of his office. A study of council minutes and voting patterns in 1971 found only 3 percent race voting, or in other words, relatively few cases in which black city council members unilaterally opposed white council members. Across New Jersey, even when city councils were evenly split between white and black members, political analysts did not find racial blocs in voting patterns, except on symbolic issues such as major appointments of blacks to high-rank-ing positions. For example, after Anthony Imperiale's election to the city council in 1968, the United Brothers and other black activists organized a recall election against the longtime South Ward council member, Lee Bernstein, because he consistently voted conservatively with the Italian American bloc and supported the so-called police K-9 program, Imperi-ale's initiative to arm the Newark police with attack dogs. They voted Reverend Horace Sharper in, only the second black council member in Newark history.[43]

Also, a residual white nationalism kept alive by Imperiale and his hangers-on hindered the full implementation of a more pluralistic gov-ernment. When the mayor proposed a number of black appointments to the Newark Housing Authority (NHA), Imperiale attempted to block several. But the reign of the notorious Louis Danzig was coming to an end. In exchange for dropping the opposition to his choice for a new di-rector, Gibson promised Imperiale two judgeships and some positions on the Model Cities project, but the white maverick refused to relent. He charged that the mayor's decisions violated the law, and pressed the district attorney to convene a grand jury at which both Imperiale and Gibson testified.[44] But it discovered no evidence of malfeasance, and Gibson's nominee for head of NHA was confirmed by the city council.[45] At one point, Imperiale called upon the mayor to open communications with him and other conservatives, but Gibson's initial reluctance re-flected again his desire to steer clear of racial polarization.[46] In response, reported the dailies, Imperiale again "declared a 'war' on the adminis-tration." He rallied his core constituency, including supporters of former Alabama governor George Wallace, and said he "was calling the Birch-ers and everybody else."[47] Yet less than a week after the declaration of war on the mayor, Imperiale posed with Gibson for a news photo, prom-ising to "attempt to open the channels of communication."[48]

Gibson tapped the popular enthusiasm for Black Power to gain lever-age against the state and federal government. Across the nation, local black elected officials joined national networks, attempted to build a na-tional black political party to increase political representation in Con-gress, and planned to petition the U.S. Congress for statehood for Wash-ington, D.C. Gibson supported a movement for local reapportionment in order to elect a congressional representative from Newark, to under-cut white suburban interference with black political initiatives, and to help defeat the white conservative, Peter Rodino, in the Tenth District.[49]

Fig. 9.1. In the local elections in 1968 and 1970, blacks and whites organized various constituencies to reclaim political power. The newly elected black mayor, Kenneth Gibson (right), attempted to broker political peace with conservative white ethnics such as Anthony Imperiale. (Courtesy of New Jersey News Service and Newark Public Library)

Gibson's ally on the city council, Donald Tucker (elected to an at-large seat in 1974), not only joined the National Black Leadership Round-table, the outreach program for the Congressional Black Caucus, but was elected president of the National Black Caucus of Local Elected Officials, dispersing concentrated black power in Newark through national political networks. Under the old patronage system, black political figures relied on white clients for access to the municipal government, but now, according to black political analysts, black leaders initiated "an ongoing dialogue with Black professionals, civic, social and economic organizations" as a way to reconstruct African American civic culture from the bottom up.[50]

Gibson's practice of Black Power revealed his interest in building a black political machine, including the recruitment of a higher percentage of minorities to serve in major posts and in the rank-and-file municipal workforce. For years, white elected officials had delivered the best jobs to their constituents, reproducing a municipality that disadvantaged black Newarkers. Gibson called on the Human Rights Council (HRC), which monitored racial discrimination, to address employment disparities when they announced a new pluralistic image in which they sought to "broaden its scope," including plans for a Fair Employment Practices

Cities	Black Population	Total Black Police	Percent Black Police
Washington, DC	71.1	1797	35.9
Newark	54.2	225	15
Gary, IN	52.8	130	31
Atlanta	51.3	260	28
Baltimore	46.4	420	13
New Orleans	45	83	6.1
Detroit	43.7	567	12
Wilmington, DE	43.6	32	11.5
Birmingham	42	13	1.9
St. Louis	40.9	326	14
Portsmouth, VA	39.9	14	7.5
Jackson, MS	39.3	17	6.2
Memphis	38.9	55	5
Cleveland	38.3	191	7.7
Mobile, AL	35.5	36	13.3
Oakland, CA	34.5	34	4.7
Winston-Salem, NC	34.3	20	6.6
Shreveport, LA	33.9	25	7.2
Philadelphia	33.6	1347	18.6
Chicago	32.6	2100	16.5
Dayton, OH	30.5	22	4.1
Hartford, CT	27.9	60	12
Pittsburgh	20.2	105	6.4
Dallas	24.9	32	1.9
Miami	22.7	74	10
New York City	21.2	2400	7.5
Los Angeles	17.9	350	5.2
Boston	16.3	60	2.1
Milwaukee	14.7	50	2.3
San Francisco	13.4	90	5.5

Fig. 9.2. Black police in key cities. *Source*: *Ebony* (May 1971), p. 124.

division that authorized the aggressive study of personnel statistics.[51] Like municipal governments across the nation, in 1975 Newark's HRC established a plan for affirmative actions—the Affirmative Action Review Council—to monitor both municipal employment and service and construction contracts.[52] By the 1970s, a string of Supreme Court decisions had upheld some preferences in hiring, and permitted the revision of personnel tests that evinced racial bias.[53] At the same time, the mayor and the white majority on the city council passed affirmative action ordinances covering all corporations that contracted with the city. The HRC and other offices at City Hall monitored minority percentages in the major airlines, car rental agencies, airline sales offices, freight companies, restaurants, and parking facilities, and ordered local businesses as well as national and international corporations to comply with affirmative action policies if they intended to use the airport. When minority percentages lagged, the city investigated.

By 1977, the HRC and City Council summoned a contractor with the city, Computer Sciences Corporation (CSC), to defend its employment record and answer charges that they harassed ethnic minorities. The representatives of CSC explained several personnel decisions as the result of unsatisfactory work performance, absenteeism, and insubordination.[54] The HRC had gained new powers beyond a passive commission model of the Division Against Discrimination (DAD) that reviewed and litigated complaints, and wrote policies that required the investigation of racial quotas and corporate compliance with nondiscrimination statutes, including the employment of timetables and plans.[55] The plans ensured fair hiring in the municipal government but failed to enforce its objectives with private investors who refused to comply. In 1983, a project jointly sponsored by the Port Authority of New Jersey and New York to build "a 400 room-hotel" at the Newark International Airport closed after city authorities discovered that the Port Authority lowered the goal set by the city for minority hiring.[56]

Mayor Gibson defended affirmative action as a tool for administrative oversight and accountability, but also admitted that he desired "a fairer representation" of black employees.[57] Conservatives had criticized that such initiatives, when applied to higher education, benefited only minorities in the middle class and neglected the truly disadvantaged, but its implementation in cities affected primarily working-class and even poor black residents. Before such measures, in a city that was 60 percent African American, records indicated that white employees dominated the upper-level categories. One survey at City Hall indicated that twenty-seven white men were listed in the category of "professionals," but there were only five black men, three white women, one black woman, and no Hispanics. As the Puerto Rican population increased as a percentage, the HRC noted "the urgent needs" of the Hispanic community, what they called the "bottom-rung minority." Also, although the program was promoted as a tool of black empowerment, the monitoring system highlighted gender imbalances. Before affirmative action at City Hall, no white or black women worked in skilled municipal employment, a category dominated by black men. Black men topped the service/maintenance categories at close to four hundred, but again personnel surveys indicated no black female employees.[58]

Records had always shown the racial composition of the public housing projects in changing neighborhoods, but what if analysts also examined statistics for employment in the housing authority? Although white males comprised only 3.8 percent of all public housing residents, they held 32.7 percent of jobs in the Newark Housing Authority (NHA). Under Gibson, 23.3 percent of residents were black males, and their numbers increased to 43.1 percent of staff. But the social problem of the truly disadvantaged was that of single-parent-headed households and black female poverty. According to one survey, black females comprised 51.7 percent of residents, but only 11.6 percent of employees. By employing affirmative action, the city hired more black women, helped raise average per capita income in public housing complexes, and positively assisted in the transition of African Americans and their families into private rentals or home ownership. By 1973, total minority employment at the municipality increased to 33 percent, and after another HRC initiative and affirmative action plans in 1977, African Americans increased to 66 percent of both the temporary and professional employees, with especially sharp increases in the pools of temporary workers, including 87 percent of skilled crafts, and 74 percent of maintenance employees.[59] By 1978, the HRC plan imposed per diem fines on companies that did not comply with the relatively modest goal of employing 25 percent minorities in contracts with the government.[60]

By the early 1970s, partially in response to the implementation of affirmative action, the public confrontation between Imperiale and Baraka on the margins of debate in the post-riot period gave way to full-blown culture wars at City Hall. As the Black Power mayor implemented new policies that elevated poor and working-class African Americans, more whites were mobilized against both black radicals and their former bastion of civic power, City Hall. By the 1970s, advancing on the terrain of civil rights by inverting its tactics, Imperiale endorsed a fair employment practice ordinance for the city of Newark, which he believed could protect the new white minority from affirmative action and other apparent injustices of reverse racism, invoking color blindness against the advances of the black political machine, to serve, he said, the "people regardless of race, color or religion."[61] In the mid-twentieth century, liberal intellectuals such as Horace Kallen debunked the myth of the Puritan or any other single ethnic national heritage, and celebrated a kind of white pluralism that valued positively the expression of diverse backgrounds. But their assumptions still reflected very specific tenets of middle-class individualism. According to historian Jerold Podair, the Black Power activists "objected to a white, Western, and European-dominated civic culture" and advocated the idea that "the city was not made up of contributors to a coherent whole but a series of communities unto themselves."[62] Because of the rise of Black Power mayors, the ceremonial and civic construction of ethnicity that animated municipal politics shifted in meaning, including for the first time the public expression of an African-American presence.

When Baraka was asked to measure the importance of the mayor's race to the goals of Black Power, he once replied that "in Newark we've overcome the first obstacle by gaining political power. What we have to do now is to create, and build, a culture."[63] Twenty-five years after Italian Americans attempted to block African Americans from moving into their neighborhoods, in 1972 Baraka and other black activists in his Congress of African People lobbied city and federal government for tax breaks and loans with which to build the Kawaida Towers housing project, a sixteen-story complex to celebrate the presence of an African heritage in the North Ward. Like the Italian Columbus Homes from the first generation of public housing, the Kawaida project boasted modern amenities, such as a community center, child-care facilities, and library. The nationalist architects produced a design they claimed followed the African principles of unity and harmony and that the decorative façade was no more foreign to Newark than the Walsh Homes or the Columbus Homes (named for white ethnic officials and patrons). Back in the 1950s, Turner, the mainstream black council member, had weathered the storms of black popular opinion when he loyally supported the old Irish political machine in its plan to erect a statute of former Mayor

Callaghan in the Central Ward. Even then, black residents objected to the valorization of yet another white figure.[64]

From the start of construction, local white residents resisted the African-inspired name and decoration, and vowed to halt the project. But Baraka's design for Kawaida Towers promised ninety one-bedroom and seventy-four two-bedroom apartments at a time of shortages in the housing stock, and Mayor Gibson appeared with Baraka at a groundbreaking ceremony in the area, displacing white protest by officially lending his civic authority to the project.[65] But the white city council members decided to challenge Baraka's documentation and licensing, and investigated the original tax abatement hearings that underwrote the loan for more than $6 million. Within months of breaking ground, Imperiale, now a state senator, organized demonstrations in which one thousand residents crowded onto the construction site.[66] Baraka tried to diffuse the nationalist signification of Kawaida, and promoted the modern appearance and technological advancements, "amenities like libraries, community rooms and a closed circuit television security system." But Baraka also out and said that "blacks have held land in the Central Ward since 1967 but we have been stopped from developing it."[67] Italian council members Giuliani and Abudato moved to revoke the tax breaks on Kawaida, accused Baraka of fraud, and claimed that he concealed his name on the application to the city council.[68] White opponents argued that Afrocentricism conflicted with the core civic values of Newark. Though Italian symbols or iconography could honor their heritage, Kawaida was a "racist philosophy" which was "diametrically opposed to the vast majority of the North Ward." Some doubted if any project bearing its name was "eligible" for federal funding.[69] Others charged that the design would "overwhelm the area, architecturally and racially," and Imperiale predicted that Kawaida Towers would result in "all-black management" and "an all black tenant population."[70] Within a week, approximately three hundred white protesters gathered at the site to picket and chant, inaugurating what was to be two years of endemic ethnic conflict.

In the wake of the Italian American's loss of the mayor's office and several seats on the city council, like the silent white majority in other cities, the North Ward embraced the tactics of civil disobedience and chained and padlocked themselves to the entrance of the construction site.[71] They demanded new public hearings, and made the national news.[72] Mobilizing the moribund Citizens' Council, Imperiale lobbied further to rescind the tax abatement, and by now, stopping Kawaida was a sign of masculine Italian American pride. "You cannot force something down people's throats these days. You can't do it in the black community and they shouldn't do it in the white community," testified a white resident. Black nationalists espoused self-determination as necessary to reverse a long history of racist oppression, but now white Newarkers invoked the same rhetoric to mobilize their interests. It was argued that the "white community" should receive as much liberation and autonomy as the black community.[73]

Like Baraka's inflammatory writing on the inferiority of Italian Americans and Jews, the conservative white ethnics insulted the followers of Kawaida, speaking of African Dashikis and the "people with lampshades and do do dads on their heads."[74] Every morning at 6:30 A.M., white picketers resumed their protest, and the only workers to cross the pickets were "four black laborers, who entered under heavy police guard," it was reported. The war of signs harkened back to the days of Hayden, Curvin, and Colonel Hassan. Drawing on a powerful trend in white suburbs, the North Ward Italians proclaimed "Tax Revolt" and linked this to "Stop the Kawaida Monster," according to one sign. Black and progressive whites fought back: "Build it, fight racism, and let new housing lead the way." But the opponents of Kawaida not only rejected the project but also the public display of black culture, and they rejected Baraka's claim that his design could represent the civic pluralism that had evolved since the white immigrants landed in Newark. And despite Baraka's claim that the project represented the aspirations of people of color, some Puerto Ricans, reportedly some 30 percent of the North Ward, marched under the banner of "Puerto Ricans Against Kawaida," perhaps because most were Catholic and unlikely to convert to another religion.[75] At the same time, the North Newark Committee Against Racism, comprised of holdovers from NCUP, protested against Imperiale. In retracing political rituals of antiracism built into the terrain of Newark a quarter century before, the white youth invoked Double V, chanting, "Hitler Rose, Hitler Fell, racist Tony go to hell." But unlike their interracial activist predecessors, the white youth message of "Black and White United" was rejected by both whites and blacks. At one point, Baraka demanded that white supporters of his project withdraw from the site and stop demonstrations.[76]

Across the nation, readers expectantly awaited the next battle in the war of parades.[77] While marchers at an "Afrikan Liberation" demonstration chanted, "We are African people, we are African People," almost on cue, one thousand white onlookers responded, "We are Americans, we are Americans."[78] The black and Puerto Rican demonstrators who favored Kawaida staged a procession up Meeker Avenue to Bergen Street, onto Clinton Avenue to Belmont Avenue, and then to the city's main business district and along Broad Street to the Kawaida site. At the parade ceremonies at the Scudder Homes housing project in the heart of the Central Ward, newly elected council member Dennis Westbrooks justified the construction, declaring "we are an oppressed people," and denounced "oppressive conditions here at Scudder Homes." Then, another contingent of protesters paraded against "racist policies" toward Angola in Africa by demonstrating outside the Portuguese consulate in Newark.[79] Despite Baraka's decision to reshape black cultural nationalism into a kind of civic pluralism acceptable to whites in the North Ward, eventually Gibson faulted him for the extremism of his rhetoric. In weekly meetings he advised Baraka on how to appeal to a broader constituency—"don't let anybody take the American flag," Gibson told him. "If the whites played a record of Kate Smith singing 'God Bless America,' you play Ray Charles singing 'America the Beautiful.'"[80] Angered by what he perceived as advice to sell out, Baraka denounced the mayor in the press, and later charged that "Gibson smiled his little Amos & Andy smile. . . . His whole role has been to warehouse, use, cool out the militants, to buy off who can be bought off."[81] As the battle between Italians and black nationalists entered a stalemate, Gibson called on his supporters to drop Kawaida and rename the building—one suggestion was the name of Martin Luther King, Jr.—because it honored the theme of "striving" toward the ideals of King and Robert Kennedy. But in the end the project was never completed.[82]

Was the *New York Times* correct when it commented that the unfinished foundation of Kawaida "stands like a raw wound"?[83] Baraka's stature had suffered a blow from its failure, for he had not successfully adapted his model of Black Power to the operation of the city. For better or worse, Gibson was serving urban nationalism to Newarkers in ways that marginalized Baraka.[84] By the early 1970s, Baraka moved on to call for an international struggle involving decolonization, Afrocentrism, and socialist economics, but he failed to mobilize large numbers in the community. When Baraka wrote to Gibson of the "need for closer contact between Africans in Africa" by developing an office of "African Affairs" at City Hall, the mayor simply ignored the request.[85] Although

Fig. 9.3. In urban machine politics, the ethnic group in control of City Hall was reflected in the operation of the police force. By the 1970s, the African American fraternal society, the Bronze Shields, signaled the changing of the guard with a parade. (Courtesy of the Newark Public Library)

Gibson flatly rejected Imperiale's argument that Baraka's Black Arts culture was "racist," he also rejected black nationalism as a viable policy.[86] When the city council voted to pass a resolution that all schools that enrolled a majority of black students could display the famous red, black, and green "Black Liberation flag," requiring the purchase of some two thousand flags, a white member of the city council stormed out of the meetings after the vote.[87] When Italians attacked the Irish in their fight to reach City Hall in the 1940s and 1950s, or when the middle-class reformers attacked the Italian Americans to push them back and protect their numbers in civil service, observers tended to view this kind of ethnic conflict as part and parcel of the political process. Was Black Power merely a stage in ethnic succession, fated to decline and fade away?

By Gibson's second term as mayor, Baraka had indeed lost influence as well as popularity, and the *New York Times* declared that "Baraka's Power Is Said to Wane," while black elected officials reportedly rejected him because they felt a duty to "represent a broader spectrum of opinion."[88] By the mid-1970s, the celebration of Black Power symbols had as much to do with the current popularity of the television miniseries

Fig. 9.4. By the 1990s, the main public forums of the city, such as Military Park in the Central Ward, were open to more cultural diversity than ever before, hosting an African-inspired festival with imported wares, books, and international cuisine. (Author's photograph)

Roots, which had "rekindled an interest" and "respect for the long road traveled by black people," as the victory of Gibson over the Italian machine.[89] Schools, churches, and organizations now celebrated Black History Month, with an array of "films, concerts, and other special programs detailing Afro-Americans' rich past and hopes for the future." Like the national designation of Columbus Day twenty-five years before, the governor declared an official holiday for the teaching of the African American experience.[90] The state legislature responded with the assertion of U.S. nationalism, passing a bill banning the flying of any other flag than the American. Two weeks after Gibson's public statement on the matter at a local meeting to plan for the National Black Convention, a white group picketed to express its sense that the new emphasis on Black Power did not represent all views and ethnic backgrounds of the city, causing a kind of civic alienation. At one point, Baraka astutely replied that for the white ethnics like "Imperiale to be upset about Afrikan Liberation Day is like for me to be upset by Columbus Day."[91]

As Baraka's popularity waned in the 1970s, his supporters attempted to revive ethnocentric Black Power with a Black Heritage Day parade.[92]

As an expression of his dissatisfaction with its co-optation by black mayors, Baraka criticized cultural nationalism as superficial and reaffirmed his commitment to socialism in analytical writings that elevated class over race, prompting reports that "Baraka Drops Racism for Socialism of Marx." (The national media continued to misrepresent the politics of Black Power, caricaturing it as movement that "blamed American society and the white power structure for economic and social problems of black people.") In the aftermath of the Italian American victory in 1968, Baraka pursued the unification of the community by any means necessary, but by 1974 Baraka reportedly dropped the African wedding ceremonies at his Temple of Kawaida on Belmont Street and traded in his African dress for blue jeans and sweatshirts.[93]

In what ways would the new ethnic groups settling into the city respond to surviving tenets of Black Power incorporated into the civic culture at City Hall? Since the 1960s, the fastest-growing group was no longer Italian American but Puerto Rican, a community with a fairly strong affinity for the cultural radicalism of nationalists like Baraka. The Puerto Rican community had participated in the Community Choice Convention and won influence in the appointment of a Puerto Rican deputy mayor, but they did not elect a city council representative until 1978. And despite Baraka's claim that Kawaida represented the aspirations of people of color, some Puerto Ricans marched under the banner of "Puerto Ricans Against Kawaida."[94]

In political negotiations, in 1974 Gibson found himself calling for law and order after the eruption of Puerto Rican riots, which caused the death of one, shooting of three, and injuries to at least thirteen.[95] Puerto Rican protesters tossed Molotov cocktails, complained of police misconduct, and demanded more representation, while Mayor Gibson warned against violence on the streets and canceled the Puerto Rican street festival the following year. After the riots subsided, he authorized more than half a million dollars for overtime of 7,500 hours for police and fire rescue.[96] Even under Gibson, some Puerto Ricans felt as alienated as black Newarkers under Addonizio on issues of access, responsiveness, and conflict with police. In the wake of the Puerto Rican riots, a group of Latinos from several neighborhoods organized a meeting with the mayor and later formed the Hispanic Emergency Council. Their demands included an independent mayoral commission, the Division of Hispanic Affairs, and consideration for the appointment of Latinos to the bench and to administrative office. Like black Newarkers before them, the new Latino minority demanded fair hiring and cultural recognition, including a promise from the mayor that all city documents would be published in Spanish as well as English.[97]

By the beginning of the new century, ethnic succession and the arrival of a greater diversity of civic values tested the relevance and representative nature of the old Black Power regime. By 2000, in the famous North Ward, ethnic patronage passed from the Italian, Anthony Carrino, who had served for twenty-eight years on the city council, to the Latino challenger, Hector Corchado. The Latinos had gained as a percentage of the population in the city (30 percent), tipping to a majority in the North Ward—more than 39,000—an increase of more than 3,000 between 1990 and 2000.[98] Although Corchado had served as deputy mayor, the majority of Latinos broke with the traditional black leadership and supported a fresh young candidate for mayor who spoke Spanish during the campaign. Many in the Latino community believed that the administration that came into power after the riots had stayed largely the same for more than twenty-five years, representing the black community and not the diversity of Newark.[99] Despite the decline of Baraka, the public culture of Newark maintained its reputation as a Black Power city. But the triumph against racism at the polls had not taught the black community how to reach out beyond the borders of race. This was to be the challenge of the future.

Epilogue

In 1997, the city daily, the *New Jersey Star-Ledger*, ran a story that encapsulated the span of Newark's modern political history. A ten-day commemoration of the 1967 riots was about to begin. A former physical education instructor, and victor in the historic city council races against the Italian Americans in 1970, Sharpe James, was now serving as mayor and presided over a somber ceremony to remember and exonerate civil disobedience. Though Newark was engulfed in fiscal and social crises, the parade glowed with pride. They marched from the Fourth Precinct (the place where the riots erupted), along Military Park (where organizers planned countless rallies), past a church (where groups like the Newark Community Corporation and the NAACP met to plan and strategize), and then onward to Irvine Turner Boulevard (the namesake of the first black city council man), and literally inscribed the memory of African American political perseverance on the civic sphere.[1]

The pioneers of Black Power at the head of the parade had defeated segregation and disenfranchisement, but the irony was that their reward, the metropolitan terrain, had suffered from seemingly irreversible decline. Whether it was unemployment, crime, abandoned housing, single-mother births, or homicide, Newark consistently led the nation in the indices of social distress. A survey heaped more ridicule with the news that the number of reported venereal diseases "placed Newark in undisputed first place in the nation among all major cities reporting."[2] Across the nation, from Baltimore and Charlotte to Los Angeles and Newark, the black mayors now focused on economic issues, rather than racial or cultural identity conflicts. In one survey in the 1990s, sixty-three of sixty-seven African American mayors (94 percent) had developed new plans for economic development, enterprise zones, and government-business partnerships. Yet separating the struggle for race empowerment from economic conditions proved a challenge in the face of powerful suburban whites who commuted to City Hall, and, one study quipped, ducked out of work early ("on Friday afternoons the offices are nearly empty") to get out of town.[3]

To a far greater extent than before, Newark felt the disparities and unpredictability of an economy of flexible accumulation that produced socially disastrous patterns of underemployment and transience. Deindustrialization had accelerated sharply, and by the mid-1970s both Mutual Insurance and Prudential Insurance cut employees, with Prudential scaling down from 14,000 to 4,000, while several major manufacturers, including Spring Air Mattress, J. Swill and Sons Cutlery, the Barton Press, and Wilbur Driver Company closed their operations. With 478 fewer employers in 1976 than when the riots erupted, payroll taxes dropped by 8 percent, or, put another way, job rolls declined from 202,000 to 145,000 in a ten-year period. In Newark and nearby black-majority suburbs, the electrical-machinery industry, another major part of the city's economy, declined with gains by Japanese imports.[4] By the 1970s, black youth unemployment increased to an annual average of 45–50 percent, compared to the already high average unemployment rate of 12 to 14 percent for the city.[5] Most African Americans were employed in the public sector, but between 1973 and 1980 the U.S. cities lost approximately 25,000 municipal jobs, and the number of blacks on urban payrolls in Newark increased only by an estimated 9,000.[6]

Despite the devastation left behind the flow of capital into the suburbs, many economic analysts attributed urban decline to the tax structure.[7] For reasons that few could explain, Newark assessed the highest property tax in the nation. Home owners were already paying $8.47 per $100 of assessed value of their property, which meant that every twelve years they were paying the assured value of their home. To stimulate new investment, city hall had granted tax-exempt status to two-thirds of the area, which was now reserved for public housing, urban renewal, or private investment and development. According to the *Newark News,* business was paying at the same tax rate it had paid in 1963, while local home owners were experiencing larger and larger tax increases.[8] To stave the flow of capital, Mayor Gibson had proposed a commuter tax on payroll income on all city employees who resided outside of Newark, but legislators from the largely white suburbs defeated the proposition in the state legislature. By 1974, Newark's property tax base had decreased by 21 percent since 1963.[9] Because the State of New Jersey tax structure used property taxes to fund public education, the budget created a wide disparity between suburban and inner-city school systems, and Newark's educational system slipped to one of the worst in the nation.[10]

Into the 1970s, according to the city's application to the Departments of Housing and Urban Development (HUD), the estimated housing deficit in Essex County exceeded 64,000 units, with the projected number of families (12,000) in need of shelter expected to increase with the arrival of another 10,000 new families each year. At the same time, a second report indicated that some 57,019 individual residences failed to meet building codes, and, the mayor's office applied for a demonstration cities grant, the Great Society program under HUD. Like the earlier Area Boards of the mid-1960s, the new HUD program relied on leadership and civil society to foster maximum feasible participation in the implementation processes.[11]

Upon receipt of the funding, Mayor Gibson appointed Junious Hedgepath, a former black nationalist member of the Area Board from the Central Ward, to the position of director of the program, bridging Black Power with municipal administration.[12] The percentage of families that spent more than one-quarter of their income on rent increased from 38.6 in 1970 to 43.5 in 1974, and the pool of rental apartments also deteriorated rapidly. It was more economical for home owners to accrue large back taxes and abandon their property than it was to try to sell, remove liens, and meet their tax debt, and even middle-class homeowners "torched" their property to remove their tax debt and collect insurance. In the decade after the riots, when two thousand homes were razed in the Interstate 78 highway project for speedier commuting, one study indicated that taxable property items had declined by 14 percent.[13] As the number of private residences declined and public housing residents increased, the city built only about four thousand new units, but in the late 1970s twice that number were demolished.[14]

The new administrations of black-majority cities were riddled with internecine cultural conflict and declining approval rates, and the first generation of black mayors, including Richard Hatcher of Gary, Carl Stokes of Cleveland, and then Gibson went down to defeat by black opponents, and later the black majority in Gary even elected a white mayor.[15] The defeat of Black Power mayors signaled a rightward turn in the political climate in the midst of the rise of the New Right and Reaganism, portending disaster for the people in trouble in the nation's cities. Recall that at the beginning of the postwar era, the Supreme Court handed down *Shelley v. Kraemer* and *Brown v. Board of*

Education, pressuring local housing authorities to implement integration policies, dispersing African Americans into middle-class neighborhoods. But the poorest black Newarkers, especially the recent arrivals from the South, had fallen into homelessness at least at some point in their settlement from the 1950s to 1980s.[16] As a result, more tenants in public housing such as Hill Manor Apartments, Brick Towers, and Douglas Harrison Apartments testified before the press and government, and demanded better maintenance, running water, heat, and elevators.[17] Although they probably did not recognize their antecedents, they drew from the same tradition forged by black and white activists since the rise of the Division Against Discrimination in World War II, and a related protest traditions built by groups such as the NAACP, NCUP, and CFUN. Like activists in the interracial movement before them, in the 1980s organizers attacked lax city oversight, poor housing management, and a biased municipal court. In the 1990s the indefatigable Amiri Baraka resurrected plans for a Kawaida housing project, only this time proposing the Central Ward as the site. When the proposal collapsed again, he accused the city council of voting it down because he refused to pay kickbacks and payoffs.[18] It was striking that at a time when the dominant image of Newark was that of a city ravaged by economic crisis and social pathology, black citizens continued to mobilize grassroots protests against housing discrimination in the name of improving the quality of their lives.[19]

By the end of the 1980s, surveys estimated that the total homeless population in Newark had climbed to 8,000–11,000, and that this group had recently changed "from the traditional single adult male to women and children."[20] As temporary service work replaced the eight-hour day, the safety net had dropped out of the social welfare services of cities.[21] By 1990, estimates showed that 25,000 homeless individuals or 10,000 homeless families were living in shelters, welfare hotels, train stations, church basements, and abandoned buildings across the state.[22] Newark was widely perceived as a "dumping ground," with the homeless in the southern part of the state reportedly given bus tickets to the city, arriving in disarray and bearing their disempowerment.[23] Since at least the 1980s, advocates for the homeless protested for and sometimes received relief, such as a commitment to shelter the homeless in unused space in public hospitals, nursing homes, and mental health facilities.[24]

The homeless represented a public nuisance—sitting in doorways, urinating in public, or ignoring traffic signals when crossing the street—

and thus kindled a kind of low-intensity disacknowledgment of their plight. But few possessed the resources with which to stage direct actions or organize a political group. As the figure of the homeless person entered the late-1980s avant-garde and popular culture, and circulated in urban community newsletters, the voices of homeless people suggested new directions in American political history.

Although New Jersey newspapers reported random incidents of protest and agitation, few advocates for the homeless were mobilized in the more conservative 1980s. One homeless Newark resident placed a mattress next to a wall and set it on fire at 3 A.M., and in another case a homeless person who was denied admittance into a shelter for the night tried to burn it down.[25] In 1987, four activists "barricaded themselves in an empty hospital floor at the Jersey City Medical Center" in a Christmas Eve protest of the home shortage crisis, in which they "unfurled a banner outside the window of the 16th story room and showered passers-by with red and green leaflets." Another group of protesters gathered at City Hall and chanted in English and Spanish to demand unused public facilities for the shelter of the homeless population. In nearby Jersey City, homeless activist Edward Paquin complained that "we have been listening to all the people say what they can do for us and we are sick and tired of hearing what they can't do." At the age of 51, he lived in the Journal Square Transportation Center, midway between Newark and Manhattan, serving as an itinerant leader of a movement to claim a place for themselves.

As both black nationalism and interracial liberalism failed to protect people in trouble from the enormous attack by Reagan's America, in which the material base for human survival had been repossessed by the state, what strategies in the political tradition of African Americans were effective? In 2000, officials from HUD announced that one of Newark's largest public housing complexes, Brick Towers, which housed more than 1,100 residents, was slated for demolition. A new grass-roots activist arrived in the city to work in a nongovernmental organization that concentrated on housing issues. The young maverick was Cory Booker, a privileged graduate of Stanford and Yale, and a Rhodes Scholar. Combining both the strategies of activism and electoral empowerment, Booker utilized canvassing and face-to-face campaigning to win a seat on the city council, representing the Central Ward. But unlike his great predecessor, Irvine Turner, Booker opposed rather than helped to build the political machine, staging many demonstrations against the status quo in the administration at City Hall, making himself a nuisance rather than a patron. For some, Booker was the political future to watch, perhaps destined to become the first black president. For others, Booker represented the political outsider, a stranger, to be distrusted. Booker had charged both the Newark Housing Authority and federal officers with creating a neighborhood of homeless, and after he was elected began living in a van in an abandoned lot, and later moved into the Brick Towers public housing to protest recently announced HUD plans for demolition. Booker's residency in the dilapidated housing evoked the kind of personal commitment that NCUP activists demonstrated in Clinton Hill thirty years before.[26]

In 2002, Booker decided to challenge the four-term incumbent mayor Sharpe James, in a contest that received national attention, challenging received wisdom and changing the terms of the debate by reconstructing race as a political signifier. Before the rise of the black elected officials in the 1970s, black activists had organized to unseat the white power structure, to defeat the Italians, Portuguese, or more recent white immigrants. Now, black community organizations funded with thousands, and eventually millions, of dollars fought one another, as professional promoters joined the local campaign organizations, staged black public events, and spoke of black empowerment. At the end of integration, Turner had tangled with Amiri Baraka, who accused him of Uncle Tomism. But neither Booker nor James accepted the conservative label. Much of the debate focused on the depth of Booker's racial allegiance and the authenticity of his racial identification. If Sharpe James campaigned positively on the platform of the "Real Deal"—which implied, the *New York Times* correctly stated, "Mr. Booker was somehow inauthentic"—he negatively portrayed Booker as a Republican, not a traditional urban Democrat; as a Jew; as possibly gay; and most visibly painful for Booker, as white. At one point, a quote from James ran in an inch-high headline, in which the mayor exhorted Booker: "You have to learn to be an African-American! And we don't have time to train you all night."[27]

In a prize-winning documentary on the mayor's race, *Street Fight,* the director Marshall Curry captured Booker speaking before an informal gathering of what appear to be public-housing residents, who provoke the candidate with jibes and queries. Did he really live in the public-housing project? To which the candidate replied that the inquisitor ought to inspect his apartment and look at his mess and dirty laundry on the floor. But then a young boy brought the boisterous conversation to a dead silence: "Are you white?" the boy asked? Booker was enigmatic to many black Newarkers not only because he was light skinned and visibly strained to speak the local black vernacular, but because his campaign proved difficult to interpret and locate on the political landscape. Booker courted whites and other minorities, as well as appealing to the black political machine. By contrast, from the first, James identified his campaign with his life in the South Ward, and thus with the history of African American empowerment.

History repeated itself in the speeches and campaign battles by revealing the political tension traced over and over again in this book between the civic culture and civil rights. On the one hand, Booker frequently justified his campaign and election to the office of mayor by invoking his parents' participation in the civil rights movement, including his memory of white supremacist assaults on his father while growing up in the South. On the other hand, James campaigned for his election on the basis of his identity as the native son of Newark. He appealed to a sense of civic pride, or what one observer criticized as "civic chauvinism." James repeatedly referred to Booker as a carpetbagger, despite the fact that he was born only two counties away.[28] In responding, Booker failed to disentangle criticism of James and his administration from the perception that he was attacking the pride of the city. How to win on the merits of policies without insulting the residents who not only voted for James but identified him as an embodiment of Newark?[29]

Both candidates advanced claims of their entitlement to the civic culture in ways that revolved around the question of class, and both attempted to capitalize on the virtues of their economic background and demonize the class privileges of the opponent. James's attack on Booker for being "un-black" rarely gained ideological coherence until quite late in the race, but from the start voters questioned his identification with poor people. What did a native of the white New Jersey suburbs, a graduate of the Ivy League, and a newcomer to Newark know of black urban decline and the economic obstacles to mobility? When Booker attempted to appeal to these very constituents, poor black men in the worst neighborhoods, he did so by attacking the economic background of James. He criticized James for raising his salary dramatically during his tenure and ridiculed him in television advertisements for his ostentatious lifestyle. For the elite Democrats, because Booker had won election in the Central Ward and lived in public housing, this proved that he had "great empathy for the poor," to quote the *New York Times* endorsement of Booker.[30] Yet some observers noted that although Booker studied books on the problem of black urban poverty, James cared about the poor because he had risen from among them.

Not until near the end of the campaign did full-fledged racial confrontation really overtake this sort of politics.[31] The press pointed out the ways in which the strength of Booker's challenge had pressed James into an ethnic campaign, in which he literally ignored the white vote while seeking to mobilize the black constituency. James signified continuity in the sense of recuperating and maintaining black rule and pride —"We didn't struggle for so many years just to have some rich kid and his friends ride into town and take over City Hall."[32] Not surprisingly, James ran strongly among senior citizens, the group that most clearly remembered the rise of black politics in the city.[33] In an interview, Booker once described the mere existence of a political network as a vice of patronage. But he failed to appreciate the extent to which the black community once needed massive efforts to gain representative inclusion into the democracy.[34] Even as his reform message reached Latino and white voters clamoring for a piece of the pie, he indiscriminately criticized the rank and file that had struggled mightily for civil rights as nothing but cogs in a machine.[35]

Perhaps one of the most important continuities was the continuing critical necessity of an open public sphere in Newark. One of the main points of Marshall Curry's documentary was that the civil liberties of the public sphere were under attack. The opening shots of the film reveal a director who has discovered the sort of political rites detailed in this book: a street-level sphere of deliberation that intersected with government and municipal power. Curry spent more than a year filming the Booker campaign, from the dilapidated offices to Booker's apartment in public housing, to heated confrontations with his staff. In 2002 as in 1967, the city space of rallies and marches, publicity and public speaking served to mobilize the citizenry, but also succumbed to official repression. The visceral impact of scenes of African American bodyguards, representing themselves as members of the Newark Police Department, grabbing Curry's camera and threatening him with physical harm harkened back to white police intimidation of the Tom Hayden days and the persecution of black nationalists like Colonel Hassan. As these improprieties in the campaigns unfolded, observers and reporters who recalled the civil rights movement now alleged the culprits were not white racist throwbacks to the Ku Klux Klan but other African Americans.[36]

The documentary criticized the James campaign for employing intimidation tactics against Booker supporters, for removing campaign publicity from the public sphere, and for breaking into the Booker headquarters. If the director sometimes betrayed a bias for the Booker campaign, the scenes of police and fire department officials obstructing justice proved the point. The press reported that Mayor James had filed charges with federal investigators against the Booker campaign for advertising in illegal places, but the Booker campaign pointed out that "the law is being selectively enforced, since the city is full of Sharpe James signs."[37] At the end of it all, the *New York Times* blamed James for tolerating the "strong-arm tactics" of his supporters.[38] Finally, because of the number of violations reported by both sides, the United States attorney dispatched election monitors to the city of Newark, not unlike any number of delegations of monitors sent to foreign destinations undergoing democratic transitions, perhaps most similar to the ethnic ravages in the Balkans.[39]

In the end, James soundly defeated Booker, outpolling him by some 3500 votes, 53 percent to 47 percent. Booker had captured the new Latino vote by a convincing margin as well as the white ethnics, holding his election-day party to await the returns in the upwardly mobile Ironbound district. But James trounced Booker in the two largest black areas, reflecting the interconnections between the political machine and what might be termed the "black ethnic" vote.[40] These wards and their black constituents had long fought on the battleground of elections against white domination and injustice in city affairs, and their experience had told them to vote for Sharpe James. But for the first time since their ascension to power, African Americans were deeply divided among themselves at the polls.[41]

Four years later, in 2006, Sharpe James announced his decision not to seek a fifth term, virtually assuring the election of Booker in May. With national attention on Newark after Curry's documentary received a nomination for an Academy Award, the press followed Booker's victorious bid for office closely, and recently a long editorial on his first days in office ran in the *New York Times*. To signal just how much had changed since the first elections of African Americans, Booker no longer contended with a hostile white police force, but with corruption in a black-appointed and black-majority force. Black leadership no longer opposed the law-and-order campaigns associated with the white nationalists, but instead called for better and more law enforcement and protection from crime and violence. The death of young black men at the hands of other black Newarkers, and the very construction of black-on-black crime, fundamentally reconstructed the ideology of urban politics. The new black public sphere had ritually and frequently commemorated the deaths of young black men with funerals, music, and mementos—but a young resident of Newark was calling for a new direction: "We've got to stop the killing because I'm tired of putting pictures of black brothers on T-shirts." In the end, Mayor Booker proposed not only an increased police force and tougher enforcement, but "plans for restructuring civic life in New Jersey's biggest city."[42]

Notes

NOTES TO THE INTRODUCTION

1. Important studies include Susan Hirsch, *The Roots of the American Working Class: The Industrialization of Crafts in Newark, 1800–1860* (Philadelphia: University of Pennsylvania Press, 1978); John Cunningham, *Newark* (Newark: Newark Historical Society, 1966).

2. Thomas Bender, "Wholes and Parts: The Need for Synthesis in American History," *Journal of American History* 73 (1986), pp. 120–36.

3. Kevin Mumford, "Double V in New Jersey: African-American Civic Culture and Rising Consciousness Against Jim Crow, 1938–1966," *New Jersey History*, 119, nos. 3–4 (Fall/Winter 2001), p. 50.

4. Kenneth Jackson, *Crabgrass Frontier: The Suburbanization of the United States* (New York: Oxford University Press, 1985); Lizabeth Cohen, *A Consumer's Republic: The Politics of Mass Consumption in Postwar America* (New York: Knopf, 2003).

5. On the ghetto synthesis, see Robert A. Beauregard, *Voices of Decline: The Postwar Fate of U.S. Cities* (New York: Routledge, 2003), pp. 150–78; David Roediger, *Working toward Whiteness: How America's Immigrants Became White* (New York: Basic, 2005), pp. 163–68.

6. Nicholas Lemann, *The Promised Land: The Great Black Migration and How It Changed America* (New York: Knopf, 1991); Mike Davis, *City of Quartz: Excavating the Future in Los Angeles* (New York: Verso, 1990).

7. Lemann, *The Promised Land*; Thomas Sugrue, *Origins of Urban Crisis: Race and Inequality in Postwar Detroit* (Princeton: Princeton University Press, 1996); Robert Self, *American Babylon: Race and the Struggle for Postwar Oakland* (Princeton: Princeton University Press, 2003); Wendell Pritchet, *Brownsville, Brooklyn: Blacks, Jews, and the Changing Face of the Ghetto* (Chicago: University of Chicago Press, 2002); Craig Wilder, *A Covenant with Color: Race and Social Power in Brooklyn* (New York: Columbia University Press, 2000).

8. Robin D. G. Kelley, *Race Rebels: Culture, Politics, and the Black Working Class* (New York: The Free Press, 1994); Kimberley L. Phillips, *AlabamaNorth: Migrants, Community, and Working-Class Activism in Cleveland, 1915–1945* (Urbana: University of Illinois Press, 2000); Matha Biondi, *To Stand and Fight:*

The Civil Rights Movement in Postwar New York City (Cambridge, MA: Harvard University Press, 2003); also see Matthew J. Countryman, "Civil Rights and Black Power in Philadelphia, 1940–1971," (Ph.D. dissertation, Duke University, 1998); Winston James, *Holding Aloft the Banner of Ethiopia: Caribbean Radicalism in Early Twentieth Century America* (New York: Verso, 1998); Gerald Horne, *Black Liberation/Red Scare: Ben Davis and the Communist Party* (Newark: University of Delaware Press, 1994); Tera W. Hunter, *To 'Joy My Freedom: Southern Black Women's Lives and Labor after the Civil War* (Cambridge, MA: Harvard University Press, 1997); Joe W. Trotter, Jr., *Black Milwaukee: The Making of an Industrial Proletariat, 1915–1945* (Urbana: University of Illinois Press, 1985).

9. Studies that examine black migration in the context of politics include Adam Cohen and Elizabeth Taylor, *American Pharaoh: Mayor Richard J. Daley and His Battle for Chicago and the Nation* (New York: Back Bay, 2000); Buzz Bissinger, *A Prayer for the City* (New York: Random House, 1997); Randall Kenan, *Walking on Water: Black American Lives at the End of the 21st Century* (New York: Random House, 1999).

10. On the cultural politics of social movements and radical politics more generally, see Waldo E. Martin, Jr., *No Coward Soldiers: Black Cultural Politics and Postwar America* (Cambridge, MA: Harvard University Press, 2005), p. 7; see also Michael Denning, *The Cultural Front: The Laboring of American Culture in the Twentieth Century* (London: Verso, 1996); Kelley, *Race Rebels*; William Van Deburg, *New Day in Babylon: The Black Power Movement and American Culture, 1965–1975* (Chicago: University of Chicago Press, 1992); Paul Gilroy, *The Black Atlantic: Modernity and Double Consciousness* (Cambridge, MA: Harvard University Press, 1993); on traditional politics see Harvard Sitkoff, *The Struggle for Black Equality, 1954–1992*, rev. ed. (New York: Hill and Wang, 1993); Manning Marable, *Race, Reform, and Rebellion: The Second Reconstruction in America* (Jackson, MS: University Press of Mississippi, 1991).

11. Michael C. Dawson, *Black Visions: The Roots of Contemporary African-American Political Ideologies* (Chicago: University of Chicago Press, 2001).

12. Michael J. Sandel, *Public Philosophy: Essays on Morality in Politics* (Cambridge, MA: Harvard University Press, 2005).

13. Jürgen Habermas, *The Structural Transformation of the Public Sphere* (Cambridge, MA: MIT Press, 1987); Etienne Balibar, *We, The People of Europe? Reflections on Transnational Citizenship* (Princeton: Princeton University Press, 2004), p. 119.

14. Chris Rhomberg, *No There There: Race, Class, and Political Community in Oakland* (Berkeley: University of California Press, 2004), p. 9. Robert Putnam, "Bowling Along: America's Declining Social Capital," *Journal of De-*

mocracy 6, no. 1 (January 1995), pp. 60–65; Doug McAdam, *Political Process and the Development of Black Insurgency* (Chicago: University of Chicago Press, 1982).

15. *The Black Public Sphere: A Public Culture Book,* ed. The Black Public Sphere Collective (Chicago: University of Chicago Press, 1995); Nancy Fraser, "Rethinking the Public Sphere: A Contribution to the Critique of Actually Existing Democracy," in *Habermas and the Public Sphere,* ed. Craig Calhoun (Cambridge, MA: MIT Press, 1992), pp. 109–42; *Civic Engagement in American Democracy,* ed. Theda Skocpol and Morris P. Fiorina (New York: Russell Sage, 1999), esp. pp. 70–71, 469; a multicultural approach to the public that errs by eliminating race as a substantial democratic problem while deliberating on the polity and gender, the polity and class, is Nancy Fraser, *Justice Interruptus: Critical Reflections on the "Post-Socialist" Condition* (New York: Routledge, 1997); on the fractious city, see Mary Ryan, *Civic Wars: The People and Public in the Nineteenth Century* (Berkeley: University of California Press, 1996); Gary Gerstle, *American Crucible: Race and the Nation in the Twentieth Century* (Princeton: Princeton University Press, 2000); revisioning public culture is David Henkin, *City Reading: Written Words and Public Spaces in Antebellum New York* (New York: Columbia University Press, 1998); Vanessa Schwartz, *Spectacular Realities: Mass Culture in Fin de Siècle Paris* (Berkeley: University of California Press, 1997); Jane Jacobs, *The Death and Life of Great American Cities* (New York: Modern Library, 1961, 1993); for an important discussion of Jacobs, see James Scott, *Seeing Like the State* (New Haven: Yale University Press, 1997); on the interracial public sphere, see St. Clare Drake and Horace Cayton, *Black Metropolis: A Study of Black Life in a City* (Chicago: University of Chicago Press, 1944, 1994); on interracial liberalism in postwar public life, Walter Jackson, *Gunnar Myrdal and America's Conscience: Social Engineering and Racial Liberalism, 1938–1987* (Chapel Hill: University of North Carolina Press, 1988); Gunnar Myrdal, *An American Dilemma: The Negro Problem and Modern Democracy* (New York: Harper and Row, 1944); on federalism and localism, a central and pervasively argued thesis is Morton Keller's *Affairs of State: Politics and Society in the United States, 1865–1917* (Cambridge, MA: Harvard University Press, 1984); for a critique of popular democracy, see Jean Baudrillard, *The Illusion of the End* Stanford, CA: Stanford University Press, 1995); on De Tocqueville, see Claude Lefort, *Democracy and Political Theory,* trans. David Macey (New York: Polity, 1988), esp. pp. 190–97.

16. The most eloquent writing on this point is Dipesh Chakrabarty, *Habitats of Modernity* (Chicago: University of Chicago Press, 2004).

17. On the disintegration of the traditional black public sphere, see Dawson, *Black Vision,* pp. 36–40.

18. Pioneering in the public sphere in relation to African American history is

Evelyn Brooks-Higginbotham, *Righteous Discontent: The Women's Movement in the Black Baptist Church, 1880–1920* (Cambridge, MA: Harvard University Press, 1993); an early example of conceptualizing organizations as activism is Rosalyn Terborg-Penn, "African-American Women's Networks in the Anti-Lynching Crusade," in *Gender, Class, Race, and Reform in the Progressive Era,* ed. Noral Lee Frankel and Nancy S. Dye (Lexington: University Press of Kentucky, 1991); Glenda Elizabeth Gilmore, *Gender and Jim Crow: Women and the Politics of White Supremacy in North Carolina, 1896–1920* (Chapel Hill: University of North Carolina Press, 1997); Elsa Barkley Brown, "Negotiating and Transforming the Public Sphere: African-American Political Life in the Transition from Slavery to Freedom," *Public Culture* 7 (1994), pp. 107–46; on white women, see Mary P. Ryan, *Women in Public: Between Banners and Ballots, 1825–1880* (Baltimore, MD: Johns Hopkins University Press, 1990).

19. Anthony Appiah, *The Ethics of Identity* (Princeton: Princeton University Press, 2005), pp. 60–61.

20. The difference between Barbara Fields's first and revised interpretation of racial ideology concerns this very point of citizenship as a contested, not merely mediated, terrain. See Barbara Jeanne Fields, "Slavery, Race, and Ideology in the United States," *New Left Review* 181, no. 1 (1990), pp. 95–118.

21. Seyla Benhabib, *The Claims of Culture: Equality and Diversity in the Global Era* (Princeton: Princeton University Press, 2002), pp. 60–61; on black nationalism in Newark, see Komozi Woodard, *A Nation within A Nation: Amiri Baraka and the Politics of Black Nationalism* (Chapel Hill: University of North Carolina Press, 1999).

22. Exhaustive research on World War II northern civil rights legislation is Sidney Fine, *Expanding the Frontier of Civil Rights: Michigan, 1948–1968* (Detroit: Wayne State University Press, 2000).

23. The phrase informs a study of middle-class experience by Sheryl Cashin, *The Failures of Integration: How Race and Class Are Undermining the American Dream* (New York: Public Affairs, 2004).

24. Attempts to overcome the effect of what I term "post-riot reconstruction" include the deeply thoughtful philosophical analysis of interracial trust (though in ways that ignore interracial communities or what they were up against in the past) by Danielle S. Allen, *Talking to Strangers: Anxieties Since Brown v. Board of Education* (Chicago: University of Chicago Press, 2004).

NOTES TO CHAPTER I

1. Lewis Mumford, *The City in History: Its Origins, Its Transformations, and Its Prospects* (New York: Harcourt, Brace, and World, 1961), p. 474.

2. *Newark's 250th Anniversary* (Newark, 1916), Newark Historical Society (NHS); other early writing on the origins of the city include Wilmer Kennedy,

Board of Education, *Newark* (1911), NHS; Frank Urquhart, *Newark: A Short History* (Newark: Baker, 1908).

3. On Leroi Jones and the Great Society programs at Robert Treat, see *Newark News* (2-6-68); on the naming controversy, see the *New York Times* (9-8-71).

4. Mary P. Ryan, *Civic Wars: Democracy and Public Life in the American City during the Nineteenth Century* (Berkeley: University of California Press, 1997), pp. 78–84, 108–10.

5. On civic culture, see John Ehrenberg, *Civil Society: The Critical History of an Idea* (New York: New York University Press, 1999), 109–43; Robert Putnam, "Bowling Alone: America's Declining Social Capital," *Journal of Democracy* 6, no. 1 (January 1995), pp. 65–78; Charles Taylor, "Modes of Civil Society," *Dissent*, Spring 1991, pp. 293–304; Garbiel Almond and Sidney Verba, *The Civic Culture* (Boston: Little, Brown, 1965); on Tocqueville and membership organizations, see Theda Skocpol and Morris Fiorina, eds., *The Civic Engagement in American Democracy* (New York: Brookings Institution Press, 1999); on race, ethnicity, and legal definitions of national inclusion, see Rogers Smith, *Civic Ideals: Conflicting Visions of Citizenship in the United States* (New Haven: Yale University Press, 1997).

6. Classic accounts of the New York machine, which do not yet emphasize immigration, begin with Harold F. Gosnell, *Boss Platt and His New York Machine* (Chicago: University of Chicago Press, 1924); Harold Zink, *City Bosses in the United States: A Study of Twenty Municipal Bosses* (Durham, NC: Duke University Press, 1930); Alex Gottfried, *Boss Cermak of Chicago: A Study of Political Leadership* (Seattle: University of Washington Press, 1962), p. 355; John M. Allswang, *Bosses Machines, and Urban Voters* (Baltimore: Johns Hopkins University Press, 1977), pp. 60–65.

7. For this formulation, see Ryan, *Civic Wars*, p. 90.

8. Tom Flemming, *A Real History of Newark and Notable Newarkers* (Newark, 1916), pp. 62–68; John Cunningham, *Newark* (Newark: Newark Historical Society, 1966).

9. Lee Calligaro, "The Negro's Legal Status in Pre-Civil War New Jersey," *New Jersey History* (Spring, 1971), pp. 155–66.

10. *Newark: Chronological and Documentary History*, ed. Arnold Rice (Dobbs Ferry, NY: Oceana, 1977). The first large industrial manufacturer opened in 1803, and the number of plants increased steadily from 80 to 163 to 730 between 1830 to 1860. Finally, by the beginning of the twentieth century, according to a manufacturer's report, the Newark industrial economy employed 59,995 of a total population of 347,469.

11. Marion Thompson Wright, "The Early Years," *Journal of Negro History* 26, no. 2 (April 1943), pp. 159–161. Free black men found work in Newark as day laborers and in skilled trades, and black women found domestic work in

wealthy white homes, but returned to their families in the evening rather than live in. See Graham Russell Hodges, *Root and Branch: African-Americans in New York and East Jersey, 1613–1863* (Chapel Hill: University of North Carolina Press, 1999), p. 238; Calligaro, "The Negro's Legal Status," p. 176.

12. Marion Thompson Wright, "A Dramatic Historical Event (in Negro Suffrage in New Jersey, 1776–1875)," *Journal of Negro History* 33, no. 2 (April 1948), pp. 168–71; idem, "The Early Years of the Republic (in Negro Suffrage in New Jersey, 1776–1875)," *Journal of Negro History* 33, no. 2 (April 1948), pp. 223–24; idem, "A Period of Transition, 1804–1865," *Journal of Negro History* 33, no. 2 (April 1948), pp. 177–83; idem, "Early History (in New Jersey Laws and the Negro)," *Journal of Negro History* 28, no. 2. (April 1943), pp. 159–61.

13. Calligaro, "The Negro's Legal Status," p. 166; Frances D. Pingeon, "Dissenting Attitudes toward the Negro in New Jersey—1837," *New Jersey History* 89, no. 1 (Spring 1971). In 1837, at the height of abolitionist ferment, a bill entitled "A further Supplement to an Act entitled an Race Respecting Slaves" passed the New Jersey Assembly on January 26 by 32 to 12.

14. City of Newark, *Know Your City Government, City of Progress* (1965), NHS; Douglas P. Seaton, "Colonizers and Reluctant Colonists: The New Jersey Colonization Society and the Black Community," *New Jersey History* (Spring–Summer 1978), pp. 16–19.

15. Craig Steven Wilder, *In the Company of Black Men: The African Influence on African American Culture in New York City* (New York: New York University Press, 2001); Patrick Rael, *Black Identity and Black Protest in the Antebellum North* (Chapel Hill: University of North Carolina Press, 2002); James Oliver Horton and Lois E. Horton, *In Hope of Liberty: Culture, Community, and Protest among Northern Free Blacks, 1700–1860* (New York: Oxford University Press, 1997).

16. John Anderson, *Black Education in the Nineteenth Century* (published by New Jersey Urban History Association, 1976), NHS; Robert Turk, "Public Schools in the City of Newark" (Ph.D. dissertation, Rutgers University, 1967), pp. 83–88; Hodges, *Root and Branch*, p. 220; on Baptists in Newark, see Rev. Edgar M. Levy, *Newark Baptist Mission* (Newark, 1869), NHS, which does not mention black issues or worshipers; Spencer Crew, "Black New Jersey before the Civil War: Case Studies," *New Jersey History* 99 (Summer 1981), pp. 82–84. According to Crew, African American children attended Colored School No. 1, Latin Grammar School in 1774, the Newark Academy, and the Elizabethtown Free School Association (1815); on the black counterpublic, see the critical theorizing in Joanna Brooks, "The Early American Public Sphere and the Emergence of a Black Print Counterpublic," *William and Mary Quarterly* 62, no. 1 (January 2005), pp. 72–73.

17. Hodges, *Root and Branch*, p. 256; quoted in William B. Gravely, "The

Dialectic of Double Consciousness in Black American Freedom Celebration, 1808–1863," *Journal of Negro History* 67, no. 4 (Winter 1982), p. 311.

18. Rice, ed., *Newark: Chronological History;* Carl Hatch, "Trenton's David Naar: Profile of the Anti-Negro Mind," *New Jersey History* 86, no. 2 (Summer 1968), p. 69.

19. Hodges, *Root and Branch,* p. 269; Marion Thompson Wright, "Extending the Suffrage," *Journal of Negro History* 33, no. 2 (April 1948), pp. 205–7.

20. On African American male population and voting, see Wright, "Extending the Suffrage," pp. 90–95; David Roediger, *The Wages of Whiteness: Race and the Making of the American Working Class* (London: Verso, 1990); on white industrialization in Newark, see Susan Hirsch, *Roots of the American Working Class.*

21. Marion Thompson Wright, "Extending Civil Rights in New Jersey through the Division against Discrimination," *Journal of Negro History* 38, no. 1 (January 1953), pp. 96, 101; Marion Thompson Wright, *The Education of the Negro in New Jersey* (New York: Columbia University Press, 1941). Interracial meetings convened in the mid-1940s promoted desegregation of state schools; on a meeting convened for desegregation in Atlantic City, see *New Jersey Afro-American* (3-9-46); Wright, "Extending Civil Rights," p. 101; *New Jersey Afro-American* (6-7-47); *New Jersey Afro-American* (4-6-45); *New Jersey Herald* (9-18-43).

22. On sex ratios, see *Thirteenth Census of the Unites States* (1910), part 1, p. 281; sex ratios declined slightly, reflecting increase of females in 1920 and 1930. See *Fifteenth Census of the United States* (1930), vol. 3, part 2, p. 177; Irving T. Busch, *Recommendation of Irving T. Busch* (Newark, 1912), p. 13.

23. E. Marvin Goodwin, *Black Migration in America from 1915 to 1960: An Uneasy Exodus* (New York: Mellen, 1990), p. 21.

24. Paul Stellhorn, "Depression and Decline, Newark, New Jersey, 1929-1941," (Ph.D. dissertation, Rutgers University, 1982), pp. 7–8; Clement Alexander Price, "The Afro-American Community of Newark, 1917–1947: A Social History," (Ph.D. dissertation, Rutgers University, 1975), p. 72.

25. On ethnic groups population and employment, see summary of census and relief census for 1937 in Charles W. Churchill, *The Italians of Newark: A Community Study* (New York: Arno, 1975), appendix 6.

26. *The Neighborhood House,* NHS, pp. 3–8.

27. On work in World War I, see Price, "Afro-American Community," tables 2.2, 2.3, pp. 28, 29; *The Neighborhood House,* pp. 8–10, NHS.

28. Goodrich, ed., *Report of Newark Manufacturing,* p. 20; whites were 96 percent or higher of residents in rural or urban areas and black New Jerseyans were 3.7 to 4 percent. On migration work statistics for black men, see Price, "Afro-American Community," p. 22, 30; *Fourteenth Census of the United States*

(1920), vol. 2, part 2, p. 95; *Sixteenth United States Census* (1940), vol. 2, part 4, p. 821; *Seventeenth Census of the United States* (1950), part 3, p. 30.

29. On school segregation, see *New Jersey Afro-American* (10-16-43); *Annual Report of the Urban League of New Jersey* (1946); *Annual Report of Urban Colored Commission* (7-31-45), NPL; the commission was created by Senator Hargraves from Essex County, by Assembly Bill 184, on 2–17–41. See *Program of the New Jersey Negro Welfare Commission Report* (1942–1943), NPL.

30. Kelly Miller, *Race Adjustment: Essays on the Negro in America* (New York: Neale, 1909), pp. 171–81; U.S. Department of Commerce, Bureau of the Census, *Negroes in the United States, 1920–1932* (Washington, D.C.: Government Printing Office, 1935); Arnesen, *Black Protest and Migration,* pp. 3–34; Deborah Gray White, *Ar'n't I a Woman: Female Slavery in the Antebellum South* (New York: Norton, 1985); Elizabeth Fox-Genovese, *Within the Plantation Household: Black and White Women of the Old South* (Chapel Hill: University of North Carolina Press, 1988); Hazel Carby, "Policing the Black Women's Body in an Urban Context," *Critical Inquiry* 13 (Summer 1993), pp. 739–52.

31. Price, "Afro-Americans in Newark," p. 128 (table 5.5).

32. Price, "Afro-Americans in Newark," p. 127; Mary White Ovington, *Half a Man: The Status of the Negro in New York* (New York: Negro Universities Press, 1911), pp. 152–53.

33. See "Reports from the Convention" (8-3-1920), Rev. J. W. Locke, quoted in Robert Hill, ed., *The Marcus Garvey and UNIA Papers,* vol. 2, pp. 522–23.

34. On ethnic composition, see Thomas Philpot, *The Slum and the Ghetto: Neighborhood Deterioration and Middle-Class Reform, Chicago, 1880–1930* (New York: Oxford University Press, 1978), pp. 147–48; for the racial discrimination synthesis, see Alan Spear, *Black Chicago: The Making of a Negro Ghetto, 1890–1920* (Chicago: University of Chicago Press, 1967), pp. 91–110.

35. Planning Board in Essex, *North Jersey—Prospects and Development Problems 1949,* p. 1, Frances Loeb Library, Harvard. See Charles Allan Baretski, "Newark Public Library," in Stanley Winters, ed., *From Riot to Recovery: Newark after Ten Years* (Washington, D.C.: University Press of America, 1979); Harold Kaplan, *Urban Renewal Politics: Slum Clearance in Newark* (New York: Columbia University Press, 1963), p. 149; *Urban Atlas,* Newark, New Jersey, UA-SMSA 5640-1 (U.S. Census Bureau, 1970).

36. *New Jersey Governor's Commission on Civil Disorders, Final Report,* NJSA (1968), pp. 58–60; *Economic Development of the Greater Newark Area: Trends and Prospects Report,* Frances Loeb Library, Harvard, p. 95.

37. Price, "The Afro-American Community of Newark," p. 31

38. Michael Dawson, "A Black Counterpublic? Economic Earthquakes, Racial Agenda(s), and Black Politics," in *The Black Public Sphere,* ed. The Black Public Sphere Collective (Chicago: University of Chicago Press, 1995), p. 201.

39. Kenneth Kusmer, *A Ghetto Takes Shape: Black Cleveland, 1870–1930* (Urbana: University of Illinois Press, 1975), pp. 78, 136–37.

40. Paul Stellhorn, "Depression and Decline, Newark, New Jersey, 1929-1941" (Ph.D. dissertation, Rutgers University, 1982), pp. 7–8; Price, "Afro-American Community," p. 72.

41. *Historical Statistics of Black America,* vol. 2 (New York: Gale Research, 2000), pp. 361, 407–9.

42. Spear, *Black Chicago,* pp. 12–14, 24–27; Goodwin, *Black Migration,* p. 23; Sugrue, *The Origins of the Urban Crisis,* p. 44.

43. Harry Davis, "Alpha Lodge, No. 116. New Jersey: An Extract," *Journal of Negro History* 20, no. 2 (April 1935), pp. 180–89; C. G. Woodson, "The Negro in Banking," *Journal of Negro History* 14, no. 2 (April 1929), pp. 156–201; on African American and black Caribbean organizations and community formation, see Irma Watkins-Owens, *Blood Relations: Caribbean Immigrants and the Harlem Community, 1900–1930* (Bloomington: Indiana University Press, 1996), pp. 57–74, 127–35; on accommodation entrepreneurs in the North, see Kusmer, *A Ghetto Takes Shape,* pp. 135–39; Spear, *Black Chicago,* pp. 106–10.

44. Clement Price, "The Beleaguered City as Promised Land: Blacks in Newark, 1917–1947," in *Urban New Jersey since 1870,* ed. Willliam C. Wright (Trenton, NJ: The New Jersey Historical Commission, 1975), pp. 14–17.

45. Warren Grover, *Nazis in Newark* (New Brunswick: Transaction, 2003), pp. 143–44; William Ashby, *Tales without Hate* (Newark: Upland Press, 2001), pp. 71–74, 78. According to one report, "next to Detroit in advance of colored women in industry during the war comes Newark" see Forrester B. Washington, "Reconstruction and the Colored Woman, Life and Land" (January 1919), reprinted in *Arnesen, Black Protest and the Great Migration,* pp. 152–53.

46. *Newark Herald* (6-11-38); Donald Henderson, "The Effects of the Migration upon the Migrants Themselves," *Journal of Negro History* 6, no. 4 (October 1921), pp. 445–57. Father Divine does not regularly appear in the press or in politics, however. The membership report was printed in *Newark Afro-American* (9-28-36); on NAACP, see *Newark Afro-American* (11-1-46); on uplift theory and practices, see Higginbotham, *Righteous Discontent.*

47. See "Summary on Newark," August 1924, in Robert Hill, ed., *Marcus Garvey and UNIA Papers,* vol. 5, p. 659.

48. On Father Divine, see Jill Watts, *God, Harlem, USA: The Father Devine Story* (Berkeley: University of California Press, 1992).

49. *New Jersey Afro-American* (10-1-49).

50. Grover, *Nazis in Newark,* pp. 223–24.

51. "All in A Week," *Italian Tribune* (3-14-56); see the paparazzi of civic and union functions in the *Italian Tribune*. For example, "Pictorial Reflections by Frank Cuva," *Italian Tribune* (1-11-52); "Pictorial Reflections by Frank

Cuva," *Italian Tribune* (1-16-53); "Pictorial Reflections by Frank Cuva," *Italian Tribune* (1-25-52).

52. *New Jersey Afro-American* (10-23-43).

53. Charles W. Churchill, *The Italians of Newark: A Community Study* (New York: Arno, 1975), p. 25.

54. Quoted from *Sunday Call* (5-30-1885), in Michael Immerso, *Newark's Little Italy: The Vanished First Ward* (Newark: Newark Public, 1997), p. 11.

55. "All in a Week," *Italian Tribune* (n.d.).

56. Churchill, *The Italians of Newark*, pp. 27, 33; Alan H. Spear, *Black Chicago: The Making of a Negro Ghetto, 1890–1920* (Chicago: University of Chicago Press, 1967), pp. 159–64; William Tuttle, *Race Riot: Chicago in the Red Summer of 1919* (New York: Atheneum, 1970), pp. 156–83; for example, see "Free Assistance for Alien Registration Is Offered By Vaca Travel," *Italian Tribune* (1-16-53).

57. They constituted 22 percent of the population but 42 percent of the relief clients in 1937. See Churchill, *The Italians of Newark*, pp. 58–59; "Foreign-Born White, by Country of Birth, Sex, for the City of Newark: 1940 and 1930," *Sixteenth Census of the United States, Characteristics of the Population*, vol. 11, part 4, p. 927.

58. Stellhorn, *Depression and Decline*, pp. 8–9; Price documents employment discrimination and the vigilance of the Urban League and discovered protean protest against Jim Crow accommodations in connection to employment discrimination locally. See Clement Price, "The Struggle to Desegregate Newark: Black Middle Class Militancy in New Jersey, 1932–1947," *New Jersey History* (1980–81), pp. 215–28.

59. Price, "The Afro-American Community of Newark," pp. 116, 122; *Sixteenth Census of the United States, Population*, vol. 11, part 4, table 13, pp. 205–6, 209–10.

60. "J.C. Sisters in Silver Jubilee," *Italian Tribune* (1-18-52); women's auxiliaries played a role in philanthropic and public institutions, bridging ethnicity and municipal power. See "Elect Mrs. Norman Cogliati President of Women's Auxiliary Columbus Hospital," *Italian Tribune* (1-15-54).

61. Robert Orsi, "The Religious Boundaries of an In-Between People: Street Fetes and the Problem of the Dark-Skinned Other in Italian Harlem, 1920–1990," *American Quarterly* 44, no. 3 (September 1992), pp. 313–347; on the culture of the Italian procession, see the excellent work of Joseph Sciorra, " 'We Go Where the Italians Live': Religious Processions as Ethnic and Territorial Markers in a Multi-ethnic Brooklyn Neighborhood," in Robert Orsi, ed., *Gods of the City: Religion and the American Urban Landscape* (Bloomington: Indiana University Press, 1999), pp. 330–32; a pioneering study is Susan Davis, *Parades and Power: Street Theatre in Nineteenth Century Philadelphia* (Philadelphia: Temple University Press, 1986), pp. 2–22, and Alessandro Falassi, "Festival: De-

finition and Morphology," in *Time Out of Time: Essays on the Festival,* ed. Alessandro Falassi (Albuquerque: University of New Mexico Press, 1987), pp. 173–80.

62. "Solemn Rites for L. Russomanno," *Italian Tribune* (1-3-58).

63. This school applied to Newark; see Peter I. Rose, *Racial and Ethnic Tensions: Racial and Ethnic Relations in the United States* (New York: Random House, 1964), pp. 97–99; Robert Penn Warren, *Segregation: The Inner Conflict in the South* (New York: Random House, 1956); Talcott Parsons, *The Social System* (Glencoe: Free Press, 1951); Everett V. Stonequist, *The Marginal Man* (New York: Scribner's, 1937); Brewton Berry, *Race and Ethnic Relations* (Boston: Houghton Mifflin, 1958); Oscar Handlin, *The Newcomers: Negroes and Puerto Ricans in a Changing Metropolis* (Cambridge, MA: Harvard University Press, 1959).

64. "Italian Institute to Present Opera," *Italian Tribune* (4-16-54); "Megaro Welfare Club Dance Proceeds, Will Send Boys to Camp," *Italian Tribune* (3-12-52).

65. "Names Chairman for American Day," *Italian Tribune* (2-12-54); "I Am an American Day Fete Planned," *Italian Tribune* (4-24-53).

66. "Important Accomplishments of Congress of Special Interest to Nationality Groups," *Italian Tribune* (8-19-55); "Award to Be Made at Annual I Am an American Day," *Italian Tribune* (5-6-55).

67. "Solemn Rites for L. Russomanno," *Italian Tribune* (1-3-58).

68. "Rodino Bill to Reach Committee," *Italian Tribune* (3-27-53); "Amerigo D'Agostino Calls for Revision of Bills on Immigration in Congress," *Italian Tribune* (3-21-52).

69. "First Ward C.C. Elect Officers," *Italian Tribune,* (3-14–58); "Columbus Club 50th Anniversary," *Italian Tribune* (5-18-56).

70. "Twenty Colorful Floats to Be Featured in Newark's Columbus Day Parade," *Italian Tribune* (10-7-55);"Columbus Day," *Italian Tribune* (6-6-52); "Addonizio Plans New Legislation," *Italian Tribune* (1-9-53); "Thousands to March in Gala Parade in Honor of Columbus October 12," *Italian Tribune* (10-8-54).

71. "Addonizio Backs Columbus Day Bill," *Italian Tribune* (1-14-55); "First Immigration Law Based on Fear; McCarran Act Based on Hate," *Italian Tribune* (1-9-53); "Addonizio against Immigration Act," *Italian Tribune* (1-23-53).

72. Grover, *Nazis in Newark,* pp. 5, 21, 119, 124.

73. Clement Price, "The Struggle to Desegregate Newark: Black Middle Class Militancy in New Jersey, 1932–1947," *New Jersey History* (1980–81), p. 234; Grover, *Nazis in Newark,* pp. 238, 258.

74. Komozi Woodard, *A Nation within a Nation: Amiri Baraka (Le Roi Jones) and Black Power Politics* (Chapel Hill: University of North Carolina Press, 1999), pp. 33, 35; Cheryl Greenberg, *Or Does It Explode: Black Harlem*

in the Great Depression (New York: Oxford University Press, 1991); Winston James, *Holding Aloft the Banner of Ethiopia: Caribbean Radicalism in Early Twentieth Century America* (New York: Verso, 1998); Mark Naison, *Communists in Harlem during the Depression* (Urbana: University of Illinois Press, 1983); Tony Martin, *Race First: The Ideological and Organizational Struggles of Marcus Garvey and Negro Improvement Association* (Westport, Conn.: Greenwich, 1976); Depression-era Newark was not particularly a rich site of labor organizing much less a labor-led civil rights movement. On Detroit, see Beth T. Bates, "Double V for Victory Mobilizes Black Detroit, 1941–1946," in Komozi Woodard, ed., *Freedom North: The Civil Rights Movement in the North* (New York: Palgrave, 2002); and Beth T. Bates, "A New Crowd Challenged the Agenda of the Old Guard in the NAACP, 1933–1941," *American Historical Review* 102, no. 2 (April 1997), pp. 340–77.

75. William L. O'Neill, *A Democracy at War: America's Fight at Home and Abroad in World War II* (New York: The Free Press, 1993); *Newark Evening News* (1-10-41); *New Jersey Afro-American* (3-13-43); Price finds little in the way of militancy in the 1930s in "Afro-American Community," pp. 134, 153; *New Jersey Afro-American* (10-30-43).

NOTES TO CHAPTER 2

1. It was in a letter to the *Pittsburgh Courier* in which a twenty-six-year-old cafeteria worker in the Cessna Aircraft Corporation introduced the slogan Double V; but the exact origins of Double V are a matter of historical debate. Patrick Washburn, *A Question of Sedition* (New York: Oxford University Press, 1986), p. 100–120; Robert Hill, The FBI's *RACON: Racial Conditions in the United States during World War II* (Boston: Northeastern University Press, 1995), p. 689; *Pittsburgh Courier* business stationery advertised the slogan with brightly colored print on its borders, on stickers for buildings, and on automobile windshields, spreading the idea to newspapers across the nation; *New Jersey Afro-American* (3-10-45); from W. F. Bayless to Walter White (4-20-42), file "Double V," Box A239, Group II, NAACP.

2. For example, see Philip Klinker with Rogers Smith, *The Unsteady March: The Rise and Decline of Racial Equality in America* (Chicago: University of Chicago Press, 1999), pp. 189–90; Alan Brinkley, *American History: A Survey* (New York: McGraw-Hill, 1999), p. 939; Beth Bailey and David Farber, "The 'Double V' Campaign in World War II Hawaii: African-Americans, Racial Ideology, and Federal Power," *Journal of Social History* 26, no. 4 (Summer 1993), pp. 817–43; Peter J. Kellog, "Civil Rights Consciousness in the 1940s," *Historian* 42, no. 1 (November 1979), pp. 18–41; Patrick Washburn, "The Pittsburgh Courier's Double V Campaign in 1942," *American Journalism* 3, no. 2 (1986), pp. 73–86.

3. From Jesse Jettr to Roy Wilkins, Box B:8, file "Civil Rights, NJ," Group II, NAACP, Library of Congress.

4. On public accommodations, see Joseph Singer, "No Right to Exclude: Public Accommodations and Private Property," *Northwestern University Law Review* 90, no. 4 (Summer 1996), p. 1485; Marion Wright Thompson, "Extending Civil Rights in New Jersey through the Division against Discrimination," *Journal of Negro History* 38, no. 1 (January 1953), pp. 93–96; and Marion Thompson Wright, "Intensified Battles for Emancipation and the Rights of Citizenship (in Negro Suffrage in New Jersey, 1776–1875)," *Journal of Negro History* 33, no. 2 (April 1948), pp. 184–223.

5. Thompson, "Extending Civil Rights in New Jersey"; idem, "A Dramatic Historical Event (in Negro Suffrage in New Jersey, 1776–1875); *Journal of Negro History* 33, no. 2 (April 1948), pp. 168–71; idem, "Intensified Battles for Emancipation and the Rights of Citizenship (in Negro Suffrage in New Jersey, 1776–1875), *Journal of Negro History* 33, no. 2 (April 1948), pp. 168–71; idem, "The Early Years of the Republic (in Negro Suffrage in New Jersey, 1776–1875)," *Journal of Negro History* 33, no. 2 (April 1948), pp. 223–24; idem, "A Period of Transition, 1804–1865," *Journal of Negro History* 33, no. 2 (April 1948), pp. 177–83; idem, "Early History (in New Jersey Laws and the Negro)," *Journal of Negro History* 28, no. 2 (April 1943), pp. 151–61.

6. The NAACP endorsed the Double V in May 1942; see telegram (5-12-42), Box A:239, Group II, NAACP, the Library of Congress. The NAACP led a membership drive for five thousand members during the war years, but correspondence suggests that ineptitude hindered the organization's effectiveness. From Madison Jones to Bert Bland (5-23-42), Box C 110, File "Newark 1940–1942," Group II, NAACP, LOC.

7. On the black press, see David Scott Domke, "The Press, Social Change, and Race Relations in the Late Nineteenth Century" (Ph.D. dissertation, University of Minnesota, 1996). Before Double V, the press covered equal protection legislation and schooling in particular; see Penelope Laconia Bullock, "The Negro Periodical Press in the United States, 1838–1909" (Ph.D. dissertation, University of Michigan, 1971); Reginald Lee Owens, "The African American Press as a Response to Oppression: Trends in Formation and Circulation" (Ph.D. dissertation, University of Texas—Austin, 1993).

8. Illiteracy rates for males and females in 1900 indicated by the census suggest 1,183 who could read but not write; the number who could neither read nor write was 10, 532; by 1920, for the urban population of New Jersey, Negro illiteracy was 6.5 percent and declined to 5.7 percent in 1930; native white illiteracy was .04 percent, and foreign born was 13.4 percent in 1930. *See U.S. Federal Census, Fifteenth Decennial Census,* vol. 3, part 2, p. 182.

9. Additional smaller newspapers include the *Newark Appeal* (1902–1910), the *New Jersey Observer* (1914–1923), the *New Jersey Informer* (1919–1923),

the *New Jersey Record* (1933–1943), the *New Jersey Guardian* (1934–1942). See Price, "Afro-American Community," p. 133.

10. *Newark Afro-American* (10-23-46).

11. Lee Finkle, "The Conservative Aims of Militant Rhetoric: Black Protest during World War II," *Journal of American History* 60, no. 3 (December 1973), p. 694.

12. *New Jersey Herald* (7-25-42); on Randolph's Double V and fascism in the 1940s, see Robert Hill, *RACON*, p. 434; *New Jersey Afro-American* (11-4-44); *New Jersey Afro-American* (7-22-44).

13. The Daughters of the American Revolution was founded in 1890 by four women. By the late 1890s women were joining at the "rate of three, four and five" thousand a year. By 1931 the Daughters were 173,525 strong. Peggy Anderson, *The Daughters: An Unconventional Look at America's Fan Club—The DAR* (New York: St. Martin's, 1974), p. 46; Barbara Truesdell, "God, Home, and Country: Folklore, Patriots, and the Politics of Home" (Ph.D. dissertation, Indiana University, 1996). Why the DAR rejected Anderson exactly, since the organization had previously rented to Roland Hayes, a black opera star, and later invited Anderson during the war, without amending the charter is a matter of speculation. On Hayes, see Allan Keiler, *Marian Anderson,* p. 187; *The Interracial Movement in Newark,* pp. 10–12, NPL.

14. *New Jersey Herald* (2-25-39).

15. *New Jersey Herald* (1-14-39).

16. *Newark Herald News* (6-24-39).

17. *New Jersey Herald* (3-14-39).

18. Marian Anderson, *My Lord, What a Morning: An Autobiography* (New York, 1956), p. 207; from Secretary, office of White, to Emory Jackson (1-29-51), Box A18, File "Anderson, General 1951–55," Group II, NAACP, LOC. (Ironically, black activists boycotted Anderson when she performed for segregated audiences in the South in 1951. Anderson then agreed to sing only at integrated auditoriums.)

19. On the convergence of anti-Semitism and racism, see George Fredrickson, *Racism: A Short History* (Princeton: Princeton University Press, 2002), pp. 103–38; *The National Urban League of Newark, Annual Report* (1940), p. 7, NPL.

20. "Doctor Refused Cup of Coffee," *New Jersey Afro-American* (1-23-43); *New Jersey Afro-American* (1-23-43).

21. *New Jersey Herald* (2-22-41); the white American repose to Nazi anti-Semitism was not prominently used in the American ideology for mobilization and combat. See Peter Novick, *Holocaust in American Life* (Boston: Houghton Mifflin, 1999), pp. 24–30; and major intellectuals followed rather than led the newspaper discourse, such as Du Bois's experience with Nazism during the 1930s; see Werner Sollors, "W.E.B. Du Bois in Nazi Germany, 1936," *Amerikastudien/American Studies* 44, no. 2 (1999): 207–22.

22. *Pittsburgh Courier* (2-15-41); *New Jersey Afro-American* (2-13-43).

23. From Clarence Derwent to Addison V. Pinkney, Actors Equity, New York, NY (1947), Box B66, File "Discrimination in Theatres," Group II, NAACP, LOC; Walter White, telegram (2-13-47), Box B66, File "Discrimination in Theatres, Group II," NAACP, LOC.

24. *New Jersey Afro-American* (2-13-43); see signed affidavit, from Thurgood Marshall to Mrs. Bernice Johnson, Chicago, Ill. (10-6-43), Box B66, File "Discrimination," Group II, NAACP, LOC; *New Jersey Afro-American* (12-10-49). For example, see the comparison between American political tradition and Nazism. Both dwelled on the evil of racism and compared the methods and practices of U.S. white supremacists with analogues in Germany, such as racial classification. The *Newark Herald* regularly published a "Jim Crow Guide to U.S.A.," to "bring forcibly to the attention of the nation a few of the essentially fascistic limitations on human freedom which exist in America today."

25. James W. Ford, *The War and the Negro People* (New York: Worker's Library, 1942), pp. 9, 12.

26. Clement Price, "The Struggle to Desegregate Newark: Black Middle Class Militancy in New Jersey, 1932–1947," *New Jersey History* (1980–81), p. 234.

27. *Newark Directory* (Price and Lee Co., 1947), p. 276. Among the department stores, 5c to 100: A & E Department Stores, 484A Hawthorne; Altman B. & Co., 576 Central Avenue, East Orange; Altman's Wm Dept. Store, 82 Broadway; Bamberger's, L. and Co., 109–131 Market, and 220 and 242 Washington; Fairmont Department Store, 396 Springfield; Franklin Stores, 66 Pacific; Gates Dept. Store, 508 Broadway; Kresge Dept. Store, 709 Broad Street; Sears Roebuck, 168 Elizabeth; Kresge S. S. & Co., 151 Market Street; 5 and 10 Cent Store, 697–703 Broad Street.

28. *The New Jersey Herald* (12-24–38).

29. When refused service at 125 South Orange Street, two Jersey City residents brought a suit, and the proprietors were "hailed into court." See *New Jersey Herald* (12-9-44); *New Jersey Afro-American* (9-24-49); another incident occurred on 9-16-49.

30. *Newark Evening News* (1-10-41).

31. *New Jersey Afro-American* (12-1-43); *New Jersey Afro-American* (10-12-46); originally appeared in *New Jersey Afro-American* (5-10-43); Phillip McGuire, *Taps for a Jim Crow Army: Letters from Black Soldiers in World War II* (Santa Barbara: ABC-CLIO, 1983), p. 170. For example, Corporal Russell Banks requested help from the black press, because "we have no convenient place to eat our dinner, No decent latrine. We would appreciate it very much if you would put this to the proper authorities. Please send a reporter to city of Newport News, VA."

32. *New Jersey Afro-American* (4-1-44); on low morale among black sol-

diers due to segregation, *New Jersey Afro-American* (6-24-44). "No doubt the average colored soldier is of the opinion that he is the least thought of and the most unappreciated member of our nation's armed forces." On the USO, see *New Jersey Afro-American* (7-1-44); *New Jersey Afro-American* (4-21-45), "Jim Crow Officers Clubs Expressly Barred by Army." "No Officers Club, mess, or other similar social organization of officers will be permitted by the post commander to occupy any part of any public building"; *New Jersey Afro-American* (11-20-43), p. 1. See anonymous memo (11-22-48), Box A15, File "American Red Cross," Group II, NAACP.

33. On the politics of Truman and civil rights, see Robert Ferrell, *Harry S. Truman: A Life* (Columbia: University of Missouri, 1994), p. 293; Steve Lawson, *To Secure These Rights: The Report of President Harry S. Truman's Committee on Civil Rights* (Bedford: St. Martin's, 2004). The South warned against "ramming miscegenation down their throats." When Truman proposed federal civil rights legislation, southern legislators invoked Rule 22 (passed in 1917 allowing filibusters on civil rights issues), and several proposals were defeated, most notably a permanent Federal Employment Practices Commission. However, by 1950 the armed forces were basically integrated. See *Blacks in the United States Armed Forces, Basic Documents,* vol. 12, p. 43.

34. "Material for State Librarian," memo, "Staff Activities" (November–December 1942), pp. 2–3, Box 3, Urban Colored Commission Papers, NJSA.

35. See Annual Reports that focus on wartime measures and civil rights, *Annual Reports of Urban Colored Commission, 1942–1949,* NPL; *Fourth Annual Report, Urban Colored Commission* (1946); "Discrimination in Public Places and the Civil Rights Laws of New Jersey," Box 2, File 11, Urban Colored Commission, NJSA.

36. For the stress on 1949, see Biondi, *To Stand and Fight,* pp. 70–80; "Antidiscrimination Law of 1945," chapter 11, *Laws of 1949, State of New Jersey* (Trenton: MacCrellish, 1949); for the use of "civil rights" in the white press, see "Holderman Warns on Discrimination," *Italian Tribune* (6-24-55); "Discrimination in Public Places and the Civil Rights Laws of New Jersey," *Fourth Annual Report* (1946), Box 2, File 11, Urban Colored Commission, NJSA.

37. That women led the drives was emphasized in postwar news; see "Red Cross Starts Membership Drive," *Italian Tribune* (3-7-52).

38. Spencie Love, *One Blood: The Death and Resurrection of Charles B. Drew* (Chapel Hill: University of North Carolina Press, 1996), pp. 150, 159; the meeting occurred between Wilkins and the Red Cross in 1937; see *NAACP Annual Report* (1937), pp. 19–20.

39. *Urban Colored Commission Report* (1945), pp. 5–6, NPL.

40. *New Jersey Herald* (1-22-44).

41. *Municipal Report of Newark* (1947), p. 86, NPL.

42. *American Junior Red Cross* (1950), NPL.

43. *NAACP Annual Report* (1937), pp. 19–20.

44. Robert Hill, ed., *RACON* (March 23, 1943), p. 429.

45. "State of Policy Regarding Negro Blood Donors," (1-21-42), Box A15, Group II, NAACP, LOC; *NAACP Annual Report* (1939), p. 31; *NAACP Annual Report* (1942); from unsigned to T. M. Smith (8-20-42), Box A15, File "Red Cross policy," Group II, NAACP, LOC.

46. *Annual Report, American Red Cross of Newark* (April 25, 1946).

47. From Norman Davis, to Henry R. Smith (World Council of Churches) (12-7-42), Box A15, File "Red Cross," Group II, NAACP, LOC.

48. See memo of 8-10-44, Box A15, File "Red Cross," Group II, NAACP, LOC.

49. From Roy Wilkins to Norman Davis (2-21-44), Box A15, Group II, NAACP, LOC.

50. *Annual Report, American National Red Cross Newark Chapter,* 343 High Street (1939), p. 11; *New Jersey Afro-American* (3-27-43). Boston plasma centers refused to separate blood that was shipped overseas; see Robert Hill, ed., *RACON*, p. 434.

51. 5-16-42, "Use of Negro Blood from Blood Banks," Box A15, File "Red Cross Donor Policy," Group II, NAACP, LOC.

52. From Henry Smith Leiper to G. Canby Robinson, Blood Donor Services, American Red Cross (1-15-42), Box A15, File "Red Cross Donor Policy, 1942–44."

53. See Eileen Boris, " 'You Wouldn't Want One of 'Em Dancing with Your Wife: Racialized Bodies on the Job in WW II," *American Quarterly* 50.1 (March 1998); Mica Nava, "Wider Horizons and Modern Desire: The Contradictions of American and Racial Difference in London, 1935–1945," *New Formations*, no. 37 (Spring 1999), pp. 71–91; on the varied responses to interracial activity, see Sonya Rose, "Sex, Citizenship, and the Nation in World War II," *American Historical Review,* 103, no. 4 (October 1998), pp. 1155–57; similar anxiety surfaced in the form of antimiscegenation in World War I France, connected to labor strikes; see Tyler Stovall, "The Color Line behind the Lines: Racial Violence in France during the Great War," *American Historical Review* 63, no. 3 (June 1998), pp. 1737–69.

54. *New Jersey Afro-American* (5-5-45). On the labeling controversy, see from Madison Jones to Manes M. Brittain, Citizens Council on Democratic Rights (7-31-50), Box A15, Group II, NAACP; from Louis Boochever, Dir. of Public Relations, to Madison Jones (2-5-51), Box A115, Group II, NAACP. Why southern resistance to Jim Crow failed remains something of a mystery. On unorganized civil rights movements in Birmingham, see Robin D. G. Kelley, *Race Rebels: Culture, Politics, and the Black Working Class* (New York: The Free Press, 1996), pp. 72–75.

55. On the decline of scientific racism, see Hamilton Cravens, *The Triumph*

of Evolution: American Scientists and the Heredity-Environment Controversy, 1900–1941 (Philadelphia: University of Pennsylvania Press, 1978).

56. David Roediger, *Working toward Whiteness: How America's Immigrants Became White* (New York: Basic Books, 2005), pp. 23–26.

57. Josef Barton, *Peasants and Strangers: Italians, Rumanians, and Slovaks in an American City, 1890–1950* (Cambridge, MA: Harvard University Press, 1975), pp. 166–69.

58. Charles W. Churchill, *The Italians of Newark: A Community Study* (New York: Arno, 1975; original published 1942), pp. 58–59, 74–75, 87.

59. *National Collegiate Athletic Association, Swimming Guide* (Nat. College Athletic Assoc., 1941); Richard Peterson, "How I Have Included Christian Emphasis on Teaching Young Boys to Swim," *Journal of Physical Education* 56, no. 1 (1958), p. 3.

60. By 1962 it was estimated that Los Angeles was the city with the highest density percentage of pools. A report published by the Outdoor Recreation Commission estimated 11,000 pools across the nation in 1947, and by 1964 more than 310,000; see *United States Outdoor Recreation Commission* (1965); Thomas Leeuwen, A.P., *The Springboard in the Pond: An Intimate History of the Swimming Pool* (Cambridge, MA: MIT Press, 1998).

61. *Newark Directory* (Price and Lee Co., 1947).

62. *Newark Municipal Yearbook* (1945–49), p. 133.

63. *Newark Herald* (6-18-38).

64. NAACP, *Annual Report*, 1939, p. 21; *New Jersey Herald* (7-1-39).

65. *New Jersey Afro-American* (7-28-45). When private swim clubs segregated, black victims appealed to local government authorities, yet the conflicts frequently ended in a stalemate, with the licenses suspended or the clubs closed, rather than operators changing the policy to accommodate all residents. "Charged with Denying Admission to Colored Bather," *New Jersey Herald* (8-20-38); "Natatorium Which Was Closed after Race Friction," *NAACP Annual Report*, 1936, p. 22. Though swimming was a favorite pastime both of black and white residents before U.S. involvement abroad, the *Newark Herald* reported disruptions in pools and swimming as "old timers here describing it as one of the poorest in many years." Little more is known about the incident. The medium-sized city of Summit witnessed conflicts over the integration of swimming pools, and the municipal authorities were "smarting under protests against drawing the color line at the YWCA's swimming pool." The YWCA issued a statement to the African American applicants "notifying the colored girls that they would not be accepted in the swimming class along with an apology because the distinction was not indicated when the invitation was given to the class." Rather than boycotting and withdrawing from public confrontation, black residents knew enough to assert their rights and demanded access immediately. In addition to contacting the black newspapers, the girls turned to the lo-

cal NAACP, and the branch wrote directly to the national secretary to report the case of discrimination. When the girls and their representatives met with the YWCA board and again appealed for integrated access, they lost the case. The black girls were not permitted to attend classes with white girls.

66. *Newark Herald* (7-23-38).

67. From F. Berman to Franklin Williams (8-2-46), Box B66, File "Discrimination, 1945–49," Group II, NAACP, LOC.

68. *New Jersey Afro-American* (3-27-43).

69. Ibid.; To Lucille Black from A. C. Farleyh Colicitory (11-25-1947), Box C105, File "Asbury Park," Group II, NAACP, LOC. See from Madison Jones, campaign director, to Bert Bland (5-23-42), Box C:110, File "Newark 1940–1942," Group II, NAACP.

70. Before the new civil rights law was written in 1949, the exact scope of the 1945 discrimination law was contested; in one case a state court held that swimming pools were not covered by state accommodation laws. From Clifford Moore, Louis E. Saunders, 28 Concourse East, Jersey City 6, New Jersey, to Louis E. Saunders (6-17-48), Box B66, File "Discrimination in NJ Swimming Pools," Group II, NACCP, LOC; see the decision in the opinion of the Rosecliff case in *Valle v. Stengel*, 71 *New Jersey Law Review* 3 (6-10-48).

71. *Newark Herald* (8-27-38); *Newark Directory* (1964–65), p. 926.

72. "Mayor Raps Gang Attack," *Newark Evening News* (8-29-47).

NOTES TO CHAPTER 3

1. *New Jersey Afro-American* (9-27-47); *New Jersey Afro-American* (1-5-51). Mumford, "Double Vin New Jersey," p. 48.

2. *Official Master Plan of the City of Newark* (1947), pp. 20–22.

3. *North Jersey—Prospects and Development Problems, 1949*, pp. 1, 46.

4. *Newark News* (3-1-41); *Newark News* (10-30-37); *Newark News* (6-25-53); *Newark News* (3-10-53); traditional mortgages had required 25 percent as cash down payment, another 25 percent in trust, and 50 percent loaned at a high rate. During the New Deal, FHA guaranteed loans in New Jersey reached $1 million and by 1941, New Jersey was seventh in loans received, with California leading the nation. See *Newark News* (3-1-41).

5. Robert Burchwell, James Hughes, and George Sternlieb, "Housing Costs and Housing Restraints: Newark, New Jersey" (New Brunswick, NJ: Center for Urban Social Research, 1970), *report*, p. 25; *Economic Development of the Greater Newark Area* (1956), pp. 54–56, 73–75; on zoning, see State Planning Section, New Jersey Division of Planning, *Model Ordinance for Creating Municipal Government* (December 1953), Frances Loeb Library, Harvard University, p. 3; New Jersey State League of Municipalities, *Conference Issue Report* (November 1953), Frances Loeb Library, Harvard University, pp. 7–8; *New Jer-*

sey County and Regional Planning Enabling Act, Laws of 1935; New Jersey County and Regional Planning instructed the election of freeholders at a county planning board in 1953, *Housing Costs and Housing Restraints*, p. 25, Loeb Library, Harvard University.

6. *Municipal and County Planning Legislation and Procedures in New Jersey*, (March 1936), p. 11, 14, 52, Frances Loeb Library, Harvard University; *Economic Development of the Greater Newark Area* (1957), p. 26.

7. *Economic Development of the Greater Newark Area* (1956), pp. 54–56, 73–75, NHS.

8. New Jersey, Department of Commerce, *Rutgers BERC* (1975), table 47, p. 85.

9. Per capita income increased by 39.7 percent in the Greater Newark area; by 65.6 percent in the rest of New Jersey; and by 52.5 percent in the state. See *Economic Development of the Greater Newark Area*, pp. 42, 35, Frances Loeb Library, Harvard University.

10. "Characteristics of the Population," *Seventeenth Census of the United States*, vol. II, part 30, pp. 260–63. Hence, approximately 38 percent of African American residents earned less than $4,000 in 1959, whereas only 17 percent of white residents fall into that category; "Census of the Population," *Eighteenth Census of the United States*, vol. 1, pp. 32–68. On decline of white collar work in Newark, see Division of City Planning, *Master Plan of Newark* (1964); Clark Taylor, "Newark's Parasitic Suburbs," *Society* 9, no. 10 (19XX), p. 39.

11. *Economic Development of the Greater Newark Area: Trends and Prospects*, p. 95; *Governor's Commission on Civil Disorders* (final report, 1968), pp. 58–60; *Atlantic Monthly*, November 1956, pp. 12–13.

12. *Newark News* (1-19-35).

13. *Newark News* (2-26-35).

14. *Census of Housing*, table 18, (1950), vol. 30, part 4, p. 22; *Census of Housing* table F-12 (1970), pp. 150–80.

15. Thomas M. Shapiro, *The Hidden Cost of Being African-American: How the Wealth Perpetuates Inequality* (New York: Oxford University Press, 2004), pp. 106–7. Recently, the *New York Times* reported that black applicants—39.2 percent versus 12.9 percent of white—received far worse mortgage rates and terms than whites. See "Blacks Hit Hardest by Costlier Mortgages," *New York Times* (7-14-05).

16. *Newark News* (7-16-1950).

17. "Survey of Negro World War II Veterans and Vacancy and Occupancy of Dwelling Units Available to Negroes in Newark, New Jersey" (January–February 1947), pp. 2–6, University of Iowa Main Library, Government Documents; also see tables 1 and 3, pp. 4–5, ibid.

18. "Home Loan Act of 1949" (HH 1.7, H78), 81st Cong., 1st sess. (July 20, 1949).

19. *Newark News* (4-24-56).

20. Jackson, *Crabgrass Frontier,* pp. 110–30. Housing Authority of the City of Newark, "Public Housing Pays Dividends"(1945), NPL.

21. See Stanley Sangful, Investigative Report (4-10-60), Levittown Files, Lett Papers, NPL.

22. Investigative Record (4-13-60), Levittown Files, Lett Papers.

23. Investigative Record (3-27-60), Levittown Files, Lett Papers; Investigative Report (3-27-60), Levittown Files, Lett Papers. Investigative Record (3-28-60) and (3-29-60). See also John P. McGarrigle (salesman), Invesigative Record (4-15-60). On accepting integration in small doses, see comments on Investigator Record (3-13-60), (4-18-60), and (3-28-60).

24. On *Shelley,* see "Anti-Discrimination Policy," *Rutgers Law Review* 12, no. 4, pp. 574–75.

25. "Tentative Policy Statement" (10–11–51), Box 12, Folder 19, August Meier Papers, Schomburg Manuscripts, New York City.

26. *Newark News* (7-14-45); Arnold Hirsch, "Choosing Segregation: Federal Housing Policy between Shelley and Brown," in *From the Tenements to the Taylor Homes,* eds. John F. Bauman, Roger Biles, and Kristin M. Szylvian (University Park: Pennsylvania State University Press, 2000), pp. 206–25; Ronald Tobey, Charles Wetherell, and Jay Brigham, "Moving Out and Settling In: Residential Mobility, Home Owning, and the Public Enframing of Citizenship, 1921–1950," *American Historical Review* 95, no. 5 (December 1990), pp. 1395–1421.

27. *Newark News* (9-15-50).

28. *Newark News* (10-12-50).

29. *Newark News* (7-16-50); also see *Newark News* (2-8-53); "More Non-Whites," *Newark News* (1-23-66).

30. On ethnic groups, see summary of census and relief census for 1937 in Churchill, *Italians of Newark,* appendix 6; Kaplan, *Urban Renewal Politics,* pp. 151–52; on Clinton Hill response to dispersion, see "The New Jersey Housing Anti-Bias Law: Applicability to Non-State-Aided Developments," *Rutgers Law Review* 12, no. 4, p. 563.

31. *Newark News* (10-10-49); *Newark News* (10-12-50).

32. *Newark News* (10-12-50).

33. Legal scholarship at the time argued that *Shelley v. Kraemer* not only decided that racial covenants violated the Fourteenth Amendment but also denied legal redress in state action. William R. Ming, Jr., "Racial Restrictions and the Fourteenth Amendment: The Restrictive Covenant Cases," *University of Chicago Law Review* 16, no. 2 (Winter 1949), pp. 203–38; "Anti-Discrimination Policy," *Rutgers Law Review* 12, no. 4, pp. 574–75.

34. *Newark: A City in Transition,* vol. 2, p. 35. In Vailsburg, 54 percent reported there are "many things they dislike or would dislike about having these minority groups as their neighbors."

35. "Characteristics of the Population," in *Census of the Population* (1950) vol. 11, part 30, pp. 268–70; table 2, "Nativity and Citizenship of the Experienced Civilian Labor Force," in *Census of the Population* (1950), *Special Reports*, pp. 1B–28; "Rodino Predicts Public Housing for Non-Citizens," *Italian Tribune* (6-17-55); "Mayor Carlin Plans Job Boost by Speeding Newark Projects," *Italian Tribune* (4-11-58).

36. Quoted in *Newark News* (1-21-52); "NHA to Rebuild Newark's First Ward," *Italian Tribune* (1-25-52); Churchill, *Italians in Newark*, pp. 122–25, 150; "1st and 14th Ward Housing," *Italian Tribune* (4-18-52).

37. Quoted in Dominic J. Capeci, "Black-Jewish Relations in Wartime Detroit: The Marsh, Loving, Wolf Surveys and the Race Riot of 1943," in Maurianne Adams and John H. Bracey, eds., *Strangers & Neighbors: Relations between Blacks and Jews in the United States* (Amherst: University of Massachusetts Press, 1999), p. 398; *Newark: A City in Transition*, vol. 2, tables 5, 8. On rates of high school graduation for black youth moving into Weequahic, see *Newark: A City in Transition*, vol. 2, p. 44.

38. Sherry Ortner, *New Jersey Dreaming: Capital, Culture, and the Class of '58* (Durham, NC: Duke University Press, 2003), pp. 53, 60.

39. Ibid., p. 72.

40. "1st and 14th Ward Housing," *Italian Tribune* (4-18-52); "Italian Societies Support 1st Ward Housing Project," *Italian Tribune* (3-7-52).

41. "Housing Project to Be Named after Columbus," *Italian Tribune* (1-14-55). On Addonizio's promotion of federal urban renewal, see "All in a Week," *Italian Tribune* (1-23-53).

42. "Columbus Hospital Dedicates Its New $7,000,000 Building," *Italian Tribune* (5-8-55).

43. *Newark News* (7-31-55); Kaplan, *Urban Renewal Politics*, pp. 78–80.

44. *Newark Evening News* (6-30-66).

45. On Chicago, see Arnold Hirsch, "Massive Resistance in the Urban North: Trumbull Park, Chicago, 1953–1966," *Journal of American History* 82, no. 2 (September 1995), pp. 522–49; on Detroit, see Thomas Sugrue, "Crabgrass-Roots Politics: Race, Rights, and Reaction against Liberalism in the Urban North," *Journal of American History* 82 (September 1995), pp. 551–78; "Columbians," *Italian Tribune* (2-6-53), p. 9; "Rodino, Addonizio, Matturri, Vilanni Support Housing," *Italian Tribune* (2-8-52); on negative fallout, see "All in A Week," *Italian Tribune* (7-2-55).

46. See correspondence with Louis Danzig, who balances between liberal integrationists, white ethnic segregationists, and the hegemony of federal policy. From Arnold Harris to Louis Danzig (10-10-52), Box 12, Folder 4, August Meier Papers, Schomburg Manuscripts.

47. From Arnold Harris to Louis Danzig (11-10-52), p. 2, Box 12, Folder 4,

August Meier Papers, Schomburg Manuscripts New York City; "Study Wee-quahic Interracial Moves," *Newark News* (4-29-60), Box 12, Folder 11, ibid.

48. *City in Transition,* p. 1, NPL.

49. Ibid., p. 28, NPL.

50. "Talk to Greater Newark Council CIO re Endorsement of NAACP drive" (3-9-48), Box 11, Folder 3, August Meier Papers, Schomburg Manu-scripts; on the efforts for federal FEPC in 1950, see "Report on Civil Rights Mobilization" (January 15–17, 1950), pp. 1–3, Box 11, Folder 3, ibid.

51. "Mayor Carlin Host to City for Brotherhood Film Showing on Feb. 16," *Human Relations News* (February 1959), p. 1, Box 12, Folder 20, ibid.; "New-ark Points the Way to National F.E.P." (1950), memo, Box 12, Folder 20, ibid.

52. "Newark Presbytery Urges Non-Segregated Housing," *Newark News* (April 10, 1957), Box 12, Folder 4, August Meier Papers, Schomburg Manu-scripts.

53. "Holderman Warns on Discrimination," *Italian Tribune* (6-24-55),

54. "N.Y. Mayor Assails Libeling of Italians," *Italian Tribune* (3-13-53).

55. "Mayor Villani Will Proclaim Fair Employment Practice Week," *Italian Tribune* (2-13-53); *Italian Tribune* (2-27-53).

56. "Resident's Views on Inter-Group Relations and Statistical Tables," in *Newark: A City In Transition,* vol. 2.

57. Self, *American Babylon,* pp. 23–57; Heather Ann Thompson, *Whose Detroit? Politics, Labor, and Race in a Modern American City* (Ithaca, NY: Cor-nell University Press, 2001), pp. 9–27.

58. Memo (n.d.), Box 2, File 11, Urban Colored Commission Papers, NJSA.

59. Benjamin J. Davis, "The McCarran Act and the Negro Freedom Move-ment," *Freedomways,* vol. 3, no. 2 (Spring 1963), pp. 198–201.

60. On rent control, see "A Rent Control," *Italian Tribune* (12-10-54); "Clippings" (n.d.), Box 69, Folder 7, August Meier Papers, Schomburg Manu-scripts; "Richardson Slave Dies," *Newark News* (7-6-64); "Richardson Ticket," *Newark News* (7-9-64); "Demise of Frontier Ticket Causes More Speculation," *Newark Evening News* (7-10-64).

61. "Newark Branch" (1-10-52), p. 2, Box 11, File 2, Meier Papers, Schom-burg Manuscripts.

62. Harold Lett, biography, Harold Lett Papers, NPL; *Newark Afro-Ameri-can* (9-4-38). As early as the New Deal, Lett had called for the reform of sub-standard housing as a way to address "the root of the many evils of my race's social and economic existence," to quote a *Newark Afro-American* story on him; see *New Jersey Afro-American* (3-22-47). In the same manner, he pressed for the integration of the National Guard when it formed in 1947; see *New Jer-sey Afro-American* (1-13-45). Lett facilitated the integration of rental units in a transitional neighborhood, and showed pride when the "color bar [was] lifted";

see *Newark Afro-American* (12-24-45). Harold Lett, Assistant Director, Division Against Discrimination, N.J. Department of Education, 1060 Broad Street, Newark, NJ, memo, p. 2, Lett Papers; "Conference Announcement" (6-28-1956), Box 3, Lett Papers; flier for meeting at Moorestown Community House, at 16 East Main Street (May 17, 1960).

63. *Newark: A City in Transition*, vol. 2, p. 35. See note 34.

64. Andrew Wiese, *Places of Their Own: African-American Suburbanization in the Twentieth Century* (Chicago: University of Chicago Press, 2004), pp. 52, 53, 56, 140. Wiese finds the black female population higher than the male by 6 percent in Orange and by 18 percent in East Orange in 1920. In Montclair, he reports that 22 percent of men were employed in manufacturing, distinguishing it as a middle-class, albeit segregated, suburb since the beginning of migration there.

65. "Age of Employed Persons by Occupation, Color, and Sex for the State and for Standard Metropolitan Statistical Areas," in *Eighteenth Census of the United States,* "Characteristics of the Population," vol. 32, p. 524.

66. Kenneth Clark, *Dark Ghetto: The Dilemmas of Social Power* (New York: Harper, 1965); Alice O'Connor, *Poverty Knowledge: Social Science, Social Policy, and the Poor in Twentieth-Century U.S. History* (Princeton: Princeton University Press, 2001), pp. 200–4; for those promoting liberal policies, see *Daryl Michael Scott, Contempt and Pity: Social Policy and the Image of the Damaged Black Psyche, 1880–1996* (Chapel Hill: University of North Carolina Press, 1997), pp. 150–55.

67. "Newark Branch" (1-10-52), pp. 2, Box 11, Folder 2, August Meier Papers, Schomburg Manuscripts; "Resolution on Peace and against UMT and Peace-Time Conscription" (4-13-48), Box 11, Folder 3, ibid.; on fund-raising in the late 1940s, from Harry Hazlewood, Jr., to Fellow Workers (6-12-48), Box 11, Folder 3, ibid.; "Regular Monthly Meeting" (6-12-51), Box 11, Folder 5, ibid.

68. "Report of the Regional Conference, Philadelphia" (4-6-57), Box 12, Folder 9, ibid.

69. "Conversation with Philip Hoggard" (2-22-58), Box 139, Folder 1, ibid.

70. "Group Finds No Racial Bias in Tests for Vice Principals," *Newark News* (6-29-60), Box 12, Folder 11, ibid.; "Newark Branch, NAACP, Regular Monthly Meetings" (1-10-57), p. 1, Box 12, Folder 5, ibid.; "Branch Meeting" (1-10-57), p. 1, Box 12, Folder 5, ibid.

71. "Call to All New York City," memo (2-15-??), pp. 1–2, Box 84, Folder 4, ibid.

72. On Italian patronage at the NHA, see "NHA Nomination Stirs Protest," *Italian Tribune* (3-25-56); "Branch Meeting" (1-10-57), Box 12, Folder 5, August Meier Papers, Schomburg Manuscripts.

73. On Central Ward politics, see Price, "Afro-American Community," p.

161; Stanley B. Winters, "Charter Change and Civic Reform in Newark, 1953–1954," *New Jersey History* 118, nos. 1–2 (Spring/Summer 2000), pp. 35–65.

74. "Turner Faces Stiff Fight from Westbrooks," *Newark Evening News* (6-10-70).

75. "Potential Voting Population By Citizenship, Race, Nativity, and Sex For the City of Newark: 1930 and 1940," in *Sixteenth Census of the United States,* vol. 2, part 4, p. 925; Winters, "Charter Change and Civic Reform in Newark, 1953–1954," pp. 35–65.

76. Kaplan, *Urban Renewal Politics,* p. 52.

77. "All in a Week," *Italian Tribune* (4-16-54).

78. Ibid. (7-13-56).

79. Ibid.

80. From Mr. George Slaten, 51 South Munn Avenue, Newark, to Harold Lett (9-7-56), Box 3, Lett Papers, NPL. Legal scholars have not written extensively on housing racism between *Shelley* and *Jones v. Mayer.* On racial master narrative that assumes black inferiority, see Reginald Leamon Robinson, "The Racial Limits of the Fair Housing Act: The Intersection of Dominant White Images, the Violence of Neighborhoods, and the Master Narrative of Black Inferiority," *William and Mary Law Review* 37 (1995–96), pp. 68–159; Chris Bonastia, "Why Did Affirmative Action in Housing Fail during the Nixon Era? Exploring the 'Institutional Holes' of Social Policies," *Social Problems* 47, no. 4, pp. 536–539; Hugh Graham Davis, *The Civil Rights Era: Origins and Development of National Policy, 1960–1972* (New York: Oxford University Press, 1990); Thomas W. Hanchett, "The Other 'Subsidized Housing': Federal Aid to Suburbanization, 1940s–1960s," in Bauman, ed., *From Tenements to Taylor Homes,* pp.163–75; R. Allen Hays, *The Federal Government and Urban Housing: Ideology and Change in Public Policy,* 2d ed. (Albany, NY: SUNY Press, 1995).

81. Curvin, "The Persistent Minority," pp. 16–20; Robert Curvin, "Black Ghetto Politics in Newark before World War II," in Joel Schwartz and David Prosser, eds., *Cities of the Garden State: Essays in the Urban and Suburban History of New Jersey* (Dubuque, IA: Kendall/Hunt, 1977), p.147; for a critique of black politicians in the machine as more conservative than their constituency, see William J. Grimshaw, *Bitter Fruit: Black Politics and the Chicago Machine, 1931–1991* (Chicago: University of Chicago Press, 1992), pp. 107–112.

82. "Turner Urges Meeting to Spur Newark Housing," *Newark Star-Ledger* (1-22-64).

83. "Turner Eyes Rent-Strike for Newark," ibid. (5-20-64); "Council to Act on Bill Next Week," ibid. (6-9-65).

84. Douglass S. Massey and Nancy A. Denton, *American Apartheid: Segregation and the Making of the Underclass* (Cambridge, MA: Harvard University Press, 1993), p. 76.

85. Massey and Denton, *American Apartheid,* p. 48.

86. Douglass S. Massey and Shawn M. Kanaiaupuni, "Public Housing and the Concentration of Poverty," *Social Science Quarterly* 74, no. 1 (March 1993), pp. 109–22; on white resistance in Chicago, see Peter Rossi and Robert A. Dentler, *The Politics of Urban Renewal: The Chicago Findings* (New York: Free Press, 1961), pp. 180–81. On segregation due to FHA/Public Housing distribution in Chicago, see Edwin Berry and Walter Stafford, *The Racial Aspects of Urban Planning* (Chicago: Chicago Urban League, 1968), pp. 54–55; William Julius Wilson, *The Truly Disadvantaged: The Inner City, the Underclass, and Public Policy* (Chicago: University of Chicago Press, 1987).

87. *Newark News* (6-13-63); also see ibid. (6-14-63); this law was challenged in court and upheld by the State Supreme Court of New Jersey. See ibid. (11-14-63), (4-28-64), (5-19-64).

88. On Zion Towers, see Burchell et al., "Housing Costs and Housing Restraints," pp. 135–86; *Newark News* (7-25-50); Kaplan, *Urban Renewal Politics*, p. 65; "Non-Whites in Low-Rent Housing Projects Increase," *Newark News* (11-1-66); "Racial Ratio in City Homes Reverses Itself since 1950," ibid. (2-5-66).

89. *Newark: A City in Transition*, vol. 3, p. 39.

90. *Newark: A City in Transition*, vol. 2, p. 81.

91. "See "The Third V," Box 2, File 11, Urban Colored Commission, NJSA.

92. Membership list (4-5-57), Box 12, Folder 5, August Meier Papers, Schomburg Manuscripts.

NOTES TO CHAPTER 4

1. "Robert Curvin Interview" (4-23-71), Box 56, Folder 4, August Meier Papers, Schomburg Manuscripts.

2. Evelyn Brooks-Higginbotham, "Foreword," in Jeanne F. Theoharis and Komozi Woodard, eds., *Freedom North: Black Freedom Struggles in the North, 1940–1980* (New York: Palgrave, 2003), pp. viii–xiv.

3. Clayborne Carson, *In Struggle: SNCC and the Black Awakening of the 1960s* (Cambridge, MA: Harvard University Press, 1981); Barbara Ransby, *Ella Baker and the Black Freedom Movement: A Radical Democratic Vision* (Chapel Hill: University of North Carolina Press, 2003), pp. 344–52.

4. Thomas Bender, *Toward an Urban Vision: Ideas and Institutions in Nineteenth-Century America* (Lexington: University of Kentucky Press, 1975), pp. 151–57. On the genealogy of the new activist and their tactical repertoires, a number of literatures pertain. On Saul Alinsky's influence in ERAP and GROIN activism, see Jennifer Frost, *Interracial Movement of the Poor: Community Organizing and the New Left in the 1960s* (New York: New York University Press, 2002), pp. 170–71; for civil rights roots, such as "situational democracy" and the "outsider within," see Barbara Ransby, *Ella Baker*, pp. 105–46, 366–70; on

the organizing tradition and formal political systems, see Andrew Sable, *Ruling Passions: Political Offices and Democratic Ethics* (Princeton: Princeton University Press, 2001), pp. 266–76; the vast literature on the New Left has not really paid attention to the ERAP and "interracial movement of the poor" impulse; for example, SDS recruited students with announcements and application forms that read "Organize the Organized," NCUP application (n.d.), reel 14, SDS Papers.

5. A classic account of the rise of class politics in urban racial formations is the argument that individual organizing failed to build a "mass movement," but "collective action" succeeded. See Frances Fox Piven and Richard A. Cloward, *Poor People's Movements: Why They Success, How They Fail* (New York: Vintage, 1977), pp. 301–5; for the argument that white liberals demobilized black protest, see Thomas F. Jackson, "The State, the Movement, and the Urban Poor: The War on Poverty and Political Mobilization in the 1960s," in Michael Katz, ed., *The Underclass Debate: Views from History* (Princeton: Princeton University Press, 1993), pp. 403–39; Current synthesis of labor and civil rights focuses not on Old Left–style community organizing but bread-and-butter unionization and elections; see Bruce Nelson, *Divided We Stand: American Workers and the Struggle for Black Equality* (Princeton: Princeton University Press, 2001), pp. 246–50.

6. In Philadelphia and New York, the NAACP led many of the major campaigns for civil rights, rather than CORE. In Philadelphia, the NAACP, not CORE, debated the feasibility of adopting sit-ins, and eventually the new president of the branch embraced cultural nationalism and even rejected the programs of the Great Society. See Matthew Countryman, "Civil Rights and Black Nationalism in Philadelphia, 1940–1975" (Ph.D. dissertation, 1998, Duke University), pp. 73–75, 144–50, 460–65.

7. "Amended Constitution of the Congress of Racial Equality" (7-1-56), CORE Papers, reel 2; NAC memo (2-21-64), ibid., reel 1. CORE added regional representatives to the field representatives as its membership increased; policy statement (1965), ibid., reel 10.

8. "Some Audiences Which James Farmer Has Spoken to in Past," James Farmer Press Release (1961), ibid., reel 5.

9. "Fr. Carey Calls Freedom Rides 'An Experiment in Love' at Rally" (undated news clipping), ibid., reel 3; Rabbi Theodore Friedman, Cong. Beth El, South Orange (July 1961), ibid., reel 4; from Marian Hitner to James Farmer (6-17-62), ibid., reel #4.

10. Memo to James Farmer from Clara Coleman (undated), ibid., reel 4; from Paul Izenberg and Richard Max to James Farmer (8-20-62), ibid., reel 2; from Charles J. Hayes to James Farmer (1-3-62), ibid., reel 3; from John Ernest to James Farmer (11-4-61), ibid., reel 3; from Charles Sowell, Bethany Lodge, to James Farmer (7-20-61), from Robert Bender to James Farmer (11-5-1962), from Robert Bender to James Farmer (12-24-62), ibid., reel 1; "State Conven-

tion, Americans for Democratic Action of New Jersey" (12-1-62), ibid., reel 1. Also see Meier and Rudwick, *CORE*, pp. 58–59.

11. "Northern Negro Is Forum Topic" (undated newspaper clipping), CORE Papers, reel 3. Individuals from around New Jersey corresponded with national CORE and many applied to go south and work for civil rights. See from David Dennis to Robert Coleman (5-10-65), ibid., reel 9.

12. "Testimony of Robert Curvin" (10-17-67), Box 5, N.J. Gov. Comm., NJSA.

13. From Cardinal Cushing to James Farmer (8-30-62), CORE Papers, reel 3.

14. "Attendance: National Core Convention," Hampton House, Miami (6-28-62), ibid., reel 2; "1964 Convention Minutes, Election of Officers," ibid., reel 2. In Bergen County, Shirley Lacey, an African American woman, was elected chair. See Meier and Rudwick, *CORE*, p. 197. No religious affiliates were listed in a national directory for Newark, but for Trenton, Cranford, and Summit, see CORE Papers, reel 10.

15. "Robert Curvin" (July 1971), Box 56, Folder 4, August Meier Papers, Schomburg Manuscripts.

16. "Newsletter: Essex CORE," (n.d.), Box 87, Folder 3, ibid.

17. To Patricia Hainey, chairman of Northern New Jersey Chapter CORE (2-13-62), CORE Papers, reel 5; Meier and Rudwick, *CORE*, pp. 239–40; to Miss Edythe M. Jones (May 31, 1964), CORE Papers, reel 5, pp. 1–2.

18. "Robert Curvin Interview" (4-23-71), Box 56, Folder 4, August Meier Papers, Schomburg Manuscripts.

19. "Seattle CORE and A&P Reach Sweeping Employment Accord," memo, (n.d.), Box 84, Folder 12, ibid.; "Win Fair Job Pact with Michigan AAA," memo (1965), Box 84, Folder 13, ibid.; Black Muslims worked for the telephone company after AT&T desegregated in the mid-1960s.

20. Douglass Eldridge, "Inter-racial Action," *Newark News* (March 22, 1964); Howard A. Palley, "Community Action, Public Programs, and Youth Un-employment: A Case Study of Newark, New Jersey," *Journal of Negro Education* 36, no. 2 (Spring, 1967), p. 102.

21. "Robert Curvin Interview" (4-23-71), Box 56, Folder 4, August Meier Papers, Schomburg Manuscripts; Porambo, *No Cause for Indictment: An Autopsy of Newark* (New York: Holt, Rinehart, Winston, 1972), p. 81.

22. "2 Protests By CORE," *Newark News* (July 22 1963), Box 2, N.J. Gov. Comm.

23. "Diner Picketed," *Newark News* (7-20-63), Box 69, Folder 5, August Meier Papers, Schomburg Manuscripts.

24. On Malcolm X, see from James Farmer to Robert Shomer of Teaneck, New Jersey (9-21-62), CORE Papers, reel 5. On the Committee to Aid the Monroe Defendants, see memo to CORE Groups from James Farmer, "RE: Monroe Defense" (4–15–62), ibid., reel 5; for a different interpretation, see Simon

Wendt, "The Spirit, the People, the Courage, and the Shotguns: The Southern Black Freedom Struggle, Armed Resistance, and the Radicalization of the Congress of Racial Equality" (Master's thesis, University of Wisconsin, 2000), pp. 56–60.

25. "Parish Scouting Report," Bernice Farmerville (1964–1965), CORE Papers, reel 6, "Bogalusa, Louisiana Incident Report" (1-25 to 2-21, 1965), ibid., reel 6.

26. Meier and Rudwick, *CORE*, pp. 239–40; to Miss Edythe M. Jones (May 31, 1964), pp. 1–2, CORE Papers, reel 5.

27. "Newsletter: Essex CORE" (n.d.), Box 87, Folder 3, August Meier Papers, Schomburg Manuscripts.

28. *Newark News* (6-24-65), Box 2, N.J. Gov. Comm.

29. "CORE Sets Moves against N.J. Bell," *Newark Evening News* (n.d.), Box 87, Folder 3, August Meier Papers, Schomburg Manuscripts; "Information Bulletin" (3-23-64), Box 87, Folder 3, ibid.

30. For planning meetings, see notebook, Box 87, Folder 1, ibid.; CORE Immediate Release (6-11-64), Box 87, Folder 3, ibid.

31. From 127 Belmont Avenue, to Mrs. Patricia Hainey, Chairman, Northern New Jersey Core (2-13-62), CORE Papers, reel 5; Meier and Rudwick, *CORE*, p. 193.

32. From Ruby Doris Smith to James Farmer (12-20-62), reel 5, CORE Papers; from Robert A. Haber to Friend (5-28-62), ibid., reel 3; CORE was informed of the founding meeting at Port Huron, where SDS drafted its first manifesto, for example; estimates of membership in Meier and Rudwick, *CORE*, pp. 226–27.

33. Meier and Rudwick, *CORE*, p. 200. In interviews, both Phil Hutchings and Eric Mann have described much of Newark activism outside of NCUP as liberal and middle class.

34. "Interview with Robert Curvin" (August 2000).

35. Ibid.

36. From CORE headquarters to Mrs. Patricia Hainey, Chairman, Northern New Jersey Core (2-13-62), CORE Papers, reel 5; Meier and Rudwick, *CORE*, pp. 193, 29. CORE Statement of Purpose, for example, rejected the idea of a Negro problem, and argued rather that it was a "human problem which could be eliminated only through the joint efforts of all believers in the brotherhood of man."

37. "Robert Curvin Interview" (January 1969), Box 56, Folder 4, August Meier Papers, Schomburg Manuscripts; "Telephone Interview with Robert Curvin" (5-22-71), Box 45, Folder 4, ibid.

38. "Interview with Robert Curvin" (January 1969), Box 56, Folder 4, August Meier Papers, Schomburg Manuscripts.

39. "Interview with Robert Curvin" (April 2–3, 1971), ibid.

40. Margaret Anne Shapiro, "Race, Class, and Ideology: The Black Community's Response to Three Organizations in Newark, N.J., 1960–1970" (Senior thesis, Radcliffe College, 1977), pp. 35–40.

41. Ibid, pp. 35, 40.

42. Michael B. Katz, Mark J. Stern, and Jamie J. Fader, "The New African-American Inequality," *Journal of American History*, June 2005, pp. 100–101.

43. "Interview with Robert Curvin" (4-23-71), Box 56, Folder 4, August Meier Papers, Schomburg Manuscripts.

44. From Robert Carey to Richard Haley (4-20-65), CORE Papers, reel 12; "Position Paper by S. M. Miller" (May 1963), ibid.

45. See Lawrence Stewart's recollection of a CORE activist in *The Black Uprisings: Newark and Detroit, 1967* (New York: Merit, 1968), p. 9.

46. "Interview with Robert Curvin" (April 2–3, 1971), Box 56, Folder 4, August Meier Papers, Schomburg Manuscripts.

47. "Conversation with Bob Curvin" (11-20-65), ibid.; "Interview with Curvin" (9-17-71), p. 2, ibid.

48. "Conversation with Bob Curvin" (11-20-65), ibid.; "Interview with Curvin" (9-17-71), p. 2, ibid.

49. Meier and Rudwick, *CORE*, pp. 73–73.

50. "Robert Curvin Interview" (April 2–3, 1971), Box 56, Folder 4, August Meier Papers, Schomburg Manuscripts.

51. Wini Breines, *Community Organization and the New Left, 1962–1968: The Great Refusal* (South Hadley, MA: Praeger, 1982), p. 26; for a similar analysis, see Sara Evans, *Personal Politics: The Roots of Women's Liberation in the Civil Rights Movement and the New Left* (New York: Knopf, 1979).

52. David Milton Gerwin, "The End of Coalition: The Failure of Community Organizing in Newark in the 1960s" (Ph.D. dissertation, Columbia University, 1998), p. 10.

53. Alan Haber, "Non-Exclusionism: The New Left and the Democratic Left" (n.d.) reel 37, SDS Papers; From Michael Padwee to Helen Gray (2-27-65), reel 7, ibid. For a concise summary, see Gerwin, "The End of Coalition," pp. 19–20.

54. Al Haber and Sandra Carson, "Civil Rights in the North," pp. 2, 3, 4, reel 37, SDS Papers.

55. "Newark" (1965), reel 10, ibid.

56. "Meeting of Economic Committee of the National Council" (1-16-64), ibid.

57. From Nanci Hollander to Michael Harrington (3-31-64), reel 10, ibid.; from Michael Padwee to Helen Gray (2-27-65), reel 7, ibid.; O'Connor, *Poverty Knowledge*, pp. 135, 164.

58. "Students Organizing the Poor in North Cities," (n.d.) reel 14, series 2-B, no. 76, SDS Papers; on SDS and Michael Harrington. See also Tom Hayden,

Reunion: A Memoir (New York: Random House, 1988), pp. 89–93; *Newark News* (2-5-65).

59. Tom Hayden, *Reunion*, pp. 25–52, 98.

60. Joanne Grant published a story on Hayden that recited the almost apocryphal first encounter; see "Students Organizing the Poor in North Cities" (n.d.), reel 14, series 2-B, no. 76, SDS Papers. On SDS and Michael Harrington, see Hayden, *Reunion*, pp. 89–93; *Newark News* (2-5-65).

61. Gerwin, "The End of Coalition," p. 133, interview with Winters, p. 3; *Newark: City in Transition*, vol. 2, pp. 63–64. Opinion survey. Of course in the same survey in 1959, only 7 percent identified police brutality, an issue that would devastate the political landscape over the next decade.

62. Howard A. Palley, "Community Action, Public Programs, and Youth Unemployment: A Case Study of Newark, New Jersey," *Journal of Negro Education* 36, no. 2 (Spring 1967), p. 107; Frederich E. Ewing, *An Outline of Activity Relating to the War on Poverty in Newark, New Jersey* (Newark: Bureau of Municipal Research, 1965).

63. "1199 Drops Out," newsletter, no. 14, p. 2, reel 14, SDS Papers.

64. Gerwin, "The End of Coalition," p. 96; interview with Winters, pp. 2–3.

65. "Evaluation of Initial 6 Weeks of the Project" (1964), p. 2, reel 10, SDS Papers; "ERAP Evaluation," reel 10, SDS Papers; "NCUP Report to ERAP" (1965), p. 3, reel 10, ibid.

66. "Apartments for Rent," newsletter, no. 4, p. 2, reel 14, ibid. George Sternlieb, *The Tenement Landlord* (New Brunswick: Rutgers University Press, 1966), pp. 62, 73.

67. *Newark: A City in Transition*, vol. 3, p. 17; Sternlieb, *The Tenement Landlord*, pp. 150, 75, 131, 137. The report concluded that the black renters "may be getting poorer facilities for more money."

68. Sternlieb, *The Tenement Landlord*, pp. 180, 183.

69. Gerwin, "The End of Coalition," pp. 89, 90.

70. Kevin M. Kruse, *White Flight: Atlanta and the Making of Modern Conservatism* (Princeton: Princeton University Press, 2005), pp. 50–77.

71. "WE DECLARE WAR ON RATS AND ROACHES" (8-21-n.d.), reel 14, SDS Papers.

72. Not until quite late is Hayden swept up in his celebrity, on his way out of Newark. For the media-created radical-celebrities argument, see Todd Gitlin, *The Whole World Was Watching: Mass Media and the Making and Unmaking of the New Left* (Berkeley: University of California Press, 1980), pp. 180–204; Frost, *Interracial Movement of the Poor*, pp. 80, 115.

73. "New Left versus the Alinsky Model, memo (n.d.), Box 84, Folder 8, August Meier Papers, Schomburg Manuscripts.

74. Ibid.

75. Frost, *Interracial Movement of the Poor*, p. 72.

76. "Interview with Stanley Winters," p. 1; Gerwin, "The End of Coalition," p. 90.

77. From P. Bernard Nortman, Chief Office of Economic Development to Mayor Hugh Addonizio (8-15-67), Box 1, N.J. Gov. Hughes Comm., NJSA; News Clipping, Box 2, Hughes Comm., NJSA.

78. *Newark News* (4-21-67), Box 3, ibid.

79. From Detective Wm. Millard to Lt. Ferrente (10-21-64), Box 2, ibid.

80. Flyer, anonymous (n.d.), ibid.

81. Gerwin, "The End of Coalition," p. 111; interview with Winters, p. 3.

82. Ibid., pp. 113, 119; "Housing Demands," flyer (n.d.), Box 2, N.J. Gov. Hughes Comm., NJSA.

83. From Larry Gordon to Vernon Grizzard (n.d.), reel 37, SDS Papers.

84. "S.D.S. Worklist Mailing," vol. 1, no. 9 (10-17-64), reel 5, series 2A, no. 48, ibid.

85. On Jefferson, see Porambo, *No Cause for Indictment,* p. 206.

86. "Stand by Mary Martin," flyer (n.d.), reel 14, SDS Papers. The Brown case is summarized in "Worklist Mailing," reel 5, series 2A, no. 48, ibid.; also see "SDS Worklist Mailing, vol. II, no. 2 (1-23-65), reel 5, *SDS Papers;* from Tom Hayden to Harold K. Schultz (2-24-65), reel 14, ibid.

87. "Civil Rights and Political Action: A Case Study of Newark," Box 69, Folder 6, August Meier Papers, Schomburg Manuscripts.

88. "Stand by Mary Martin," flyer (n.d.), reel 14, SDS Papers. The Brown case is summarized in "Worklist Mailing," reel 5, series 2A, no. 48, ibid.

89. Tom Hayden and Carl Wittman, "An Interracial Movement of the Poor" (1966), reel 37, ibid.

90. Ibid.

91. Frost, *Interracial Movement of the Poor,* pp. 110, 114.

92. *Newark News* (1965), Box 2, N.J. Gov. Hughes Comm., NJSA; "Pickets Still Dissatisfied after Meeting with Mayor," *Newark Star Ledger* (April 1965), reel 14, SDS Papers; "10 Arrested in Noisy Lie-In at Newark Mayor's Office," *Newark News* (4-6-65), ibid.

93. "Newark" (1965), p. 2, reel 10, ibid.

94. "Newark Report to ERAP Executive Committee" (8–8-64), reel 10, ibid.; "Newark," "Hot Summer" (1965), ibid.

95. From Mrs. L. Patterson to Arabian Stompers, CHNC, reel 14, SDS Papers; "News," ibid.; "Let's Help Jesse" (n.d.), ibid.

96. *Newark News* (n.d., 1965), Box 2, N.J. Gov. Hughes Comm., NJSA. The city reporter Douglass Eldridge covered Hayden for the *Newark News,* and reported of the activists' criticism; see *Newark News* (2-5-65).

97. *Newark News* (2-5-65); Gerwin, "The End of Coalition," p. 133; interview with Winters, p. 3.

98. "Newark Community Union Project" (n.d., 1966), Box 2, N.J. Gov. Hughes Comm., NJSA.

99. Porambo, *No Cause for Indictment,* pp. 206–7.

100. "There Is No Law for Your Kind of People," (n.d.), reel 14, SDS Papers; "SDS Worklist Mailing," vol. II, no. 2 (1-23-65), reel 6, ibid.; NCUP report, p. 4, reel 14, ibid.

101. Douglass Eldridge, "Community Union Project Is Source of Controversy," *Newark News* (2-5-65).

102. Flyer, "WE WERE AT KLEIN'S" (n.d.), Box 2, N.J. Gov. Hughes Comm., NJSA; "NCUP Newark, No.5" (n.d.), ibid.

103. "Brutality at Klein's," series 2-B (n.d.), reel 14, SDS Papers.

104. "Rent-Strike Leader Faces Jail," *Militant* (2-15-65), ibid.; "Who Are the Outsiders," flier (n.d.), series 2-B, ibid.; "Clyde Wright Wrong: Admits Guilt in Klein's Case," reprinted by NCUP (n.d.), ibid.

105. "CORE Supports NCUP," newsletter no. 16 (n.d.), ibid. The ERAP projects typically did not enter protest of police brutality; see Frost, *An Interracial Movement of the Poor,* pp. 134–35, 124, 152, 157–58.

106. Interview with Robert Curvin (7-28-2000), in author's possession.

107. "Conversation with Curvin" (11-20-65), Box 56, Folder 4, August Meier Papers, Schomburg Manuscripts.

108. "Interview with Robert Curvin" (January 1969), ibid. From F. B. McKissick to August Meier (5-29-65), Box 84, Folder 11, ibid.

109. Interview with Phil Hutchings (6-28-2004).

110. Meier and Rudwick, *CORE,* p. 384; "Interview with Robert Curvin" (January 1969), Box 56, Folder 4, August Meier Papers, Schomburg Manuscripts.

111. Flyer (3-7-65), "A PEACEFUL NON-VIOLENT DEMONSTRATION AND RALLY; Military Park—Newark, New Jersey, Wednesday, July 21, 1965—8 P.M," Box 2, N.J. Gov. Hughes Comm., NJSA; "Newark" (1965), reel 10, SDS Papers.

112. Flyer (n.d.), Box 2, N.J. Gov. Hughes Comm., NJSA.

113. Gerwin, "End of Coalition," pp. 119, 121; "Pickets Plans Set For CORE," News, no. 14, reel 14, SDS Papers.

114. Tom Hayden, *Trial* (New York: Holt, Rinehart, and Winston, 1970), pp. 150–58.

115. *Newark: City in Transition,* table 13; Alexis de Tocqueville, *Democracy in America* (New York: Harper and Row, 1966), p. 311. On public sphere and urban democracy, see Robert A. Beauregard, "Democracy, Storytelling, and the Sustainable City," in *Story and Sustainability: Planning, Practice, and Possibility for American Cities,* ed. Barbara Eckstein and James A. Throgmorton (Cambridge, MA: MIT Press, 2003), pp. 65–77; *The Black Public Sphere: A Public*

Culture Book, ed. The Black Public Sphere Collective (New York: University of Chicago Press, 1995).

NOTES TO CHAPTER 5

1. Police Department, Newark, N.J., "Investigation into Possible Criminal Conspiracy During the Riots," p. 66, NPL; Porambo, *No Cause for Indictment,* p. 104.

2. David John Olson, "Racial Violence and City Politics: The Political Response to Civil Disorders in Three American Cities" (Ph.D. dissertation, University of Wisconsin, 1971), p. 123.

3. *Report for Action: New Jersey Governor's Commission on Civil Disorders* (State of New Jersey, 1968), p. 35.

4. *Report for Action,* p. 10.

5. Virginia M. Esposito, ed., *Conscience and Community: The Legacy of Paul Ylvisaker* (New York: Peter Lang, 1999), p. 215. From PNY to Messrs. R. Sargent Shriver (2-7-64), Box 11, PNY Papers, Harvard University Archives; on poverty, see PNY, "Black Politics" (2-13-64), Box 11, 1963-64; on poverty, see from YHWH to PNY (2-17-64), Box 11, PNY Papers.

6. From PNY to Messrs. R. Sargent Shriver (2-7-64), Box 11, PNY Papers, HUA. A few observers understood that a main problem with Ylvisaker's sociology of the riots was that it rewarded civil disobedience; see memo (1963–64), ibid.

7. "Newspaper clippings" (12-5-66), ibid.

8. "New Jersey Dept. of Community Affairs," memo (7-7-67), p. 8, Box 12, ibid.

9. Memo, New Jersey, Dept. of Community Affairs (7-7-67), p. 1, ibid.; from PNY to Hubert Humphrey (9-18-68), Box 12, Folder 11, ibid.

10. Memo (2-13-64), Box 11, ibid.; *U.S. Report of the National Advisory Commission,* p. 65.

11. E. S. Evans, "Ghetto Revolts and City Politics," in Louis H. Masotti and Don R. Bowen, eds., *Riots and Rebellion: Civil Violence in the Urban Community* (New York: Sage, 1968), pp. 398–402; Margaret J. Abudu Stark, "Some Empirical Patterns in a Riot Process," *American Sociological Review* 39, no. 6 (December 1974), pp. 872–73; Anita Monte and Gerald Leinwand, *Riots* (New York: Pocket, 1970); Peter Rossi, *Ghetto Revolts* (New York: Aldine, 1970); Edward Countryman, "Moral Economy, Political Economy and the American Bourgeois Revolution," in Adrian Randall and Andrew Charlesworth, eds., *Moral Economy and Popular Protest: Crowds, Conflict, and Authority* (London: Macmillan, 2000), pp. 158–60; E. P. Thompson, "The Moral Economy of the English Crowd in the Eighteenth Century," reprinted in E. P. Thompson, *Customs in Common* (London: Merlin, 1991), pp. 185–258.

12. Monte and Leinwand, *Riots,* pp. 17, 23.

13. Timothy Bates, "Black Economic Well-Being since the 1950s," *Review of Black Political Economy* 12, no. 4 (Spring 1984), pp. 6–8.

14. On urbanization leading to nationalism, see Woodard, *A Nation within A Nation,* pp. 10–12; on dialectic of metropolitanization and suburbanization leading to nationalism, see Self, *American Babylon,* pp. 25–35.

15. *Newark: New Jersey: Population and Labor Force* (New Jersey Department of Labor, 1967), p. 32.

16. *Newark, New Jersey: Population and Labor Force,* p. 28.

17. *Report for Action,* p. 66.

18. Ibid., pp. 70, 78.

19. *Newark, New Jersey: Population and Labor Force,* p. 13.

20. Michael B. Katz, Mark J. Stern, and Jamie J. Fader, "The New African-American Inequality," *Journal of American History* 92, no. 1 (June 2005), p. 97.

21. Timothy Bates, "Black Economic Well-Being since the 1950s," *Review of Black Political Economy* 12, no. 4 (Spring 1984), p. 17.

22. *Newark, New Jersey: Population and Labor Force,* p. 7.

23. On postwar intersection of wealth and race, see Jacqueline Jones, "Southern Diaspora: Origins of the Northern Underclass," in *The Underclass Debate: Views from History,* ed. Michael Kates (Princeton: Princeton University Press, 1993), pp. 27–54; Melvin L. Oliver and Thomas M. Shapiro, *Black Wealth/White Wealth: A New Perspective on Racial Inequality* (New York: Routledge, 1997); Dalton Conley, *Being Black, Living in the Red: Race, Wealth, and Social Policy in America* (Berkeley: University of California Press, 1999); Timothy Bates, "Black Economic Well-Being since the 1950s," *Review of Black Political Economy* 12, no. 4 (Spring 1984), p. 17.

24. *Report for Action,* pp. 130–131.

25. Ibid., p. 62. On the Great Society, spending, and riots, see Robert Dallek, *Flawed Giant: Lyndon Johnson and His Times, 1961–1973* (New York: Oxford University Press, 1998), pp. 403, 412.

26. *Report for Action,* p. 65.

27. Ibid., p. 86.

28. For a sampling of the sociological analysis, including social service and education, see T. M. Tomlinson, "The Development of a Riot Ideology among Urban Negroes," *American Behavioral Scientist* 11, no. 4 (March–April 1968), pp. 20–28; N. S. Caplan and J. M. Paige, "A Study of Ghetto Rioters," *Scientific American* 219, no. 2 (August 1968), pp. 15–21; H. E. Ransford, "Isolation, Powerlessness, and Violence: A Study of Attitudes and Participation in the Watts Riot," *American Journal of Sociology* 73 (1968), pp. 581–91; Betty Edison, "White Public Opinion in an Age of Disorder," in David Boesel and Peter H. Rossi, eds., *Cities under Siege: An Anatomy of the Ghetto Riots, 1964–1968* (New York: Basic Books, 1971), pp. 389–405.

29. Howard A. Palley, "Community Action, Public Programs, and Youth Unemployment: A Case Study of Newark, New Jersey," *Journal of Negro Education* 36, no. 2 (Spring 1967), p. 102.

30. *Report for Action*, p. 78.

31. *Newark News* (n.d.), clippings, Box 3, N.J. Gov. Hughes Comm., NJSA; quoted in Porambo, *No Cause for Indictment*, p. 86.

32. "CORE Demands as to School Board," memo (n.d.), Box 2, N.J. Gov. Hughes Comm., NJSA.

33. *Report for Action*, p. 4.

34. From Det. William Millard, Det. Junious Hedgepeth to Dominick Spina, Re: Board of Education Meeting Council, President and Chairman of the Board Harold Ashby (5-23-67), Box 1, N.J. Gov. Hughes Comm., NJSA.

35. Flyer (n.d.), Box 2, N.J. Gov. Hughes Comm., NJSA; Porambo, *No Cause for Indictment*, pp. 86–87.

36. Flyer, "Newark Community Union Project; We Were At Klein's" (n.d.), Box 2, N.J. Gov. Hughes Comm., NJSA.

37. Hayden, *Reunion*, p. 149.

38. Flyer, "Great Society" (n.d.), Box 2, N.J. Gov. Hughes Comm., NJSA.

39. Frost, *Interracial Movement of the Poor*, pp. 34, 37, 84.

40. Gerwin, "The End of Coalition," pp. 143, 166.

41. Hayden, *Reunion*, p. 145.

42. "Mrs. Billie Lassiter," in "A View of the Poverty Program," p. 16, Littauer Library, Harvard University.

43. Flyer, "Great Society" (n.d.), Box 2, N.J. Gov. Hughes Comm., NJSA.

44. On Bessie Smith, see Hayden, *Reunion*, p. 147; Glassman quoted in Frost, *An Interracial Movement of the Poor*, pp. 129–30; on the structure of CAP, see Gerwin, "End of Coalition," pp. 165–70; *Gov. Select Commission on Civil Disorder, Final Report and Summary* (1968), p. 35; *New Jersey Afro-American* (8-8-67).

45. "Mrs. Billie Lassiter," in "A View of the Poverty Program," p. 16.

46. "Mrs. Joyce Wells," in ibid., p. 18; for a summary of Plainfield disturbances, see *U.S. National Advisory Commission Report*, pp. 41–45; similar dynamics shaped the United Community Corporation, headed by Cyril Tyson and partly funded by Kenneth Clark's HARYOU project.

47. Hayden, "A View of the Poverty Program," p. 20.

48. "Civil Rights and Political Action: A Case Study of Newark," Box 69, Folder 6, August Meier Papers, Schomburg Manuscripts.

49. Hochschild, *Facing Up the American Dream*, p. 139.

50. Ibid., pp. 74–75.

51. Quoted in Michael Belknap, ed., *Civil Rights, the White House, and the Justice Department, 1945–1968* (New York: Garland, 1988), pp. 23–26; Olson, "Racial Violence and City Politics," p. 2; *Newark Evening News* (9-29-64).

52. Frantz Fanon, *The Wretched of the Earth* (New York: Evergreen, 1963), pp. 36–37, 88, 43, 93.

53. Stokely Carmichael, "Toward Black Liberation," *Massachusetts Review* 7 (Autumn 1966); Charles Hamilton, "Another Definition," *New York Times Magazine,* April 14, 1968.

54. "Newark to Hear Stokely Carmichael," *Newark News* (8-19-66); "Princeton Students Hear Carmichael," *Newark News* (9-23-66); "Carmichael Bids Negroes Take Control of Newark," *Newark News* (8-26-66); "At Fund Raiser," *Newark News* (8-26-68): "Britain Orders Carmichael Ban," *Newark News* (7-28-67); "Carmichael in N.J. Rips Poverty Fight" (8-25-66); "Move to Bar Carmichael Unsupported," *Newark News* (8-24-68). For continuing coverage after the riots, see "Ban Carmichael Book," *Newark News* (6-23-68); "Carmichael Again Raps Role of U.S.," *Newark News* (9-8-67); "800 Hear Carmichael," *Newark News* (8-27-68). On Rustin see "Rustin Hits Carmichael," *Newark News* (12-17-66).

55. John F. Hatchett, "The Moslem Influence among American Negroes," *Journal of Human Relations* 1, no. 4 (Summer 1962), pp. 375–81; James Holden et al. v. Board of Education of the City of Elizabeth, etc., *New Jersey Supreme Court,* A-62 (1-24-66), 216 A.2d. 387, *Race Relations Law Reporter* 11, no. 1 (Spring 1966), pp. 185–188.

56. "Interview with Holman," reel 8: Komoz, Woodard and Randolph Boehm, eds., *The Black Power Movement, Part 1, Amiri Baraka, From Black Arts to Black Radicalism* (Bethesda, MD: University Publications of America, 2000), p. 3.

57. Calvin C. Hernton, "White Liberals and Black Muslims," *Negro Digest* 12, no. 12 (October 1963), pp. 3–9; "City Apprehensive over Muhammad," *Newark News* (8-25-59), Box 69, Folder 5, August Meier Papers, Schomburg Papers Manuscripts.

58. Hernton, "White Liberals and Black Muslims," *Negro Digest,* pp. 3–9; "City Apprehensive over Muhammad," *Newark News* (8-25-59), Box 69, Folder 5, August Meier Papers, Schomburg Manuscripts; Elijah Muhammad, "What the Black Muslims Believe," *Negro Digest* 1, no. 1 (November 1963), pp. 3–7.

59. Quoted in Porambo, *No Cause for Indictment,* p. 99.

60. "Interview with Richard Wesley," p. 10, reel 8, in Woodard and Boehm, eds., *The Black Power Movement Part 1.* Newark earned a reputation among progressive whites and students as a city of change, both because of its history of white progressives in Clinton Hill and later. It maintained that reputation through the 1960s at centers of student radicalism like Columbia University.

61. See Robin Kelley, "RAM," in Eddie Glaude, ed., *Is It Nation Time? Contemporary Essays on Black Power and Black Nationalism* (Chicago: University of Chicago Press, 2002), pp. 82, 86; *Investigation into Riots,* Newark, New

Jersey Police Department (1967), p. 102, NPL.Official discussion of RAM in Newark, *Investigation into Riots*, p. 65; on small underground factions of nationalists in Newark, see correspondence with Bashir Hameed, Jericho Movement, in author's possession; RAM is not mentioned in the leading study of black nationalism in Newark by Woodard, *Nation within a Nation*; Scot Brown, "The U.S. Organization, Black Power Vanguard Politics, and the United Front Ideal: Los Angeles and Beyond," *Black Scholar* 31, nos. 3–4, pp. 21–28.

62. Nathan Wright, mss. (12–5-69); Miscellaneous Publications, p. 16, Box 1, Lett Papers, NPL.

63. Nathan Wright, mss. (12–5-69), p. 4, Box 1, Lett Papers.

64. From Detectives to Police Director Dominic Spina, Re: Blackman's Volunteer Army of Liberation (5-3-67), Box 2, N.J. Gov. Hughes Comm., NJSA; "Testimony of Dominic Spina," p. 7, Box 5, N.J. Gov. Hughes Comm, NJSA.

65. Ibid., "Investigation into Possible Criminal Conspiracy," pp. 41, 56–57, Box 5, N.J. Gov. Hughes Comm., NJSA.

66. From Det. Junious T. Hedgepeth to Dominc Spina, "We Ain't Gonna Move Rally," investigation report (5-22-67), Box 1, N.J. Gov. Hughes Comm., NJSA.

67. "Interview with Richard Wesley," reel 8, pp. 30, 28, in Woodard and Boehm, eds., *The Black Power Movement Part 1*.

68. *Report for Action*, p. 14.

69. *Newark News* (4-21-67), Box 3, N.J. Gov. Hughes Comm., NJSA.

70. *NJ Riot Chronology; Some Preliminary Signs of Discontent* (5-22-67), Box 3, N.J. Gov. Hughes Comm., NJSA.

71. "Memo" (n.d.), Box 1, N.J. Gov. Hughes Comm., NJSA; *Newark News* (5-25-67), clippings, Box 1, N.J. Gov. Hughes Comm., NJSA.

72. From Paul Caffrey, Deputy Police Chief, Re: Full Employment Practices Committee, to Dominic Spina, (7-26-64), box 2, N.J. Gov. Hughes Comm., NJSA; From Det. William Millard, Det. Junious Hedgepeth To Dominick Spina (5-23-67), box 1, N.J. Gov. Hughes Comm., NJSA.

73. Angela Dillard, "Religion and Radicalism: The Reverend Albert B. Cleage, Jr., and the Rise of Black Christian Nationalism in Detroit," in Woodard and Theoharris, eds., *Freedom North*, pp. 166–67; Scot Brown, "The Politics of Culture," in ibid., pp. 238–39.

74. *Report for Action*, p. 16.

75. "Testimony of Robert Curvin" (10-17-67), p. 80, Box 5, N.J. Gov. Hughes Comm., NJSA.

76. From Detective Junious T. Hedgepeth to Dominic Spina, Re: "We Ain't Gonna Move Rally," investigation (5-22-67), Box 1, N.J. Gov. Hughes Comm., NJSA.

77. *Report for Action*, pp. 25–26.

78. "Testimony of Benjamin Franklin" (10-23-67), vol. 4, p. 88, N.J. Gov. Comm., PUF.

79. "Interview with Phil Hutchings," pp. 1–2.

80. "Annual Report of the Legal Redress Committee," from Bertram C. Bland to Newark Branch of the National Association for the Advancement of Colored People (n.d.), Box 11, Folder 2, Meier Papers, Schomburg Manuscripts.

81. *New Jersey Afro-American* (2-23-46).

82. *Newark Evening News* (4-7-43). Clippings File (n.d.), Box 3, N.J. Gov. Hughes Comm., NJSA.

83. "Pickets Seek Spina Ouster," *Newark Evening News* (1-30-66).

84. "Testimony of Dominick Spina" (11-6-67), p. 59, Box 5, N.J. Gov. Hughes Comm., NJSA; "Press Release" (June 1962), *Newark News*, clippings file, NPL. On Newark Lions, *Newark News* (4-15-67).

85. *Newark News* (8-11-62).

86. Ibid. (11-24-63), (10-10-63).

87. *Newark: City in Transition*, vol. 2, p. 102; "Negro Detectives Spina Plans More," *Newark News* (9-10-62); on corruption in the Addonizio administration, see Porambo, *No Cause for Indictment*, pp. 75–77.

88. Cohen and Taylor, *American Pharaoh: Mayor Richard J. Daley*, pp. 326–64.

89. Porambo, *No Cause for Indictment*, p. 45.

90. Flyer, "Stop Police Brutality" (6-14-67), Box 2, N.J. Gov. Hughes Comm., NJSA; Porambo, *No Cause for Indictment*, pp. 39–41, 42, 51.

91. Porambo, *No Cause For Indictment*, pp. 42–43; interview with NGUVU, Woodard and Boehm, eds., *The Black Power Movement Part 1*, reel 8, p. 1.

92. Christopher Meeves, ed., *The Lynching of Emmet Till: A Documentary Narrative* (Charlottesville: University of Virginia Press, 2003), p. 258.

93. See notes on news clippings, *Newark News* (8-22-65); ibid. (8-24-65), (6-27-65), in Box 69, Folder 7, Meier Papers, Schomburg Manuscripts.

94. *Newark News* (12-19-65), (11-16-70). On Spina and black Muslims, see ibid. (1962), clippings files, NPL; ibid. (10-27-65).

95. *Report for Action*, pp. 25–26.

96. *Newark News* (5-25-72), (5-3-72).

97. Interview with Baraka, pp. 7–8, reel 8, in Woodard and Boehm, eds., *The Black Power Movement Part I*.

98. Ibid.

99. Leroi Jones, *Home: Social Essays* (Hopewell, N.J.: Ecco, 1966, 1998), pp. 238–50; Hettie Jones, *How I Became Hettie Jones* (New York: E. P. Dutton, 1990), pp. 222–23.

100. "Investigation into Possible Criminal Conspiracy during Riots of July 1967" (1967), N.J. Gov. Hughes Comm., NJSA, pp. 34–36; Baraka, *Raze,*

Raise, Race, Rays, pp. 59, 65; his manifesto for Newark nationalism was published as "The Legacy of Malcolm X, and the Coming of the Black Nation," reprinted in *The Leroi Jones/Amiri Baraka Reader,* pp. 161–63.

101. Stokely Carmichael (Kwame Ture), *Ready for the Revolution: The Life and Struggles of Stokely Carmichael* (New York: Scribner's, 2003), p. 537.

102. Harry J. Elam, Jr., *Taking It to the Streets: The Social Protest Theater of Luis Valdez and Amiri Baraka* (Ann Arbor: University of Michigan, 1997), pp. 56–57, 130–31.

103. Robert Curvin, "The Persistent Minority: The Black Political Experience in Newark" (Ph.D. dissertation, Princeton University, 1975), p. 62.

NOTES TO CHAPTER 6

1. *Report for Action,* pp. 138–39; *U.S. National Advisory Report,* p. 100.

2. "Investigation into Possible Criminal Conspiracy during Riots of July 1967," p. 66.

3. "The White House: Presidents Address to the Nation on Civil Disorders" (7-27-67), in Michael Belknap, ed., *Civil Rights, the White House, and the Justice Department* (New York: Garland, 1991), pp. 95, 137–138. A month before the riots, the president promised more aid and programs to prevent further "racial violence"; see *The Johnson Presidential Press Conferences,* vol. 2 (New York: Coleman, 1978), p. 779; Robert L. Galantucci, John K. Gifford, David H. Hellman, and Fern S. Seigel, "Riots and Municipal Authority," in *The Law of Dissent and Riots,* ed. M. Cheriff Bassiouini (Springfield, IL: Thomas, 1971), pp. 245–50.

4. *Report for Action,* pp. 2–3; *United States National Advisory Commission on Civil Disorders* (New York: Bantam, 1968), p. 1.

5. A survey after the riots indicated that 21 percent of the Negroes and 19 percent of the whites believed that Newark was presently a good place to live in. Fifty percent of the Negroes and 32 percent of the whites considered it average, and 25 percent of the Negroes and 47 percent of the whites considered it a poor place to live; *Survey of Attitudes, Governor's Commission* (n.d.), Box 3, pp. 2–3, N.J. Gov. Hughes Comm., NJSA.

6. *Negro and White Attitudes toward Problems and Progress in Race Relations,* N.J. Governor's Commission, Box 1, pp. 2–3, 37, N.J. Gov. Hughes Comm., NJSA.

7. Woodard, *A Nation within A Nation,* pp. 84–90; quoted in Porambo, *No Cause for Indictment,* p. 197.

8. *U.S. National Advisory Report,* p. 206.

9. Quoted in James W. Button, *Black Violence: Political Impact of the 1960s Riots* (Princeton: Princeton University Press, 1978), pp. 84–85.

10. Quoted in Porambo, *No Cause for Indictment,* p. 22.

11. "Testimony of Major General James F. Cantwell" (10-20-67), pp. 50, 68, 80, Box 5, N.J. Gov. Hughes Comm., NJSA.

12. "Testimony of Robert Curvin" (10-17-67), vol. 3, p. 17, Box 5, N.J. Gov. Hughes Comm., NJSA.

13. Donald L. Horowitz, *The Deadly Ethnic Riot* (Berkeley: University of California Press, 2001), pp. 76–77.

14. "Testimony of Robert Curvin," (10-17-67), vol. 3, pp. 7, 10, Box 5, N.J. Gov. Hughes Comm., NJSA.

15. Ibid., pp. 10–15, 15–18.

16. Sidney Fine, *Violence in the Model City,* pp. 240–41.

17. "Testimony of Robert Curvin" (10–17–67), p.19, Box 5, N.J. Gov. Hughes Comm., NJSA.

18. For the second woman's comments, see ibid.

19. *Newark Evening News* (8-12-67).

20. "Testimony of Olivia Mc Rimmon" (11-28-67), p. 35, Box 5, N.J. Gov. Hughes Comm., NJSA.

21. *New Jersey Afro-American* (7-15-67).

22. On frustration in the crowd, *see Report for Action,* p. 111; *U.S. National Advisory Commission on Civil Disorders,* p. 31.

23. "Testimony of Robert Curvin" (10-17-67), p. 29, Box 5, N.J. Gov. Hughes Comm., NJSA; "Investigation into Possible Criminal Conspiracy," pp. 68–69.

24. *U.S. National Commission on Civil Disorders,* p. 31.

25. "Testimony of Robert Curvin," p. 29, Box 5, N.J. Gov. Hughes Comm., NJSA.

26. "Testimony of Dominick Spina," p. 85, ibid.; "Testimony of Robert Curvin" (10-17-67), pp. 28, 21, ibid.

27. *U.S. National Advisory Commission,* p. 33.

28. "Testimony of Robert Curvin," p. 30, Box 5, N.J. Gov. Hughes Comm., NJSA.

29. "Testimony of John Redden" (10-31-67/11-3-67), p. 4, ibid.

30. Memo (n.d.), "Riots File," Box 3, PNY Papers, HUA.

31. "Newark Degree and Type of Damage" (n.d.), Box 1, N.J. Gov. Hughes Comm., NJSA; also see *Report for Action,* pp. 124–26.

32. "Newark Degree and Type of Damage" (n.d.), Box 1, N.J. Gov. Hughes Comm., NJSA.

33. "Testimony of Vito M. Pontrelli" (11-3-67), p. 66, Box 5, ibid.; "Newark, New Jersey Police Investigation into the Riots" (1967), pp. 58–60, Box 2, ibid.

34. "Testimony of Kenneth Melchior" (10-31-67), p. 46, Box 5, ibid.; John

Smith later expressed his sympathy for the victims of the riots. See *New Jersey Afro-American* (8-12-67).

35. "Testimony of Donald Malafronte" (9-29-67), p. 45, Box 5, N.J. Gov. Hughes Comm., NJSA.

36. Porambo, *No Cause for Indictment*, pp. 115–16; *Report for Action*, pp. 110–11.

37. From Wally Baer to Vice-President (7-14-67), reprinted in Michael Belknap, ed., *Civil Rights, the White House, and the Justice Department* (New York: Garland, 1991), p. 38.

38. *Report for Action*, p. 144.

39. Caroline Brothers, *War and Photography: A Cultural History* (New York: Routledge, 1998), pp. 117, 135–38.

40. *U.S. National Commission on Civil Disorders*, pp. 72, 189–90.

41. *Report for Action*, p. 112.

42. "Riot Kills 1, Injured 340 in Newark," *The Detroit News* (7-14-67).

43. *Report for Action*, p. 125.

44. Memo, file PNY Role in Riots (7-14-67), p. 3, Box 3, PNY Papers, HUA.

45. To Sen. John McAllen from PNY (1967), Box 3, ibid.

46. From PNY to Sen. John McAllen (1967), ibid.

47. *Report for Action*, p. 111.

48. Fine, *Violence in the Model City*, p. 249.

49. *Report for Action*, p. 111.

50. *U.S. National Advisory Commission*, p. 76.

51. Fine, *Violence in the Model City*, pp. 326–27.

52. Jeffrey Mayland Paige, "Collective Violence and the Culture of Subordination: A Study of Participants in the July 1967 Riots in Newark, New Jersey, and Detroit, Michigan" (Ph.D. dissertation, University of Michigan, 1968).

53. Paige, "Collective Violence and the Culture of Subordination," pp. 41, 54.

54. Ibid., p. 72.

55. Ibid., pp. 89, 103, 105.

56. Ibid.

57. *Time* (7-28-67), p. 31, Box 3, PNY Papers, HUA.

58. Lerone Bennet, Jr., "How to Stop," *Ebony* 12, no. 12 (October 1969), pp. 29–31.

59. *Report for Action*, pp. 138–39.

60. *U.S. National Advisory Commission On Civil Disorders*, pp. 72–73; my data on Newark refutes the social science profile of older and northern-born rioters; Leonard Zeitz, "Survey of Negro Attitudes toward Law," *Rutgers Law Review* 19 (1964–1965), pp. 288–316.

61. Paul Boutelle, ed., *The Black Uprisings: Newark 1967 Detroit* (New York: Merit, 1969), pp. 8–9.

62. "Testimony of Dennis Westbrooks" (11-17-67), p. 67, box 5, N.J. Gov. Hughes Comm., NJSA.

63. "Testimony of Major-General Cantwell" (8-17-67 to 1-4-68), vol. 3, p. 10, N.J. Gov. Comm., PUF.

64. *U.S. National Commission on Civil Disorders,* pp. 33–35, 277, 489, 498.

65. Martha Derthick, *The National Guard in Politics* (Cambridge, MA: Harvard University Press, 1965), pp. 18–19, 154–55; Jerry Cooper, *The Rise of the National Guard: The Evolution of the American Militia, 1865–1920* (Lincoln: University of Nebraska, 1997), pp. 129–52; Eldridge Colby, *The National Guard of the United States: A Half Century of Progress* (New York: Ma/ Ah Publishing, 1977), chapter 10; the essentially civic-oriented private militia formed a "social group that promised prestige, an athletic club that promoted physical vigor, and a military organization that offered an opportunity for service." Only years before the Guard received military status from the federal government, a poll of New Jersey Guardsmen in 1896 reported occupational distribution of merchants, salesmen, manufacturing and mechanical industries, and other men committed to protecting the public order

66. *U.S. National Commission on Civil Disorders,* pp. 33–35, 277, 489, 498.

67. Police reportedly discovered arms in housing projects. On Plainfield, see the "Testimony of Officer Tucker" (11-24-67), vol. 7, pp. 20–22, N.J. Comm. Civil Disorders, PUF. On the *Life* story, see Porambo, *No Cause for Indictment,* pp. 130–31.

68. "Testimony of Colonel Kelly" (9-29-67), p. 32, Box 5, N.J. Gov. Hughes Comm., NJSA.

69. Porambo, *No Cause for Indictment,* pp. 252–53.

70. "Testimony of Colonel Kelly" (9-29-67), pp. 54–55, Box 5, N.J. Gov. Hughes Comm., NJSA.

71. Ibid.

72. "Testimony of Donald Malafronte" (9-29-67), p. 45, ibid.

73. "Testimony of General Cantwell," pp. 18, 20, ibid.

74. "Testimony of Donald Malafronte" (9-29-67), p. 45, ibid.

75. "Testimony of Paul Ylvisaker" (8-16-67), Vol. 1, p. 14, N.J. Gov. Comm., PUF.

76. Ibid.

77. "Testimony," Vol. 3, pp. 19–20, N.J. Gov. Comm, PUF Princeton University Firestone.

78. The Governor's Commission did not inquire into the cause of Moran's death. See Porambo, *No Cause for Indictment,* pp. 136–38; "Firefighters Find Bullets and Jeers Biggest Hindrance," *New York Times* (7-15-67).

79. Ann Kathleen Johnson, "Urban Ghetto Riots, 1965–1968: A Compari-

son of Soviet and American Press Coverage" (Ph.D. dissertation, University of Denver, 1994), pp. 213–14.

80. Ibid., p. 268.

81. "Old-Fashioned Long, Hot Summer," *Sepia* 18, no. 9 (September 1969), pp. 78–80.

82. "Victims Identified in Newark Rioting," *New York Times* (7-15-67); "Firefighters Find Bullets and Jeers Biggest Hindrance," ibid. (7–15–67); "Newark Riot Deaths at 21 As Negro Sniping Widens: Hughes May Seek U.S. Aid," ibid. (7-16-67).

83. Douglas Eldridge, "A Betrayed City Ponders Storm: Signs of Impending Riots Cropping Up for Some Time," *Newark Evening News.*

84. *The Johnson Presidential Press Conferences,* vol. 2, p. 937.

85. Porambo, *No Cause for Indictment,* p. 240.

86. Ibid., p. 137.

87. Glenn Freese, "The Riot Curfew," in Bassiouni, ed., *The Law of Riot and Dissent,* pp. 401, 411; *Report for Action,* p. 145.

88. "Testimony of Olivia McRimmon" (11–28–67), Box 5, N.J. Gov. Hughes Comm., NJSA.

89. "Testimony of Willie Odom" (11-13-67), p. 136, ibid.

90. "Testimony of Donald Malafronte" (9-29-67), p. 45, ibid.

91. "Testimony of Leroi Jones" (11-27-67), pp. 81, 90, ibid.; Porambo, *No Cause For Indictment,* pp. 34–35

92. "Testimony of Leroi Jones" (11-27-67), p. 90, ibid.

93. "Testimony of Leroi Jones" (11-27-67), p. 91, ibid.

94. On Jack Snydor, see Sidney Fine, *Violence in the Model City: The Cavanagh Administration, Race Relations, and the Detroit Riot of 1967* (Ann Arbor: University of Michigan Press, 1989), p. 226.

95. Fine, *Violence in the Model City,* pp. 300–301.

96. The numbers were verified by tax assessors; in the case of liquor losses, they were verified by the state Alcoholic Board of Control with insurance adjusters. "The bulk of the damage was loss of stock through looting and for other reasons," but it was less than typically assumed with real property, particularly since there was "little loss due to fire." Of 250 alarms, only 13 were considered to be serious. In no case did a fire spread from its original source to other areas. On the first night of rioting, 122 fires; the second, 71; the third, 34; by the fourth night, Newark fire and police had reduced the nightly fires to 23. Of these, only 13 were considered serious. Almost 85 percent of the stores were damaged with broken windows. "Liquor stores were the most heavily looted of all types of establishments." Similarly, clothing losses amounted to 1,734,925 of which 1,412,375 were in stock losses. See "Estimated Losses," Box 1, Gov. Comm., NJSA.

97. "Testimony of Jamie Carter" (11-20-67), Box 5, p. 113, N.J. Gov. Hughes Comm., NJSA.

98. *U.S. National Commission on Civil Disorders,* p. 2.

99. Quoted in Porambo, *No Cause for Indictment,* pp. 27, 132, 149, 153.

NOTES TO CHAPTER 7

1. Mary Louise Roberts, *Civilization without Sexes: Gender and the Reconstruction of Postwar France* (Chicago: University of Chicago Press, 1994); Laura F. Edwards, "The Politics of Marriage and Households in North Carolina during Reconstruction," in Jane Dailey, Glenda Gilmore, and Bryant Simon, eds., *Jumpin' Jim Crow: Southern Politics from Civil War to Civil Rights* (Princeton: Princeton University Press, 2001), pp. 7–9; Gerald Horne, *The Fire This Time: The Watts Riots and the 1960s* (Ithaca, N.Y.: Cornell University Press, 1992), pp. 160–69.

2. "The White House: President's Address to the Nation on Civil Disorders," Press Conference Nos. 100–106 (7-27-67), p. 98, HUA; also see Joe Califano to President (7-14-67) and from Joe Califano to President (7-15-67), in Part I, *Civil Rights during the Johnson Administration, 1963–1969: A Collection from the Holdings of the Lyndon Baines Johnson Library* (Frederick, MD: University Publications of America, 1984); "Information Brief #9" (July 1967), ibid.; Dallek, *Flawed Giant,* p. 412.

3. On Harris polls of Johnson, see Button, *Black Violence,* p. 33; "Memo: Governor Hughes Reports the Following" (7-17-67), in Part I, *Civil Rights during the Johnson Administration, 1963–1969.*

4. *Report for Action,* Governor's Select Commission on Civil Disorders (February 1968), pp. 138–39.

5. Quoted in Porambo, *No Cause for Indictment,* pp. 238, 19; also see "Testimony of Richard Spellman" (11-20-67), pp. 3–6, Box 5, N.J. Gov. Hughes Comm., NJSA.

6. Porambo, *No Cause for Indictment,* pp. 20–21

7. *New Jersey Afro-American* (7-22-67)

8. Robert Carr, *Black Nationalism in the New World: Reading the African-American and West Indian Experience* (Durham, NC: Duke University Press, 2002), pp. 191, 202–4.

9. Quoted in Lewis M. Killian, *The Impossible Revolution? Black Power and the American Dream* (New York: Random House, 1968), pp. 116–117, 121.

10. *U.S. National Advisory Committee,* p. 129.

11. "Testimony of Raymond Brown" (8–16–67), vol. 4, pp. 87–88, N.J. Gov. Comm., PUF.

12. Susan D. Moeller, *Shooting War: Photography and the American Experience of Combat* (New York: Basic Books, 1989), p. 222; on gender and photography, see Judith Freyer Davidov, *Women's Camera Work: Self/Body/Other in American Visual Culture* (Durham, NC: Duke University Press, 1998), pp. 50–55.

13. On Bass, see Porambo, *No Cause for Indictment,* p. 127.

14. Russell Sackett, "In a Grim City, a Secret Meeting with the Snipers," *Life,* July 28, 1967, pp. 27–28.

15. Karen Huck, "The Arsenal on Fire: The Reader in the Riot, 1943," *Critical Studies in Mass Communication* 10 (193), pp. 42–43; Moeller, *Shooting War,* p. 222; Diana Emery Hulick with Joseph Marshall, *Photography 1900 to the Present* (New Jersey: Prentice Hall, 1998), pp. 184–85; Christopher Pinnery and Nicolas Peterson, *Photography's Other Histories* (Durham, NC: Duke University Press, 2003); Raymond P. Siljander, *Applied Surveillance Photography* (Springfield, IL: Thomas, 1975); Arthur Rothstein, *Documentary Photography* (Boston: Focal Press, 1986); on the power of signification of the image, see Roland Barthes, *Image, Music, Text* (New York: Hill and Wang, 1977), p. 45.

16. "Testimony of John Redden" (10-31-67/11-3-67), pp. 4, 101, Box 5, N.J. Gov. Hughes Comm., NJSA.

17. "Testimony of Dominick Spina" (10-30-67 to 11-6, 11-17, and 11-29-67), ibid.

18. Hayden, *Rebellion in Newark,* p. 34

19. Hannah Arendt, *Crises of the Republic* (New York: Harcourt, Brace, 1972), p. 75; Cohen, *Consumer's Republic,* pp. 372–73; Cohen located looting in the context of a national movement of "purchasers politicized."

20. Philip Roth, *American Pastoral* (New York: Vintage, 1997), p. 266.

21. Porambo, *No Cause for Indictment,* pp. 159–60; Amiri Baraka, "Black People," in *Amiri Baraka Reader,* ed. Amiri Baraka and William J. Harris (New York: Thunder's Mouth,1999), p. 224.

22. Quoted in Jerry Gafio Watts, *Amiri Baraka: The Politics and Art of a Black Intellectual* (New York: New York University Press, 2001), p. 298.

23. From P. Bernard Nortman to Mayor Hugh Addonizio (8-15-67), Box 1, N.J. Gov. Hughes Comm., NJSA.

24. From P. Bernard Nortman to Mayor Hugh Addonizio (8-15-67), "The Total Estimated Cost of the Loss," Box 1, N.J. Gov. Hughes Comm., NJSA; U.S. National Advisory Report, p. 67.

25. Jane Jacobs, *The Death and Life of Great American Cities* (New York: Modern Library, 1961, 1993); David Henkin, *City Reading: Written Words and Public Spaces in Antebellum New York* (New York: Columbia University Press, 1998); Vanessa Schwartz, *Spectacular Realities: Mass Culture in Fin de Siècle Paris* (Berkeley: University of California Press, 1997).

26. Thomas Hayden, *Rebellion in Newark: Official Violence* (New York: New York Review of Books, 1967), p. 30.

27. Porambo, *No Cause for Indictment,* p. 213; "Testimony of Boo Son Wong" (11-13-67), p. 25, Box 5, N.J. Gov. Hughes Comm., NJSA.

28. George Thomas Kurian, *Datapedia of the United States* (Lamham, MD: Berman Press, 1994), p. 86.

29. *Consumer Income,* United States Census Bureau (October 1968), table 1, "Persons below Poverty Level in 1959 to 1968," p. 22.

30. Jacobs, *The Death and Life of Great American Cities.*

31. Hayden, *Rebellion in Newark,* pp. 30–31, 61.

32. Joseph Boskin, *Urban Racial Violence in the Twentieth Century* (New York: Greenwood Press, 1969), pp. 164, 118; on garnishment, see U.S. National Advisory Commission Report, p. 140. The McCone Report on the rioting in Detroit interpreted the small amount of looting of narcotics to suggest that the motivation was retribution against discriminatory retailers rather than taking merchandise

33. Gordon Park Bloom and Marion F. Fletcher, *The Negro in the Supermarket Industry* (Philadelphia: Wharton Business School, 1972), p. 118; *Chicago Tribune* (3-8-70).

34. From Det. William Millard, intelligence unit, to Capt. Rocco Ferrant (9-13-67), Box 2, N.J. Gov. Hughes Comm., NJSA.

35. Memo on commercial areas (n.d.), Box 3, N.J. Gov. Hughes Comm., NJSA.

36. Bloom and Fletcher, *The Negro in the Supermarket Industry,* p. 118.

37. CFUN flyer, Ahadi Ya Akika (n.d.), reel 8, in Woodard, ed., *Black Power Documents.*

38. On the director of the Small Business Administration in Newark, Andrew P. Lynch, see *New Jersey Afro-American* (8-19-67).

39. Dean Kotlowski, "Black Power—Nixon Style: The Nixon Administration and Minority Business Enterprise," *Business History Review* 72 (Autumn 1998), pp. 409–45.

40. Cohen, *A Consumer's Republic,* p. 378.

41. Richard W. Thomas, "The Black Community Building Process in Post-Urban Disorder Detroit, 1967–1997," in Joe W. Trotter, Earl Lewis, and Tera W. Hunter, eds., *The African-American Urban Experience: Perspectives from the Colonial Period to the Present* (New York: Palgrave, 2004), pp. 221–25.

42. *New York Times* (8-27-74).

43. Cynthia S'thembile, "Nation Builders: Female Activism in the Nation of Islam, 1960–1970" (Ph.D. dissertation, Temple University, 1994), pp. 192, 207, 196.

44. "Ujama, Small Business, Socialism, and Capitalism," CFUN flyer (n.d.), reel 3, in Woodard, ed., *Black Power Documents.*

45. "The Black Nationalist Woman," reel 2 (1968), in ibid.

46. Audrey Olsen Faulkner, ed., *When I Was Comin' Up: An Oral History of Aged Blacks* (Hamden, CT: Archon, 1982), p. 76.

47. Ibid., pp. 109–116.

48. Ibid., p. 58.

49. Ibid., p. 142.

50. Ibid., p. 59.

51. Ula Taylor, "Elijah Muhammad's Nation of Islam: Separatism, Re-gendering, and a Secular Approach to Black Power after Malcolm X (1965–1975)," in Jeanne F. Theoharis and Komozi Woodard, eds., *Freedom North: Black Freedom Struggles Outside the South, 1940–1980* (New York: Palgrave Macmillan, 2003), p. 188.

52. S'thembile, "Nation Builders," p. 124.

53. Ibid., p. 138.

54. Ibid., pp. 144.

55. Ibid., pp. 192, 207, 196.

56. Le Roi Jones, *Home: Social Essays* (New York: William Morrow, 1966), pp. 230–31; E. Francis White, "Africa on My Mind: Gender, Counter Discourse, and African-American Nationalism," *Journal of Women's History* 2, no. 1 (Spring 1990), pp. 79, 91; on Malcolm X and gender, see Farah Jasmine Griffin, " 'Ironies of the Saint': Malcolm X, Black Women, and the Price of Protection," in Bettye Collier-Thomas and V. P. Franklin, eds., *Sisters in the Struggle: African-American Women in the Civil Rights–Black Power Movement* (New York: New York University Press, 2002), pp. 214–29. For the view that nationalists did not subordinate women, see James Edward Smethhurst, *The Black Arts Movement: Literary Nationalism in the 1960s and 1970s* (Chapel Hill: University of North Carolina Press, 2005), pp. 84–99.

57. "Interview with Amiri Baraka" (1970), General Collections, Schomburg Library, New York.

58. *Black Women's Role in the Revolution* (1970), pp. 6–8, General Collection, SCR.

59. On Baraka's education and on alienation, see interview with Baraka, reel 8, pp. 16, 23, in Woodard, ed., *Black Power Documents*; interview with NGVU, reel 8, p. 33, ibid.

60. "The Black Nationalist Woman" (1968), reel 2, ibid.

61. "Committee for Unified Newark," memo, reel 2, ibid.

62. Woodard, *A Nation within A Nation*, pp. 89, 182–84; "The Position of the Congress of Afrikan People, December 1974, Amiri Baraka, Chairman," reel 2, in Woodared, ed., *Black Power Documents*.

63. Amiri Baraka, *Raise, Race, Rays, Raze: Essays since 1965* (New York: Random House, 1971), p. 160.

64. Ibid., p. 132; "Opening Statement—Meeting of Central Council" (4-25-75), p. 2, reel 3, in Woodard, ed., *Black Power Documents.*

65. Theodore Hudson, "A Conversation between Imanu Amiri Baraka and Theodore R. Hudson," in *Conversations with Amiri Baraka,* pp. 75–76; also see 1980 interview with William Harris, in *Conversations with Amiri Baraka,* pp. 170–75.

66. Baraka, *Raise, Race, Rays, Raze,* pp. 160–61.

NOTES TO CHAPTER 8

1. An older reflection on this moment is Theodore White, *The Making of the President, 1968* (New York: Atheneum, 1969), pp. 202–30.

2. On Watts, the NAACP was critical of rioting, but attempted to capitalize on the protest energy the riots had symbolized by opening a new branch, and aiding what they termed "riot victims."

3. "Testimony of Robert Curvin" (10-17-67), p. 80, Box 5, N.J. Gov. Hughes Comm., NJSA; *Annual Report of the NAACP* (1965), pp.18–20, 41; Testimony, Gov. Comm. on Disorder (10-6-67), vol. 3, p. 9, PUF; "Explains CORE's Constitutional Move in Wake of White-Incited Controversy," *Muhammad Speaks* (8-4-67).

4. For example, see Nathan Wright, *Black Power and Urban Unrest* (New York: Hawthorn, 1967), pp. 135–55.

5. Newark NJ Police Dept., *Investigation into Riots* (1967), pp. 56–61, NPL.

6. Hayden, *Reunion,* pp. 205, 216.

7. "Testimony of Leroi Jones" (11-27-67), p. 81, Box 5, N.J. Gov. Hughes Comm., NJSA.

8. Regular civic and religious organizations toured the "riot area" and observed the "victims," while an archbishop announced a rescue effort of "slum residents," but they appeared more removed and impotent. See Clippings (9-21-67), Box 3, PNY Papers, HUA.

9. "Interview with Paul Ylvisaker" (1972), Schomburg Center for Research in Black Culture, New York.

10. "Testimony of Ylvisaker" (8-16-67), vol. 2, p. 14, N.J. Gov. Comm., PUF. Radical critics of the Kerner Commission included David Boesel, Louis Goldberg, Gary T. Marx, and David Sears. See Andrew Kopkind, "White or Black: The Riot Commission and the Rhetoric of Reform," in Anthony Platt, ed., *The Politics of the Riot Commissions, 1917–1970* (New York: Macmillan, 1971), p. 386.

11. Memo (7-28-67), p. 31, file '67–'70, Box 3, PNY Papers, HUA.

12. Memo (8-1-67), file '67–'70, ibid.

13. Testimony, State of N.J. Gov. Comm. (8-16-67), vol. 2, pp. 15–20, PUF.

14. From PNY to Hubert Humphrey (9-18-67), Box 12, PNY Papers, HUA.

15. From PNY to President-Elect Nixon (12-20-68) ibid.

16. From PNY to the President-Elect Nixon (12-19-68), ibid.

17. On white nationalism, see Carol M. Swain, *The New White Nationalism in America: Its Challenge to Integration* (New York: Cambridge University Press, 2002). For an important, yet essentialist, study of the philosophy of black nationalism, see Tommie Shelby, *We Who Are Dark: The Philosophical Foundations of Black Solidarity* (Cambridge, MA: Harvard University Press, 2005), pp. 101–35.

18. Norman Naimark, *Fires of Hatred: Ethnic Cleansing in Twentieth-Century Europe* (Cambridge, MA: Harvard University Press, 2001); Benedict Anderson, *Imagined Communities* (New York: Verso, 1991); Ernest Gellner, *Nations and Nationalism* (Ithaca, NY: Cornell University Press, 1983), pp. 7, 48, 92, 111; Paul Gilroy, *Against Race: Imagining Political Culture beyond the Color Line* (Cambridge, MA: Harvard University Press, 2000), pp. 122, 124.

19. Jürgen Habermas, "Struggles for Recognition in the Democratic Constitutional State," in Charles Taylor and Amy Gutman, eds., *Multiculturalism* (Princeton: Princeton University Press, 1994), pp. 118–19.

20. "Testimony of Dominick Spina" (10-30-67 to 11-6, 11-17, and 11-29-67), Box 5, N.J. Gov. Hughes Comm., NJSA.

21. See Gary Wills, *The Second Civil War: Arming for Armageddon* (New York: New American Library, 1968), pp. 83–84.

22. "Escalation for A Long Hot Summer," *Sepia* 17, no. 3 (March 1968), pp. 60–64.

23. "Negro and White Attitudes toward Progress" (1968), p. 43, Box 1, N.J. Gov. Hughes Comm., NJSA; Memo, "Dear Mr. Spina" (n.d.), Box 3, ibid.; from Sue La Norte to Dominick Spina (7-19-67), Box 2, ibid.; from Marlene Marsch to Dominick Spina (7-19-67), ibid.

24. David John Olson, "Racial Violence and City Politics," p. 141.

25. Gerald Horne, *The Fire Next Time: The Watts Uprising and the 1960s* (Charlottesville: University of Virginia Press, 1995), p. 139. Horne writes of the right influence: "By some estimates 2000 members in the department alone."

26. Benjamin R. Epstein, *The Radical Right: Report on the John Birch Society and Its Allies* (New York: Random House, 1966, 1967), pp. 198, 202. On the racial component of anticommunism, see Gerald Schomp, *Birchism Was My Business* (New York: Macmillan, 1970), pp. 168–69.

27. Porambo, *No Cause for Indictment*, p.135.

28. Peter L. Meyers, "Between the Lines and behind the Times: The Marginal Identities of Newark Whites," in Stanley Winters, *From Riot to Recovery*, p. 139.

29. Peter Myers, "Defining the White Population," in Winters, ed., *From Riot to Recovery*, pp. 135, 140.

30. Geoffrey Douglass, *New Jersey Monthly*, December 1976, pp. 32–37; FBI File, "Anthony Michael Imperiale," p. 3 (n.d.).

31. On Jewish and Italian American attitudes on education, for example, see Stephen Steinberg, *The Ethnic Myth: Race, Ethnicity, and Class in America* (New York: Atheneum, 1981), pp. 128–50; Michael Novak, *Unmeltable Ethnics: Politics and Culture in American Life* (New Brunswick: Transaction, 1996, 1972), pp. 232–76.

32. David Shipler, "The White Niggers of Newark: The Other Side of Prejudice," *Harpers*, August 1972, p. 83; Pete Hamill, "The Revolt of the White Lower-Middle Class," in Winters, ed., *From Riot to Recovery*, p. 19.

33. "Interview with Amiri Baraka" (1970), General Collections, Schomburg Library, New York; Myers, "Defining the White Population," in Winters, ed., *From Riot to Recovery*, pp. 142–44.

34. Geoffrey Douglass, *New Jersey Monthly*, December 1976, pp. 32–37; FBI File, "Anthony Michael Imperiale," p. 3 (n.d.); Stephen A. Buff, "Greasers, Supers, and Hippies: Three Responses to the Adult World," in Winters, ed., *From Riot to Recovery*, pp. 142–44; Herber Gans, *Urban Villagers* (New York: 1971).

35. Nathan Glazer and Daniel Patrick Moynihan, *Beyond the Melting Pot: Blacks, Jews, Italians, and Puerto Ricans in New York City* (Cambridge, MA: MIT Press, 1970), pp. 138–39; on post-riot assimilation, see Stephen Steinberg, *The Ethnic Myth: Race, Ethnicity, and Class in America* (Boston: Beacon, 2001), p. 256.

36. The best treatment of the outrageous appropriation of civil rights activism in the service of racist discrimination is Ronald P. Formisano, *Boston against Busing: Race, Class, and Ethnicity in the 1960s and 1970s* (Chapel Hill: University of North Carolina Press, 1991); Matthew Lassiter, "Suburban Strategies: The Volatile Center in Postwar American Politics," in Meg Jacobs, William J. Novak, and Julian Zelizer, eds., *The Democratic Experiment: New Directions in American Political History* (Princeton: Princeton University Press, 2003), pp. 330–31.

37. *Newark News* (5-27-68).

38. Porambo, *No Cause for Indictment*, p. 175.

39. Ibid., pp. 175, 180.

40. Ibid, p. 90; FOIA File 0977391–000, "Imperiale-File," "Alleged Caching of Firearms," p. 6.

41. Woodard, *A Nation within a Nation*, pp. 84–85.

42. One result of the post-riot Black Power national convention was a resolution to defeat Mayor Addonizio; another was Ron Karenga's involvement

with Baraka. See Brown, "US Organization and Quest for Black Unity," in Woodard, ed., *Freedom North*, pp. 233–34; Woodard, *Nation within a Nation*, p. 124.

43. "Woodard interview of Karenga," p. 13, reel 8, in Woodard and Boehm, eds., *The Black Movement Part I*. Like several successful black nationalists across the nation at the time, Baraka also founded the Committee for a United Newark (CFUN), a political front organization. CFUN offered an apparently neutral, almost civic-minded name and institutional front behind which black nationalists organized to gain political power for the black community. CFUN was similar to the Black Congress which Karenga had started in Watts.

44. "Jones in Harlem Urges Revenge for Malcolm X," *Newark News* (2-22-68); David Llorens, "Ameer (Leroi Jones) Baraka" (1968), pp. 82–84, reel 4, in Woodard, ed., *Black Power Documents*.

45. Lavern C. Hutchins, *The John Birch Society and United States Foreign Policy* (New York: Pageant Press, 1968), pp. 97–162; *Newark News* (5-17-68).

46. *Newark News* (5-25-72), (5-3-72). At the Riviera Tavern, he spoke before three hundred persons, for example, and promoted his candidacy for office and denied allegations that he was a racist; *Newark News* (5-27-68); on the FBI and Baraka, see From Director, FBI, to SAC, Newark (10-9-70), reel 2, in Woodard, ed., *Black Power Documents*.

47. FOIA File 0977391–000, Memo to Director, FBI (3-18-68), U.S. Department of Justice, "RE: Anthony Michael Imperiale, Racial Matters"(5-6-69); for racial-matters file on Baraka, see "Le Roi Jones, Racial Matters, Black Nationalist" (11-20-70), reel 2, in Woodard, ed., *Black Power Documents*.

48. *Newark News* (5-3-70).

49. "Imperiale Opens His Drive for Newark Mayoralty," *Newark News* (1-15-70).

50. "Jones' Friend Free on Bail," *Newark News* (1-11-68).

51. Ibid.

52. "Recognizing Jones," *Newark News* (11-1-67).

53. *Newark News* (10-27-67); "Negro and White Attitudes toward Progress," p. 39, Box 3, N.J. Gov. Hughes Comm., NJSA.

54. "Jones Puts Up $25,000 Bail," *Newark News* (7-18-67); "Jones Acquittal Plea Denied by Judge Kapp," *Newark News* (10-31-67).

55. "Recognizing Jones," *Newark News* (11-1-67).

56. "Jones' Convictions Upset on Appeal," *Newark News* (12–24–68). As a result of the pressure on the police and residual progressive or liberal attitudes stimulated by the riots, however, Baraka could take advantage of new civilian review mechanisms and filed a complaint against patrolman Frank Hunt, who was summoned to answer the charges before the grand jury. And eventually Hunt requested and was granted a transfer out of the First Precinct because Baraka resided there.

57. "Jones Entrapped, Lawyer Charges," *Newark News* (11-22-68).
58. "Jones Gets 60 Days, Fined $100," *Newark News* (11-26-68); "Le Roi Jones Plans Appeal," *Newark News* (11-27-68).
59. "Witnesses Back Jones at Trial," *Newark News* (11-1-68); "Racial Remarks Charged to Jones," *Newark News* (10-29-68).
60. "Retrials Ordered for Jones," *Newark News* (12-23-68); on the second trial on a weapons charge, see *Newark News* (2-25-69).
61. "Newark Detective Testifies Jones Was Abusive to Cop," *Newark News* (1-10-69).
62. "Police to Bid Court Cite Jones for Contempt," *Newark News* (12-29-67).
63. "Jones Wins Reversal of Policeman's Charge," *Newark News* (1-16-69).
64. Benjamin Epstein, *The Radical Right: Report on the John Birch Society and Its Allies* (New York: Random House, 1967), pp. 178–79.
65. Anthony Giuliano, Patrolmen's Benevolent Assoc., Local No. 3, 22 Franklin Avenue (n.d.), Box 3, N.J. Gov. Hughes Comm., NJSA.
66. *Newark News* (6-24-68).
67. Ibid.; *Newark News* (9-26-68).
68. *Newark News* (6-24-68).
69. Ibid.
70. FBI File on Imperiale, From Fred M. Vinson to Director, FBI (3-26-68).
71. *Newark News* (11-7-68).
72. *Newark News* (10-21-68).
73. FBI File, "Anthony Michael Imperiale" (8-26-68), p. 1; *Newark News* (10-21-68).
74. FBI File, "Anthony Michael Imperiale," p. 2 (n.d.).
75. *Newark News* (3-27-68); on changes in King's thought, see Alan B. Anderson and George W. Pickering, *Confronting the Color Line: The Broken Promise of the Civil Rights Movement in Chicago* (Athens: University of Georgia Press, 1986), pp. 321–37.
76. "Interview with Baraka," pp. 48–49, reel 8, in Woodard, *Black Power Documents.*
77. Porambo, *No Cause for Indictment*, p. 90.
78. *Newark News* (10-24-68).
79. Porambo, *No Cause for Indictment*, p. 203.
80. "LeRoi Jones Heads School Fund Unit," *Newark News* (2-6-68).
81. "Probe Jones Appointment," *Newark News* (2-7-68).
82. Ibid.
83. *Newark News* (11-6-68); some testimony argues that Karenga traveled to Newark in support of black candidates in the 1968 races, indicating black nationalist involvement before the Community Party in 1970. But there is factual inconsistency based on oral histories of black nationalists that credit Baraka for

the candidacies of Donald Tucker and Theodore Pinkney, since they were not necessarily members of United Brothers but received their support and ran independently, like Gibson in 1966. On the nationalist version, see Scot Brown, *Fighting for US,* pp. 103–4.

84. *Newark News* (2-5-69).

85. *Newark News* (11-6-68).

86. David John Olson, "Racial Violence and City Politics," p. 141.

87. Dawson, *Black Visions,* pp. 132–33.

88. "Interview with Paul Ylvisaker" (1972), General Collections, Schomburg Library, New York.

89. Nixon later wrote to President Eisenhower to report the warm reception given to his law-and-order rhetoric. See Stephen Ambrose, *Nixon: The Triumph of a Politician, 1962–1972* (New York: Simon and Schuster, 1989), pp. 144–45; Matthew Lassiter, "Suburban Strategies: The Volatile Center in Postwar American Politics," in Meg Jacobs, William J. Novak, Julian Zelizer, eds., *The Democratic Experiment: New Directions in American Political History* (Princeton: Princeton University Press, 2003), pp. 330–31; *Congress and the Nation,* vol. 2, (1965–68) (Washington, DC: *Congressional Quarterly*), p. 28; *Congressional Quarterly Almanac,* vol. 24 (1968), pp. 945–46. The vast scholarship on Nixon, however, downplays race in his victory over Humphrey, perhaps because Nixon's actual conduct of civil rights did not differ substantially from President Johnson's. Some biographers are loath to mention the race card, referring to law and order blue collar appeal. See Tom Wicker, *One of US: Richard Nixon and the American Dream* (New York: Random House, 1991), pp. 360–62. On ignoring Nixon's manipulation of race, see Gary Wills, *Nixon Agonistes: The Crisis of a Self-Made Man* (New York: Signet, 1969); Joan Hoff, *Nixon Reconsidered* (New York: Basic, 1994); Anthony Summers, *The Arrogance of Power: The Secret World of Richard Nixon,* (New York: Viking, 2000); *Newark Evening News* (4-2-69), (5-22-69), and (10-24-68).

90. Dan Carter, *From George Wallace to Newt Gingrich: Race in the Conservative Counterrevolution, 1963–1994* (Baton Rouge: Louisiana State University Press, 1996), pp. 13, 330–32, 435. In 1968 Wallace failed to win anything outside the South; in 1972 Wallace finished second in Wisconsin, after the Milwaukee riots, and first in Michigan, after the Detroit riots.

NOTES TO CHAPTER 9

1. "Summer Riots," *Sepia* 16, no. 8 (August 1967), pp. 22–26; "Riots, Riots, Riots," *Sepia* 16, no. 10 (October 1963), pp. 38–43.

2. Quoted in July 13, 1967, press conference, in *The Johnson Presidential Press Conferences,* vol. 2, p. 805; "How Long, Oh Lord, How Long?" *Ebony* 11 (September 1967), pp. 106–7.

3. From Malcolm X to James Forman (7-29-63), reel 3, *Papers of CORE*.

4. For an expansive definition of Black Power as militant and activist, see the introduction and bibliographic essay by Peniel Joseph, ed., *The Black Power Movement: Rethinking the Civil Rights–Black Power Era* (New York: Routledge, 2006), pp. 1–25, 251–77.

5. For the conservative response of NAACP to riots, see Thomas A. Johnson, "Newark's Summer 1967," *Crisis* 74, no. 7 (August–September, 1967), pp. 371–81.

6. Lerone Bennet, "How To Stop," *Ebony* 12, no. 12 (October 1969), p. 29; "Newark, Detroit . . . Where Next?" *Muhammad Speaks* (8-4-67); "We Want Black Power," *Muhammad Speaks* (8-18-67); "Newark: 'And They Still Ask What Causes Us to Riot," *Muhammad Speaks* (8-11-1967); "Revolutionary Political Action Front Urges Attendance of Black Activists," *Muhammad Speaks* (8-25-1967); "Wilkins Protest Anti-Riot Bill in Congress," *Muhammad Speaks* (7-28-67); "Mass Murder by White 'Guard' go Unpunished!" ibid.; "Black Struggles in American Cities Declared to be More than Mere Riots," ibid.

7. Alvin Poussaint, "A Psychiatrist Looks at Black Power," *Ebony*, March 1969, p. 151.

8. Thomas J. Joynes, "Negro Identity—Black Power and Violence," *Journal of Human Relations* 17, no. 2 (Second Quarter, 1969), pp. 204, 206.

9. "Newark Dentists Views on Causes of Upheaval," *Muhammad Speaks* (8-4-1967).

10. Stokely Carmichael and Charles V. Hamilton, *Black Power: The Politics of Liberation in America* (New York: Random House, 1967), pp. 54–55.

11. Charles V. Hamilton, "No Truce with Oppressors: Black Americans and the American Political Struggle," *Black World*, May 1970, pp. 5–9.

12. "The 'New Negro': Turner Says Understanding Needed," *Newark News* (8-31-64); for a concise chronology and analysis of the New Negro, see Henry Louis Gates, "The Trope of a New Negro and the Reconstruction of the Image of the Black," *Representations* 24 (1988), pp. 129–55.

13. "Turner Raps Malcolm X," *Star-Ledger* (9-9-64).

14. "Turner Rips CORE Aide," *Newark News* (6-27-65).

15. "Councilman Turner Enlivens Two T.V. Programs," *Newark News* (8-29-64).

16. Baraka, *Raise, Race, Rays, Raze*, p. 65.

17. Ibid., p. 67.

18. "Interview with Kenneth Gibson" (July 2000), in author's possession.

19. *New Jersey Afro-American* (9-21-74).

20. Imanu Amiri Baraka (Le Roi Jones), *Pan-African Congress: A Documentary of the First Modern Pan-African Congress* (New York: William Morrow, 1972), p. 54.

21. Carmichael and Hamilton, *Black Power*, p. 84.

22. "Interview with Amiri Baraka" (1970), Schomburg Library, New York.

23. Charles Cummings, "African-Americans in the Political Arena," *Star-Ledger* (2-24-2000). One interesting trend was that the enforcement of residential segregation in the era of the ghetto in effect removed political representation from the city to the county. In other words, several black candidates were elected to the state legislature early in the 1920s—Walter Gilbert (R, Orange) and Oliver Randolph (R, Newark), and again in the 1960s, namely Herbert Tate (D, Newark) and George Richardson (D, Newark), but never to city government, where housing, services, and federal monies were allocated.

24. Woodard, *A Nation within a Nation,* pp. 146–47. There is disagreement about who "invented" the concept of the convention: Robert Curvin has claimed credit, as has Baraka. "I thought Amiri Baraka's Committee for a United Newark was a brilliant tactical plan to force all black candidates to run against each other in a community primary and pledge that if they lost they would not run against each other in the general election." Eric Mann credits Baraka and has described the convention. "Interview with Eric Mann" (8-10-2003), p. 1 (in author's possession).

25. "Notes on Newark News," from *Newark News* (2-28-64); *Newark News* (3-13-64), Box 69, Folder 7, August Meier Papers, Schomburg Manuscripts.

26. "West Hits Rivals on Race Issue," *Newark News* (6-4-70).

27. Woodard, *A Nation within a Nation,* pp. 146–47.

28. Interview with Kenneth Gibson (1970), Schomburg Library, New York; "Gibson 3rd in Mayoral Contest," *Newark News* (5-11-66).

29. Interview with Kenneth Gibson (July 2000), in author's possession.

30. Tali Mendelberg, *The Race Card: Campaign Strategy, Implicit Messages, and the Norm of Equality* (Princeton: Princeton University Press, 2001), pp. 95–97, 211–14.

31. On Addonizio's race and legal troubles, see Porambo, *No Cause for Indictment,* p. 335.

32. Mendelberg, *The Race Card,* pp. 211–14; "Addonizio in Bitter Attack on 4 Rivals," *Newark News* (5-3-66).

33. "Gibson Wins by 12,000," *Newark News* (6-17-70).

34. "Newark PBA Votes to Back Addonizio," *Newark News* (5-27-70); "Gibson Denies Excluding Whites from Campaign" (4-16-70); "Council Veterans Hang On," *Newark News* (6-17-70); "South Ward Rivals Tangle in Bitter Personal Duels," *Newark News* (4-19-66).

35. Biographical studies of black mayors appeared just at the end of the riots, from 1967 to 1970. In Cleveland, a white labor candidate opposed a black civil rights candidate, Carl Stokes; see Kenneth Weinberg, *Black Victory: Carl Stokes and the Winning of Cleveland* (Chicago: Quadrangle, 1968), pp. 128–39. On Coleman Young, see Wilbur Rich, *Coleman Young* (New York: 1971),

pp. 186–87; "Introduction," in Colburn and Adler, eds., *African American Mayors*, p. 1.

36. David R. Colburn and Jeffrey S. Adler, eds., *African-American Mayors: Race, Politics, and the American City* (Urbana: University of Illinois Press, 2001), p. 7; Colburn, "African-American Mayors, 1967–96," in Colburn and Adler, *African American Mayors*, p. 39; "Interview with Larry Hamm," p. 8, reel 5, in Woodard, ed., *Black Power Documents*; "Black Residents Elated by Gibson's Victory" (6-17-70); political scientists theorized the transition from activism or black power to electoral office in the 1970s particularly. Influential were Ronald Walters, "The Black Politician: Fulfilling the Legacy of Black Power," *Current History* 67 (November 1974), pp. 200–210; Robert Smith, "Black Power and the Transformation from Protest to Politics," *Political Science Quarterly* 96 (Fall 1981), pp. 431–45.

37. Amiri Baraka (Le Roi Jones), *Pan-African Congress* (1973), p. 67, General Collections, Schomburg Library.

38. "Interview with Amiri Baraka" (1970), General Collections, Schomburg Library, New York.

39. Kenneth Gibson, "Newark and We," in Nathan Wright, ed., *What Black Politicians Are Saying* (New York: Hawthorn, 1972), pp. 110–11.

40. *Newark News* (10-20-70).

41. Leonard Cole, *Blacks in Power: A Comparative Study of Black and White Elected Officials* (Princeton: Princeton University Press, 1976), pp. 78–79; see Jeffrey Hadden, Louis Masotti, and Victor Thiessen, "The Making of the Negro Mayors," in *The Black Experience*, ed. August Meier, p. 149; Robert Curvin, "The Persistent Minority," pp. 94, 103, 117.

42. Curvin, "The Persistent Minority," pp. 216–18; Cole, *Blacks in Power*, pp. 76, 101.

43. Curvin, "The Persistent Minority," p. 65.

44. *Newark News* (5-3-72).

45. *Newark News* (7-11-72).

46. *Newark News* (8-4-70).

47. *Newark News* (7-23-70).

48. *Newark News* (8-4-70).

49. *Newark News*, (11–12–70).

50. Quoted in Ronald Walters and Robert C. Smith, *African-American Leadership* (Buffalo: SUNY Press, 1999), p. 160.

51. *Newark Human Rights Commission, Annual Report* (1976), NPL; *Newark Human Rights Commission* (5-1-73), NPL; *Newark Human Rights Commission,* 20th Anniversary Annual Report, p. 2, NPL.

52. City of Newark, "Affirmative Action" (7-18-75), Newark City Hall (NCH).

53. On Title VII permitting affirmative action, quotas, or preferences, see

Hanson Bratton v. City of Detroit, 712 F 2d 22 (6th Cir., 1983); *Baker v. Detroit,* 483 F. Supp. 930 (E.D. Mich., 1979), and *United Steelworkers of America v. Weber* (1979); see Rich, *Coleman Young and Detroit Politics,* p. 293.

54. From Computer Sciences Corporation to the Honorable Kenneth Gibson, Mayor; Members of the Council of the City of Newark (9-21-77), NCH; "Computer Sciences Corporation" (9-27-77), NCH.

55. City of Newark, "Affirmative Action" (7-18-75), NCH.

56. *Affirmative Action in Newark* (4-06-83),CHN.

57. "Interview with Kenneth Gibson," in author's possession.

58. "Table 1: NHRA Workforce Analysis By Job Classification," Newark Redevelopment and Housing Authority Affirmative Action Plan (1973–77), City Hall Newark.

59. Yatrakis, "Electoral Demands," pp. 258, 267.

60. *Newark News* (10-19-78); from Gabriel A. Nicholas to Gustave Heninburg, President of Newark Urban Coalition (6-27-79), Office of Affirmative Action, CHN; See "Resolution 7R-B" (10-4-78), NCH.

61. *Newark News* (3-31-72).

62. Horace M. Kallen, *Cultural Pluralism and the American Idea: An Essay in Social Philosophy* (New York: 1954), p. 83. On cultural pluralism in the context of urban politics, see Jerold Podair, *The Strike That Changed New York: Blacks, Whites, and the Ocean Hill-Brownsville Crisis* (New Haven: Yale University Press, 2002), pp. 58–60, 66–67.

63. "Le Roi Jones: An Exclusive Interview," in *Conversations with Amiri Baraka,* pp. 77–80.

64. *New Jersey Afro-American* (9-21-74); *Newark News* (4-7-68).

65. *Star-Ledger* (8-13-72).

66. Ibid. (11-10-72).

67. Ibid. (11-16-72).

68. Ibid. (10-19-72), (10-31-72).

69. Ibid. (11-6-72).

70. Ibid. (11-18-72), (11-6-72).

71. Ibid. (11-10-72).

72. *New York Times* (11-11-72).

73. *Star-Ledger* (11-12-72).

74. *New York Times* (11-14-72).

75. *Star-Ledger* (11-20-72); *New York Times* (11-20-72); *Star-Ledger* (11-22-72), (12-3-72), (11-22-72).

76. *Star-Ledger* (11-13-72); *New York Times* (1-3-72); *Star-Ledger* (1-3-73).

77. *Star-Ledger* (4-19-73).

78. Ibid. (5-27-73).

79. Ibid. (5-27-73); *New York Times* (11-13-72).

80. Interview with Kenneth Gibson, in author's possession.

81. "Interview with Baraka," p. 45, reel 8, in Woodard, ed., *Black Power Documents*.

82. *Newark Record* (8-5-74); *Herald-News*, (7-16-74); *Newark Record* (10-19-72); *Star-Ledger* (1-8-73); *New York Times* (1-6-73).

83. *New York Times* (11-14-72); Neil Leach, "Erasing the Traces: The 'De-nazification' of Post-revolutionary Berlin and Bucharest," in Neil Leach, ed., *Hieroglyphics of Space: Understanding the City* (New York: Taylor and Francis, 2001), pp. 80–85.

84. *The Student Uprising in Soweto* (1976), p. 21, McKeldin Library, University of Maryland, College Park.

85. Don Quinn Kelley, "Black Political Activity and the Formation of Public Policy on Education of Blacks in the United States—Two Eras: The State of Alabama from 1884 to 1910 and the City of Newark, New Jersey, from 1954 to June, 1972" (Ph.D. dissertation, Columbia University, 1974), p. 344.

86. *New York Times* (11-13-72).

87. Kelley, "Black Political Activity and the Formation of Public Policy," pp. 340–44.

88. From Amiri Baraka to Kenneth Gibson (10-7-70), reel 1, *Black Power Documents*; "Baraka's Power Is Said to Wane," *New York Times* (3–24–74), reel 2, *Black Power Documents*.

89. *Star-Ledger* (4-1-79).

90. *Newark Afro-American* (2-4-80).

91. Kelley, "Black Political Activity and the Formation of Public Policy on Education of Blacks in the United States—Two Eras," pp. 340–45.

92. *Star-Ledger* (4-1-79).

93. "Baraka Drops 'Racism' for Socialism of Marx," *New York Times* (12-27-74).

94. *Star-Ledger* (11-20-72); *New York Times* (11-20-72); *Star-Ledger* (11-22-72), (12-3-72), (11-22-72).

95. *New York Times* (9-3-74); Cole, *Blacks in Power*, p. 114.

96. *New York Times* (8-31-75).

97. Winters, *From Riot to Recovery*, pp. 105–7.

98. "North Ward Election Result Reflects Latino Influx," *Star-Ledger* (5-16-2002).

99. "Newark Council Veteran Carrino Ousted," *Star-Ledger* (5-15-2002).

NOTES TO THE EPILOGUE

1. *Star-Ledger* (7-10-97).

2. Demonstration Cities, *Newark Application*, part 2 (A), pp. 26–27, 36–37, Box 133, HUD, National Archives, MD.

3. David R. Colburn, "Running for Office: African-American Mayors from 1967 to 1996," in David R. Colburn and Jeffrey S. Adler, eds., *African-American Mayors* (New York: 2003), p. 33; Kathryn Yatrakis, "Electoral Demands and Political Benefits" (Ph.D. dissertation, Columbia University, 1981), pp. 258, 267.

4. Wilbur Rich, *Black Mayors and School Politics: The Failure of Reform in Detroit, Gary, and Milwaukee* (New York: Garland, 1996), p. 192; John Charles Boger and Judith Wetch Wegner, eds., *Race, Poverty, and American Cities* (Chapel Hill: University of North Carolina Press, 1996), p. 14.

5. Winters, *From Riot to Recovery*, p. 3.

6. Roger Biles, "Black Mayors: A Historical Assessment," *Journal of Negro History*, 77, no. 3 (summer 1992), pp. 117–18, 121. David Dinkins won in New York with 52 percent of the vote; Winters, *From Riot to Recovery*, pp. 10, 15, 43.

7. Winters, *From Riot to Recovery*, p. 3.

8. Ibid., pp. 6–7, 11, 13.

9. Yatrakis, "Political Benefits," p. 164.

10. Curvin, "The Persistent Minority," p. 326.

11. *Newark Model Cities*, Part 3, "First Year," pp. 49–50, 24, 33; *Newark Model Cities*, Part 2, *First Year Action Program*, pp. 7–14; Newark Application, Part 2 (A), pp. 57, 55, HUD, Demonstration Grants, National Archives, College Park, MD.

12. *Newark Model Cities*, Part 3, "First Year," pp. 2–49, 2–50, 4–24, 4–33; *Newark Model Cities*, Part 2, *First Year Action Program*, pp. 7–14; Newark Application, Part 2 (A), pp. 57, 55, HUD, Demonstration Grants, National Archives, College Park, MD.

13. See Harry L. Margulis, "Public Housing in Newark: The Struggle to Survive," and William L. Johnston, "The New Jersey Housing Finance Agency: A Decade of Housing Production in Newark," in Winters, *From Riot to Recovery*, pp. 227–46, 247–53.

14. Franklin J. James, Jr., *Race, Housing Value and Housing Abandonment: A Case Study of Newark* (New York: Columbia University Press, 1980), pp. 5–10.

15. James B. Lane, "Richard Hatcher of Gary, Indiana," in Colbern and Adler, eds., *African-American Mayors*, p. 69.

16. Arnold Hirsch, *Making the Second Ghetto: Race and Housing in Chicago, 1940–1960* (Cambridge, UK: Cambridge University Press, 1983), p. 21.

17. "Newark High-Rise Residents Are Left without Elevators," *Star-Ledger* (11-23-99).

18. "Kawaida Units Are Re-allocated," *Star-Ledger* (7-22-75); "Baraka Accuses Council on Tax Abatement Denial," *Star-Ledger* (11-19-94).

19. "Newark Tenants Seek More Action to Fix Apartment Complex Woes," *Star-Ledger* (12-20-91).

20. "Newark Agency Joins to House Homeless Families," *Star-Ledger* (7-17-88).

21. *Star-Ledger* (12-7-86).

22. "Task Force on Homeless Hears of New Strides" *Star-Ledger* (1-15-89).

23. "Newark Called Dumping Ground for Homeless," *Star-Ledger* (1-9-86).

24. *Star-Ledger* (9-25-85).

25. Kenneth Kusmer, *Down and Out, on the Road: The Homeless in American History* (New York: Oxford University Press, 2002); "New State Program Makes Strides in Curbing Homelessness," *Star-Ledger* (n.d.).

26. "Newark Council to Oppose Demolition," *Star Ledger* (4-6-2000).

27. "A Fierce Race Leaves Deep Bruises in Newark," *New York Times* (5-20-02).

28. "Poll Shows Booker and James Running Neck-and-Neck," *Star-Ledger* (4-24-02); "As Civil Rights Battles Recede, Generational Fights Replace Them," *New York Times* (5-15-02).

29. "Newark Give James His Fifth Term, Rebuffing Newcomer's Challenge," *New York Times* (5-15-2002).

30. "Cory Booker for Mayor in Newark," *New York Times* (5-6-02).

31. "Firefighters Union Stands Alone with Booker," *Star-Ledger* (4-19-02)

32. "A Fierce Race Leaves Deep Bruises in Newark," *New York Times* (5-20-02).

33. "Senior Vote Crucial in Newark Mayoral Election," *Star-Ledger* (4-15-02).

34. "Interview with Cory Booker," in author's possession (July 2000).

35. "In Newark, Newcomer's Allure Can't Topple Local Favorite," *New York Times* (5-16-02).

36. "The irony is that monitors were only used in Southern states or in places like Chicago with racial problems," *Star-Ledger* (5-11-02).

37. "Newark Mayor's Foes Face Complaints about Signs," *Star-Ledger* (4-6-02); "Mud-Slinging in Full-Swing for Mayor Race," *Star-Ledger* (3-26-02).

38. "Cory Booker for Mayor," *New York Times* (5-6-02).

39. "Federal Monitors Will Watch over Newark Election," *Star-Ledger* (5-11-02).

40. "Newark," *Star-Ledger* (5-16-02).

41. "Poll Shows Booker and James Running Neck-and-Neck," *Star-Ledger* (4-24-02); "As Civil Rights Battles Recede, Generational Fights Replace Them," *New York Times* (5-15-02).

42. "A Bleeding City, Seeking More than a Band-Aid," *New York Times* (5-21-06).

Index

About the Author

Kevin Mumford is Associate Professor of History and African American Studies at the University of Iowa. He is the author of *Interzones: Black/White Sex Districts in Chicago and New York in the Early Twentieth Century* (Columbia University Press, 1997).